ECONOMIC HISTORY *of the* UNITED STATES

ABOUT THE AUTHOR

Francis G. Walett received the degrees of Master of Arts and Doctor of Philosophy from Boston University where he was a member of the staff for ten years. He is now professor of history at State College, Worcester, Massachusetts. He has been a visiting professor at Northeastern University, University of Illinois, and Assumption College. He has contributed to numerous scholarly periodicals including *The William and Mary Quarterly, The New England Quarterly, Proceedings of the Bostonian Society, Social Science, Bostonia, Boston University Law Review, The Essex Institute Historical Collections,* and *The Proceedings of the American Antiquarian Society.*

COLLEGE OUTLINE SERIES

ECONOMIC HISTORY of the UNITED STATES

Second Edition

FRANCIS G. WALETT

BARNES & NOBLE, INC. NEW YORK

PUBLISHERS • BOOKSELLERS • FOUNDED 1873

Tenth Printing, 1966

L.C. catalogue card number: 63-22382

This book is an original work (No. 84) in the original College Outline Series. It was written by a distinguished educator, carefully edited, and produced in the United States of America in accordance with the highest standards of publishing.

PREFACE

This volume is based upon the contents of the standard college textbooks in American economic history. It presents in succinct form and in the most common organization the essential facts about the economic development of the American people. While prepared as a summary or digest of the subject, suitable for study and review in conjunction with any standard text, the book has a unity and an organization which permit its independent use.

Economic history, like other inter-disciplinary fields of study, presents a special problem to the instructor and the student. The contents of textbooks and the character of college courses in this subject area are determined to an unusually large extent by the interests of individual authors and instructors. Since historians and economists, and numerous specialists within these professional groups, teach courses in this subject, there are likely to be different emphases and methods of organization. The author of this volume, guided by some years of experience in teaching American economic history, has therefore tried to include several emphases and to summarize the points regarded as most significant by the historians, economists, and specialists.

For summaries of related subjects, the reader is urged to consult the following books in the College Outline Series:

Principles of Economics
Dictionary of Economics
History of Economic Thought
Marketing: An Introduction
Business Management
American Colonial and Revolutionary History
United States to 1865
United States since 1865
Dictionary of American Politics
Money and Banking

The author wishes to express appreciation to Dr. Samuel Smith, Editor of Barnes and Noble, Inc., and to the Editorial Staff of Barnes and Noble, Inc. for innumerable suggestions and careful supervision of the preparation of the manuscript.

FRANCIS G. WALETT

CONTENTS

TABULATED BIBLIOGRAPHY
AND QUICK REFERENCE TABLE
KEYED TO STANDARD TEXTBOOKS

TABULATED BIBLIOGRAPHY OF STANDARD TEXTBOOKS

This *College Outline* is keyed to standard textbooks in two ways:

1. If you are studying one of the following textbooks, consult the cross references here listed to find which pages of the *Outline* summarize the appropriate chapter of your text. (Roman numerals refer to textbook chapters, Arabic figures to corresponding *Outline* pages.)

2. If you are using the *Outline* as your basis for study and need a fuller treatment of a topic, consult any of the standard textbooks in the Quick Reference Table on pp. xiv-xvii.

NOTE. The student is cautioned that, because of differences in organization between this outline and some textbooks, the following tabulations are in many places far from exhaustive. The judicious use of the indexes of both this outline and the textbook used will therefore prove valuable. Some texts have not been keyed at all since their approach differs so greatly from that of this outline. Among these is *American Economic History,* by Davis, Hughes, and McDougall (Richard D. Irwin, 1961).

Bolino, August C. *The Development of the American Economy.* Columbus, Ohio: Charles E. Merrill Books, Inc., 1961.
I (7-19); II (20-37); III (38-50); IV (56-61, 75-83, 116-118); V (51-55, 84-98, 107-113); VI (99-106); VII (68-74, 124-125, 138-141); VIII (63-67, 160-162); IX (144-157); X (130-137, 209-210, 216-218); XI (162-165, 202-203, 209-216, 218-221, 231-235); XII (157-159, 209-221); XIII (173-179); XIV (180-183, 204-208, 219-220); XV (142-143, 200-201, 230); XVI (192-197, 228-232); XVII (232-236).

Faulkner, Harold U. *American Economic History.* Eighth ed. New York: Harper and Brothers, 1960.
I (1-6); II (7-10); III (11-19); IV (20-23, 25-29); V (23-24, 30-37); VI (75-77); VII (38-40); VIII (40-50); IX (51-55); X (78-83); XI (56-61); XII (91-98); XIII (84-90); XIV (68-74); XV (62-67); XVI (114-118); XVII (118-123); XVIII (124-129); XIX (130-137); XX (144-153); XXI (154-159); XXII (160-165); XXIII (138-143); XXIV (173-179);

XXV (166-172); XXVI (184-191); XXVII (192-197); XXVIII (198-203); XXIX (204-208); XXX (209-221); XXXI (222-227); XXXII (228-232); XXXIII (232-236).

Fite, Gilbert C., and Reese, Jim E. *An Economic History of the United States.* Second ed. Boston: Houghton Mifflin Co., 1965.
I (1-6); II (7-9); III-IV (11-29); V (30-37); VI-VII (38-49); VIII (51-55); IX-X (56-60); XI (68-74); XII (62-67); XIII (91-98); XIV (99-106); XV (114-123); XVI (173-179); XVII (138-143); XVIII (144-153); XIX (154-159); XX (160-165); XXI-XXII (124-137); XXIII (166-172); XXIV (180-183); XXV (184-190); XXVI (191-197); XXVII (198-201); XXVIII (201-203); XXIX (204-208); XXX-XXXI (209-221); XXXII (228-233); XXXIII (234-244).

Harris, Seymour E., ed. *American Economic History.* New York: McGraw-Hill Book Co., Inc., 1961.
IV (99-106, 174-179, 212-213); V (51-55, 173-174, 196-197, 220, 232); VI (107-113, 180-183, 204-206); VII (91-98, 167-172, 224-225); VIII (40-45, 118-122, 184-186, 193-197, 228-232, 235-236); IX (62-63, 160-161); XI (4-5, 144, 215); XII (68-74, 138-143, 200-201, 230); XIII (63-67, 160-165, 202-203, 218-219); XIV (231-235); XV (56-61, 130-137, 201-202, 216-218).

Johnson, E. A. J., and Krooss, Herman E. *The American Economy.* Englewood Cliffs, N. J.: Prentice-Hall, Inc., 1960.
II-III (7-9); VI (11-37); VII (38-53, 91-94, 99-102); VIII (68-74, 84-90, 144-153); IX (154-159); X (99-106, 174-179); XI (63-67, 160-165, 202-203, 218-219); XII (56-61, 75-83, 116-118, 124-137, 201-202, 216-218); XIII (51-55, 99-106, 158-159, 170-179, 204-208, 232-236); XIV (118-123, 193-197, 228-232); XV (107-113, 180-183, 204-208, 232-236).

Kemmerer, Donald L., and Jones, Clyde C. *American Economic History.* New York: McGraw-Hill Book Co., Inc., 1959.
I-II (1-19); III-V (20-50); VI (75-82); VII (68-74); VIII (56-61); IX (84-90); X-XI (99-106); XII (62-67); XIII (91-98); XIV (114-123); XVI (138-143); XVII (144-153); XVIII (154-159); XIX (173-179); XX (166-172); XXI (160-165); XXII (130-137); XXIII (222-227); XXIV (200-201); XXV (199-200); XXVI (230-232); XXVII (180-183, 212-213, 219-221); XXVIII (224-225); XXIX (202-203, 218-219, 231-232); XXX (216-218); XXXI (232-236).

Kirkland, Edward C. *A History of American Economic Life.* Third ed. New York: Appleton-Century-Crofts, Inc., 1951.
I (7-21, 25-28, 75-76); II (21-25, 28-29); III (30-40); IV (75-83); V (56-61); VI (91-98); VII (68-74); VIII (43-44, 51-55, 99-106); IX (84-90); X (62-67); XI (124-125, 138-142); XII (144-153); XIII (154-159); XIV (119-122, 173-179); XV (127-137); XVI (160-165); XVII (184-191); XVIII (196-

197, 212-213); XIX (201-202, 216-218); XX (202-203, 218-219, 233-234); XXI (195-196, 200-201, 224-225); XXII (193-194, 199-200, 214-216, 228-229).

Patton, Robert D., and Warne, Clinton. *The Development of the American Economy.* Chicago: Scott, Foresman and Co., 1963.

I-V (7-9); VI (11-19, 20-29, 30-37, 38-49, 51-55); VII (56-60, 68-74, 75-82); VIII (62-67, 84-90, 91-98, 99-106, 107-113); IX (114-123); X (124-129, 130-137); XI (144-153); XII (154-159, 160-165, 166-172, 173-179, 180-183); XIII (184-190, 191-197); XIV (198-203, 204-208); XV (209-221, 222-227); XVI (228-233, 234-238); XVII (238-244).

Robertson, Ross M. *History of the American Economy.* Second ed. New York: Harcourt, Brace and World, Inc., 1964.

II (7-10, 11-19); III (20-29); IV (30-37, 38-50); V (56-60, 75-83); VI (68-74); VII (99-106); VIII (84-90); IX (62-67); X (91-98, 107-113); XI (130-137); XII (138-143); XIII (173-179); XIV (144-153, 154-159); XV (166-172); XVI (160-165); XVII (180-183); XVIII (201-202, 216-218); XIX (195, 199, 200-201); XX (198-199, 212-213); XXI (199-200, 214-216, 229-230, 236-238); XXII (184-190, 222-225, 233-234, 238-241); XXIII (202-203, 218-219, 231-232); XXIV (204-208, 209-220, 241-244).

Russel, Robert R. *A History of the American Economic System.* New York: Appleton-Century-Crofts, 1964.

II (1-6, 7-10); III (11-19); IV-V (20-29); VI (30-37); VII-VIII (38-50); IX (62-63, 75-83); X-XI (68-74); XII-XIII (84-90); XIV (56-61); XV (91-98); XVI (99-106); XVII (63-67); XVIII (107-113, 114-123); XIX (124-129); XX-XXI (138-141); XXII-XXIII (144-153); XXIV (130-137); XXV-XXVI (166-172); XXVII (154-159); XXVIII (160-165); XXIX-XXXIII (192-203, 222-226); XXXV (204-208); XXXVI (209-220); XXXVII (228-233); XXXVIII (234-244).

Williamson, Harold F. (ed.) *The Growth of the American Economy.* New York: Prentice-Hall, Inc., 1951.

I (1-6); II (7-19); III (30-37); IV (20-29); V (38-50); VI (75-83); VII (68-74); VIII (56-61); IX (87); X (86-87); XI (84-88); XII (91-98); XIII (99-106); XV (88-90); XVI (51-55); XVII (107-123); XVIII (124-128); XIX (138-143); XX (129-137); XXI (126-128); XXII (149); XXIII (148-150); XXIV (149-152); XXV (152-153); XXVI (166-167); XXVII (167-172); XXVIII (173-179); XXX (160-165);

XXXI (144-146); XXXII (154-159); XXXIII (173-174); XXXIV (180-183); XXXV (195, 200-201); XXXVI (201-202, 216-218); XXXVII (193-194, 199-200, 214-216); XXXVIII (199-200, 228-229); XL (166-167); XLI (222-227); XLII (212-213); XLIV (202-203, 218-219, 233-234); XLVI (199-200, 214-215); XLVII (220, 230-231); XLVIII (199-200, 204-208, 219-220, 234-236).

QUICK REFERENCE TABLE TO STANDARD TEXTBOOKS

All Figures Refer to Pages

Chapter in This Book	Topic	Bolino	Faulkner	Fite and Reese	Harris	Johnson and Krooss	Kemmerer and Jones	Kirkland	Patton and Warne	Robertson	Russel	Williamson
I	The Physical Basis of United States Economic History		3-30	26-29			3-13					1-16
II	The European Background of American Economic History	9-10	31-41	15-24		20-67	13-14	3-12	36-116	18-29	11-19	19-22
III	The Colonization of North America	11-20	42-56	24-26		117-137	14-22	12-26	117-120	29-42	20-36	22-43
IV	Production in Colonial America	21-35	59-74 85-90	4-14		137-146	43-50	38-87	120-123	42-47	37-52 53-66	60-82
V	Colonial Commerce	35-42	75-85	63-83		146-151	54-64	88-122	123-128	48-87	67-84 85-102	44-59
VI	Economic Aspects of the Revolutionary Period	45-59	114-131	102-124	209-211		72-89	122-124	128-132	87-95	103-110	83-88
VII	Public Finance and Fiscal Policy, 1789 to 1860		152-168	84-101	130-161 212-213		64-71	262-268	133-137 169-171	69-75		296-310
VIII	Agriculture before 1860	60-83	197-217	30-45 150-167 168-184	483-521	334-345	23-32 138-153	152-191	148-157	111-115	201-224	133-153

IX	Population and Labor before the Civil War	180-195	286-305	46-61	66-69 247-254 366-384	302-312	32-37 212-226	313-338	177-183	205-222	112-132	286-294 585-591
X	Transportation Developments before the Civil War	134-167	260-285	186-206	69-70 340-348	178-184	38-42 118-137	219-261	144-148	125-146	133-153 154-170	116-132
XI	Westward Expansion before the Civil War	65-68 194-198	91-106 169-196			341-343	95-117	124-152	138-144	99-124	117-129	91-115
XII	Beginnings of American Industrialism	96-103	239-259	208-231		199-218	227-245	282-312	171-177	183-204	171-185	154-210
XIII	Foreign Trade and Maritime Industries, 1789-1860	89-93	218-235	233-250	183-195	374-377	154-173	192-218	158-169	223-246	225-235	211-226
XIV	Money and Banking, 1789-1860	108-133	155-162	251-270	101-111	268-286	174-211	264-281	169-171	147-182	237-251	227-278
XV	Performance of the American Economy, 1789-1860	434-437	162-163	128-149	162-168	416-419	265-269		133-136 181-184		268-289	311-334
XVI	Economic Aspects of the Civil War	74-80	306-346	271-292	213-218	345-347 391-412	262-264		186-262	247-249	194-197 221-224 248-251 273-274	324-327
XVII	Passing of the Frontier	153-156 248-256	347-362	394		341-343		445-460	204-212	250-254	293-308	338-365

See pages x-xiii for complete list of titles.

QUICK REFERENCE TABLE TO STANDARD TEXTBOOKS (Continued)

All Figures Refer to Pages

Chapter in This Book	Topic	Bolino	Faulkner	Fite and Reese	Harris	Johnson and Krooss	Kemmerer and Jones	Kirkland	Patton and Warne	Robertson	Russel	Williamson
XVIII	Changing Agriculture, 1860-1914	257-266	365-390	413-431	483-521	347-360	419-437	460-483	212-219 382-399	254-275	375-392	388-431
XIX	History of Transportation and Communication to 1914	153-173 483-490	477-507	324-347	69-71 349-353	178-184	291-311	339-378	205-208	276-301	324-337	366-387
XX	The Industrial Revolution	213-215	391-419	348-371		218-233	312-333	379-400	84-114 220-236	331-347	338-357 358-374	432-510
XXI	Industrial Consolidation and the Antitrust Movement	215-245 344-350	420-448	372-388		234-267 369-373	334-354	401-426	238-249 366-381	347-358	417-429	602-630
XXII	The Labor Movement, 1860-1914	195-203 280-294	449-476	389-412	373-397	313-323	398-418	484-523	249-253	382-405	430-442	585-601
XXIII	Domestic and Foreign Commerce	236-239	530-552	456-474	195-201	374-377	376-397	524-540	255-258	569-594	393-403	511-550
XXIV	Financial History, 1865-1914	392-412	508-529	475-491	111-127 130-161	286-301 379-388	355-375	427-444	258-261	302-330	404-416	551-584
XXV	The Performance of the American Economy 1865-1914	437-444	515-523	296-322	162-180	421-425	438-443		206, 214 217-218 254		266 390-391 410-411	646-662

XXVI	Economic Imperialism		553-574	469-473				540-547	257-258	377-381	401-403	541-542
XXVII	World War I and the American Economy	531-561	575-599	509-525	220-224	391-412	468-487 488-491 542-544 588-589		262-272	266-267 295-297 428-429	322 327-328 392 448	542-543 654-656
XXVIII	The Prosperous Twenties	271-272 444-454	603-635	528-550	392-397	324-327 359-360		548-558 572-592 598-605 624-637 656-671	274-288	428-470 539-568 604-626	456-469 470-482 483-498 500-519	666-681 687-699 809-816 829-843 878-890 909-910
XXIX	The Great Depression	445-454	636-653	575-591	20-21 164-170	327-329 440-444	458-459 571-572 595-599	624-637	288-291	627-634	534-545	816-817 898-899 910-914
XXX	The New Deal	272-273 297-305 360-363 368-373	654-683	592-631	397-413	329-333 360-361	459-462 572-575 595-599	558-571 592-595 606-618 656-682	292-311 348-365	634-643	546-565	666-681 689-699 817-823 832-849 881-899 914-916
XXXI	America and World Economics		684-695		201-204		462-467 558-566	637-655	311-313	594-603	585-594	785-808
XXXII	Economic Problems of World War II	273-275 417-418 531-559	696-710	632-649	204-205 224-234 420-473	391-412	491-507 578-585	595-619	316-329	439-444 514-515 576-579 640-641	566-583	681-694 823-828 902-905
XXXIII	The American Economy at Mid-Century	563-591	712-731	650-670	777-859	413-449	599-611	624-682	330-417	643-660	594-601	713-717 852-859 905-908 909-932

See pages x-xiii for complete list of titles.

1

THE PHYSICAL BASIS OF UNITED STATES ECONOMIC HISTORY

The American physical scene, however wealthy, has not by itself provided for all the needs of the people. Americans have therefore labored to adapt the gifts of nature in order to supply their needs better. United States economic history is the story not only of man's conquest of nature but also of nature's influence on man.

PHYSIOGRAPHIC INFLUENCES

Physical factors have been of importance throughout our economic development. Early settlements were located along the harbors and rivers of the Atlantic Coast; river valleys and mountain gaps pointed the way westward; natural resources facilitated the development of, and often determined the location of, certain economic activities. The struggle with nature left its mark upon the original European settlers of America and contributed to the development of the American character. Political, social, and economic attitudes have frequently reflected the physical environment; concern with the conquest of nature has produced a pragmatic and utilitarian outlook on life; extensive resources have encouraged tenacious optimism.

GEOGRAPHIC REGIONS AND CLIMATE

The United States occupies that part of North America lying roughly between the 25th and 49th parallels, an area of 3,026,-789 square miles. (In addition to Continental United States,

Physical Map of North America

there are territories and other non-contiguous areas containing about 600,000 square miles.)

Geographic Regions. There are five main geographical divisions, or natural regions of the United States.

The eastern coastal plain lies between the Atlantic Ocean and the Appalachian Mountains. Numerous rivers cross this plain, but few, except the Delaware and the Hudson, are navigable far inland. The eastern coast is interrupted by many bays, inlets, and excellent harbors. Agriculture was of some significance in this region in the early period, but commerce, business, and finance are now most important.

The Appalachian highland, just west of the coastal plain, extends from northern New England to Alabama, and is roughly 300 miles wide. It includes much good upland farm land as well as numerous fertile valleys, both east and west of the mountains. Rapid rivers provide water power, and mineral and oil deposits have facilitated the rise of industry.

The Mississippi Valley reaches from the Appalachian highland to the eastern edge of the Rocky Mountains. The central portion, the granary of America, is fed and drained by the mighty Mississippi River and its many tributaries. On the Great Plains, just east of the Rockies, the scarcity of rainfall makes agriculture difficult or impossible. Iron deposits in the western Great Lakes area have permitted the rise of manufacturing.

The Cordillera region extends from the Rocky Mountains westward to the Sierra Nevada and Cascade ranges, with an intervening arid plateau. Rainfall is insufficient to support agriculture, and dry farming and irrigation are able to make only a small fraction of the region arable. There are highly valuable deposits of copper, gold, silver, iron, coal, and uranium.

A narrow section along the Pacific Coast is made up of low mountains and a thin plain. A few rapid rivers are sources of water for irrigation and hydroelectric power. Until the recent growth of industry, this region was chiefly noted for its fruits, vegetables, timber, and fish.

Climate. All of the United States lies within the Temperate Zone and therefore enjoys the type of climate best suited to human effort. Average temperatures range from 40 to 70 degrees, insuring climatic conditions conducive to great physical and mental exertion. Conditions are similar to those of Europe, where other highly civilized societies have developed, and the conquest of the North American continent has produced a hardy, energetic, extremely self-reliant people. The average annual rainfall is 26.6 inches, with the amount in different areas varying from 5 inches in Utah to 60 inches in parts of California and the Gulf states. (The amount ordinarily essential for agriculture is 20 inches.) Conditions for agriculture are best east of the 100th meridian where rainfall averages between 20 and 60 inches annually. The arid Great Plains and the Cordillera region have less than 20 inches. Lack of rainfall is geographically the most important single factor in the economic history of the Great Plains.

NATURAL RESOURCES

The United States is blessed with abundant and diversified natural resources. These include productive soil, forests, minerals, fish and game, and water power.

Soil. Soil, the most basic resource, is varied. About 40 per cent of the land is arable, but differences in soil and climate permit the raising of a wide variety of crops. Alluvial soil along southern rivers is very fertile. Throughout northern and eastern North America, as far south as the Ohio River, glacial action did much to determine the type of soil. Glaciers sometimes scraped off the surface soil and covered the land with boulders as in New England, but at other times left very fertile land behind as in the corn belt of the Midwest, where the mixture of topsoil and subsoil resulted in highly productive land.

Forests. The luxuriant forests of the United States have been an invaluable asset throughout American history. Originally almost all of the land east of the Mississippi River was covered by thick forests. In the north the softwoods are most prevalent, but some hardwoods are found. A central hardwood belt stretches from the Great Lakes to northern Alabama, and along the Gulf of Mexico the forests produce mixed woods. West of the Mississippi River, except for scattered parts of the

Cordillera region, the land is barren of trees. Along the northern Pacific Coast there is a heavy growth of valuable fir trees.

Minerals. The United States has vast supplies of the mineral resources needed in modern industrial society. Petroleum, the most valuable mineral, is found in three main areas: the Ohio Valley and midcontinent fields; the coastal region of Louisiana and Texas; and California. Coal is second in value among minerals. The anthracite of Pennsylvania is the most important known anthracite resource in the world. Bituminous deposits have been found in the Appalachian area from Pennsylvania to Alabama and in several Mississippi Valley states. Bituminous is mined in 28 states. Known iron resources almost equal those of the rest of the world. Iron is found in every state, but the Lake Superior region produces nine-tenths of United States iron ore. The region of Birmingham, Alabama, ranks second in the production of iron. The greatest supply of copper is found in Arizona, but there are substantial deposits in many western states. Other mineral resources include zinc, lead, aluminum, gold, silver, and uranium.

Fish and Game. Abundant fish and wild game were of greater importance in our earlier history than at the present time. In the colonial period fish was the most important staple product of New England. Plentiful supplies of fish are still available in both the north Atlantic and the north Pacific. Bison and deer were once useful for their hides and as food; beaver and other fur-bearing animals were hunted for their pelts. Today we depend upon domesticated animals for meat and hides, and wild animals, greatly reduced in numbers, are valued chiefly for their furs.

Water Power. The numerous waterways of the United States have been important highways of commerce, and they also have provided an inexhaustible source of power. In early manufacturing, water power was widely used, and in the twentieth century it is being increasingly used to generate electricity.

REVIEW QUESTIONS

1. How has the physical environment proved advantageous in our economic development? In what ways has it proved disadvantageous?

2. Describe the main geographical divisions of the United States.
3. What effect have climatic conditions had on our economic life?
4. Describe and locate by regions the natural resources of the United States: soil, forests, minerals, fish, wild game, waterways.

2

THE EUROPEAN BACKGROUND OF AMERICAN ECONOMIC HISTORY

On the eve of the discovery of America, western Europe was going through a great transition period wherein medieval institutions were being transformed into early modern institutions. There were profound changes in every sphere of life—political, social, intellectual, religious, and economic.

THE TRANSITION FROM MEDIEVAL TO MODERN TIMES

Politically, the nation-state system replaced feudal localism. Socially, free society developed, and a new class, the bourgeoisie, emerged. Intellectually, the significant changes were a revival of ancient learning and a questioning of medieval authorities. In religion, the Protestant Reformation split the western Christian world in the sixteenth century. Economically, modern capitalism resulted from increased trade and business.

Revival of Trade. In the late Middle Ages (1100-1500) there was a general revival of trade and business. After the fall of the Roman Empire in the fifth century, trade and city life had declined greatly, and economic localism had characterized western Europe for at least five centuries. During this period contact with the eastern Mediterranean world had been irregular. From about 1100 on, however, there was increased interest in the East. This was stimulated by the Crusades and the tales of travelers. Although the Crusades (a series of armed pilgrimages, between 1100 and 1300, to reconquer the

Holy Land from the Turks) failed in their ostensible purpose, they increased trade and helped to revive the stagnant economy of Europe. Accounts of travel by Carpini, Rubruquis, and Marco Polo, which appeared in the thirteenth and fourteenth centuries, added to the geographical knowledge of Europeans and excited interest in the fabulous East. There developed a European market for Oriental luxuries such as spices, rugs, cutlery, gems, fabrics, and glass. In return Europe shipped woolens, tin, copper, arsenic, quicksilver, lead, gold, and silver to the East.

With the increase in trade came the rise of towns. Mediterranean cities, especially the strategically located Italian cities, led the way in the growing commercial activity. Important trading centers also developed in northern Europe. The Italian cities were logical starting places for the Crusades; Venice, Pisa, and Genoa handled much of the trade with the East. Overland passes through the Alps permitted the shipment of goods to northern Europe, but early in the fourteenth century Italian merchants began trading by an all-water route with English and Flemish towns.

Rise of Capitalism. Modern capitalism was born largely as a result of accumulation of wealth from increased trade. Surplus capital was used to open new trade routes, to subsidize nation-states, and to exploit the New World. In order to combine resources and to obtain greater protection against pirates, robbers, and unfriendly princes, merchants organized joint-stock companies (partnerships in which each partner was responsible for all debts). In these early days of capitalism, merchant princes performed many functions now associated with banking: they were the money-changers, moneylenders, and money-carriers.

Merchant capitalism found strength and support in two quarters: the nation-state and the new Protestant churches. National monarchs relied upon the wealth of the bourgeoisie to combat the influence of feudalism and the medieval Church. Capitalism derived immense benefits from the alliance with the nation-state, for the integrated state provided a wider domestic market, and protected and regularized trade. In time the public policy of mercantilism arose to strengthen capitalism as well as the nation-state. The Protestant churches contributed to the development of capitalism by providing an ethic which was compatible with the evolving economy of Europe. Many hard-working bourgeois, not content merely with reward in the next life, were attracted to the Protestant churches, which gave their blessing to capitalistic virtues.

DISCOVERY OF AMERICA

Competition for control of trade with the Orient motivated western European nations to sponsor numerous voyages of discovery and exploration.

Oriental Trade. The discovery of America was an inevitable result of the economic expansion of Europe in the late Middle Ages. Trade with the East by the Mediterranean route was expensive. The fall of Constantinople to the Turks in 1453 did not create the barrier to trade that historians formerly conceived, but it did add to the cost of trade. Merchants of Portugal, Spain, France, and England wished to trade directly with the Orient rather than through Italian and Turkish middlemen.

International Rivalry. Successful national monarchs were eager to engage in overseas ventures. Portugal, under the guidance of Prince Henry the Navigator, led in the voyages of discovery and exploration in the late fifteenth century. In 1486 Diaz rounded the Cape of Good Hope, at the southern tip of Africa; in 1497-1498 da Gama reached India. With this initial advantage and a favorable geographic location, the Portuguese created a great empire in the Far East. Spain followed the lead of Portugal and sponsored the westward voyage of Columbus in 1492. Instead of reaching Asia, Columbus discovered America. Within a few years explorers had established a magnificent Spanish empire in South, Central and North America. Navigators of other powers joined in the exploration of the New World, but in the sixteenth century Spain had a virtual monopoly in the exploitation of America. John Cabot's voyage to Newfoundland in 1497 laid the basis of England's claim to North America. France's claim rested on the voyages of Verrazano in 1524 and Cartier in 1534 and 1535.

REVIEW QUESTIONS

1. Why can the period 1200 to 1500 be called "the dawn of a new era"?
2. What caused the revival of trade and city life in the late Middle Ages?
3. How did modern capitalism originate?
4. In wbat ways did capitalism receive support from the nation-state and Protestantism?
5. Why did western Europe seek an all-water route to the Far East?
6. Describe the overseas ventures of Portugal, Spain, England, and France in the fifteenth and sixteenth centuries.

3

THE COLONIZATION OF NORTH AMERICA

Early American economic life can be understood only when considered as a frontier of the contemporary European economy. The exploration and colonization of America were natural results of the expansion of western Europe in the late Middle Ages, and colonial ventures in the New World were first of all directed to the fulfillment of the needs of the mother countries.

MOTIVES FOR COLONIZATION

A number of factors were responsible for emigration from Europe to America in the colonial period, not all of them economic.

Noneconomic Factors. Religious and political considerations were often important in colonizing ventures. In a day of great religious enthusiasm many Europeans wanted to extend their respective forms of Christianity in America: some sought to Christianize the Indians; others desired religious freedom. The French, Dutch, and English soon contested the early Spanish and Portuguese monopolies of discoveries, and intercolonial rivalries were of great influence throughout the colonial period.

Economic Motives. The economic reasons for emigration included both governmental and individual motives.

European Problems. The economic situation in Europe was most influential in the early development of America. To Europeans the New World offered many opportunities to solve some of their economic problems. Their payments of bullion to the East, because of adverse balances of trade, had caused a drainage of specie, and this explains in part the quest for gold and silver in America. Further, it was hoped that the New World would be a source of needed raw materials, a market for manufactured goods, and a convenient base of operations for the Oriental trade. Finally, the exhaustion of soil and the enclosure of land in England for pastoral purposes had limited agriculture and had caused much unemployment. It was felt that the overpopulation of Europe might be relieved by emigration to the colonies.

EUROPEAN IMPERIALISM. America provided a new field for developing European imperialism. Investments of labor and capital in the colonies greatly stimulated the expanding European economy, for the colonies needed supplies and their natural resources permitted the development of new enterprises. Colonial commodities provided greater opportunity for trade amongst Europeans and for expansion in other areas.

PRIVATE ECONOMIC MOTIVES. The desire for greater economic opportunity caused many to migrate to America. Even that staunch Puritan, John Winthrop, hoped to benefit materially by going to Massachusetts. The availability of land was probably the most tempting inducement to colonists, but the possibility of easy riches and a greater return for labor prompted many to come to America.

NON-ENGLISH COLONIZATION

Notable attempts at colonization by non-English settlers were those of the Spanish, the French, the Dutch, and the Swedes.

Spain in America. The Spanish empire began in the West Indies but soon included Central America and parts of North and South America. The discovery of gold in Mexico and Peru enriched Spain and temporarily allowed her capable rulers much influence in Europe. Although the European economy was stimulated by the influx of precious metals, Spain did not benefit greatly in the long run. Much of the gold and silver fell into the hands of Spain's rivals, the Dutch and the English, who had more highly developed commercial and manufacturing economies. The most important economic activity of the colonists of New Spain was agriculture.

GOVERNMENTAL POLICY. The Spanish colonial system was one of strict governmental regulation: only Spaniards could emigrate to the colonies; outsiders were excluded from the trade of the empire; commerce and business were strictly controlled by means of excises and import and export duties. Monopolies in the marketing of some commodities were granted: e.g., tobacco, gunpowder, salt; and colonial production of certain goods was forbidden: e.g., olives, tobacco, hemp. The English and the Dutch, however, undermined the Spanish commercial monopoly by smuggling and piratical activity.

THE ENCOMIENDA SYSTEM. The great need for labor was met in two ways: (1) enslavement of the natives, and (2) Negro slavery. In the *encomienda* system favored landholders were authorized to force natives to labor for them under conditions little better than serfdom. Although landholders were supposed to civilize and Christianize the natives, these obligations were generally neglected, and harsh treatment resulted in the practical extinction of the Indians. Negro slavery, first introduced in New Spain in 1503, spread rapidly, and the number imported annually before 1750 averaged about 3,000.

France in America. The French occupied the St. Lawrence Valley, the Great Lakes area, and the Ohio and Mississippi valleys. New France in America began with the first permanent settlement in 1605 and lasted until the final defeat by England in 1763.

ECONOMIC ORGANIZATION. Early colonization was monopolized by private commercial companies, the most important of which was the Hundred Associates. In 1663 the government took over the administration of New France and established a paternalistic mercantile system. Feudal practices characterized the economic life of the colony. Seigniories, great tracts of land, were granted to nobles, but feudal land tenure proved unsuccessful because of the availability of vacant land. The greatest source of wealth was the fur trade, and only minor attention was paid to farming and fishing.

ECONOMIC WEAKNESS. New France was never very vigorous or populous, and by 1754 the total population was only about

80,000. A relatively unfavorable geographic area and inept governmental policies contributed to the backwardness of the French colonies. Economic weakness made the eventual defeat of the French inevitable in their struggle with the English for control of North America.

New Netherland. Dutch traders and settlers occupied that part of the Atlantic coast which lies between the Connecticut and Delaware rivers. The main settlements were in the Hudson River Valley. The Dutch West India Company was granted a monopoly of the American trade as well as governing authority in New Netherland. Economic life in the colony was strictly regulated for the profit of the company, and much attention was given the fur trade. In 1629 the company introduced the patroon system, under which feudal grants of land with governmental and judicial authority were made to favored individuals. Here, as elsewhere in America, feudal land tenure proved unworkable. The English seized the Dutch colonies in 1664.

New Sweden. The Swedish South Company established Fort Christina (Wilmington) on Delaware Bay in 1638. New Sweden was a small trading colony that never numbered over 400 persons. In 1655 the Dutch took over the Swedish colony easily.

ENGLISH COLONIZATION OF NORTH AMERICA

English colonization relied upon private initiative and capital, but private activity was a response to national needs. Government resources were not adequate for the task of colonization, for Parliament in Elizabeth's time voted barely enough taxes for domestic needs, and the financial resources of the Stuart kings were never great.

Economic Motives for Colonization. England's commercial prosperity was threatened by a number of factors. The marketing of woolens was uncertain because of European competition and religious wars; and the supply of necessary imports was endangered. Unfriendly Spain was the source of dyes and vegetable oils; potash and naval stores had to be obtained from the Baltic countries; and Oriental goods were purchased from Portugal. It was hoped that the American colonies would be a source of needed supplies, and might in time be a market for English manufactures. Many felt that the overpopulation of England, which had caused an increase in unemployment, crime, and pauperism, could be relieved by emigration to America.

Joint-Stock Companies. Interested promoters sometimes organized joint-stock companies for the purpose of establishing trading posts and colonies in America. These were private organizations seeking profits for the investors. Usually they were chartered by the crown, like the Virginia companies and the Massachusetts Bay Company, but the New Plymouth settlers entered into a joint-stock arrangement without the sanction of the English government.

THE VIRGINIA COMPANIES. A royal charter of 1606 created two Virginia companies, and granted them the right to trade and colonize in America from Maine to Carolina. One of the Virginia companies, from Plymouth, England, attempted unsuccessfully to plant a colony at Sagadahoc in Maine. The other Virginia Company, from London, established the first permanent English settlement in America—Jamestown, Virginia—in 1607. New charters made the Virginia Company of London a joint-stock company in 1609 and 1612. The early years of Jamestown's history were troubled because of inadequate supplies and the fact that many of the settlers were not industrious. With the beginning of tobacco cultivation in 1612, however, Virginia had a money staple which assured the continued existence of the colony. The plantation type of economy with Negro slaves as the chief labor force soon developed. Because of disfavor with the English government and eventual bankruptcy, the Virginia Company was dissolved in 1624, and Virginia became a royal colony under the direct authority of the crown.

THE COUNCIL FOR NEW ENGLAND. This organization, a land company, was chartered in 1620 with a title to the land between the 40th and the 48th parallels. The company did not attempt to establish settlements itself, but granted land and trading rights to members and others. John Mason and Sir Ferdinando Gorges received the land between the Merrimack and Kennebec rivers. In 1630 the Pilgrims were given title to the land they had occupied in the Plymouth area. In 1632 a group of Puritans obtained a grant of land at the mouth of the Connecticut River where the Saybrook settlement was founded. The Council for New England surrendered its charter in 1635.

NEW PLYMOUTH. The Plymouth colony was promoted through a joint-stock agreement between the Pilgrim Fathers and a group of London merchants. Capital and profits were to be held jointly for seven years and then were to be divided. This communal arrangement proved unworkable, however, and in 1626 the settlers arranged to buy out their London associates. Private enterprise was established early, the main economic activities being agriculture, fishing, and the fur trade. The independent government of Plymouth had no legal basis, although title to the land occupied was obtained from the Council for New England. In 1691 Plymouth was included in the jurisdiction of Massachusetts.

THE MASSACHUSETTS BAY COMPANY. Several joint-stock companies attempted to establish settlements in the Massachusetts Bay area. Between 1623 and 1626, the Dorchester Company set up a trading and fishing colony on Cape Ann, and the New England Company, chartered in 1628, maintained a settlement at Salem. In 1629 some of the Puritan members of the latter company agreed to settle in America on condition that the charter and government be transferred to the colony. The Puritans felt that their religious, political, and economic positions in England were insecure, and they wanted to establish a Bible Commonwealth in America. In early 1630 President John Winthrop and the newly formed Massachusetts Bay Company came to Boston. Within a few months over 1,000 settlers arrived, and by 1640 the population of the Bay Colony had reached 14,000. The Massachusetts Bay Company was soon changed from a commercial organization to a political commonwealth. The company did not operate as a profit-making body, because English stockholders relinquished dividend claims in return for trade concessions and land grants. When new freemen, church members, were admitted to the general court of the Massachusetts Bay Company, the company was no longer a commercial but a political organization. Massachusetts developed a more self-sufficient economy than the southern English colonies. Agriculture was difficult and of the subsistence variety, but the forests yielded lumber, masts, and furs for export to England. Fish also proved to be a valuable export commodity, and the settlers soon began to build ships and to develop a thriving commerce.

The Expansion of New England. The other New England colonies were largely offshoots of Massachusetts Bay and Plymouth. For the most part they were not established by joint-stock companies, but by individuals who were displeased with conditions in the older settlements. Rhode Island and Connecticut, almost completely self-governing, were corporate colonies.

RHODE ISLAND. The Rhode Island settlements were begun by religious and political exiles from Massachusetts, and democratic government and freedom of conscience characterized the colony. The Indian fur trade and commerce with the Dutch were the most profitable economic activities of the colony.

CONNECTICUT. Political, religious, and economic motives were influential in the founding of the Connecticut towns. Some settlers migrated from Massachusetts Bay, and others came directly from England. Subsistence agriculture and trade with the Indians were the chief economic activities. The Dutch were rival traders on the Connecticut River until their posts were taken over in 1654.

NEW HAMPSHIRE AND MAINE. Settlers from Massachusetts founded a few fishing and lumbering villages in the region which later became New Hampshire. These outposts were under the jurisdiction of Massachusetts until 1679. The small towns along the Maine coast, merely fishing and trading posts, remained under the control of Massachusetts throughout the colonial period.

Proprietary Colonies. Later English colonization was dominated by the proprietary form of government. The crown made feudal grants of land with extensive political and economic power to individuals or to groups. Proprietors were sovereign except that laws had to conform to English law and had to be made with the consent of the freemen of the colony. Proprietors made personal investments to encourage settlement and to increase the value of the land. They expected to derive profits from feudal land tenure and through control of certain economic activities.

MARYLAND. The Maryland grant by Charles I to the Calvert family in 1632 was a model for later proprietary grants. Settlement was begun in 1634, and Maryland prospered from the start. The settlers were able to produce corn for export, but greater emphasis was placed on the production of tobacco. Except for a few years, Maryland was in the possession of the Calvert family until the Revolution.

NEW YORK AND NEW JERSEY. These colonies, created out of the Dutch possessions, were proprietary grants of the Duke of York, later King James II. New York was established on a firm economic basis with the lucrative fur trade and the valuable agricultural exports. New Jersey was granted to Sir George Carteret and John, Lord Berkeley, in 1664, but the province soon passed into the hands of a group of Quakers. A diversified agricultural economy developed in this colony. New York became a royal colony in 1685, New Jersey in 1702.

PENNSYLVANIA. Charles II granted Pennsylvania to William Penn in 1681. Settlers were quickly attracted by a liberal land policy, religious toleration, and very fertile soil. The colony increased rapidly, concentrating on the production and export of agricultural produce, and Philadelphia became an important commercial center within a few years. Except for the years 1692 to 1696, the province was owned by the Penn family until the Revolution. Pennsylvania was probably the most profitable proprietary colony.

THE CAROLINAS. North and South Carolina were settled in the late seventeenth century by Virginians and immigrants from England. All of Carolina was granted in 1663 to eight proprietors, who attempted in vain to establish an elaborate feudal state, and who finally sold their rights to the crown in 1729. The economies of North and South Carolina developed differently: North Carolina was a backward frontier community with no staple product and little commerce; South Carolina developed a prosperous plantation economy with emphasis on the staples, rice and indigo. Both provinces became important for the production of naval stores.

GEORGIA. This colony was founded in 1732 as a barrier against

Spanish Florida and as a philanthropic enterprise to care for English debtors. It was a nonprofit proprietary colony until taken over by the crown in 1752. Georgia's economy progressed slowly with concentration on rice, indigo, lumber, and the fur trade.

REVIEW QUESTIONS

1. What were the economic motives for the colonization of America?
2. Indicate how early American economic life was related to the contemporary European economy.
3. Describe the colonial systems of Spain, France, and Holland in America.
4. How successful were English joint-stock companies in planting colonies? What colonies were founded in this manner?
5. Describe the expansion of New England and the establishment of the corporate colonies.
6. What were the main characteristics of the proprietary method of colonization?

4

PRODUCTION IN COLONIAL AMERICA

The English colonists in America quickly set up an economy based on individual enterprise and private ownership of property, the early communal arrangements at Jamestown and Plymouth having proved unsatisfactory. Private enterprise provided sufficient incentive for the conquest of the new land. Hostility toward monopoly and corporate control of economic life has been a vital force in American history since the early colonial period.

LAND TENURE

The availability of land in America on cheap terms was probably the greatest inducement to settlement. Private land tenure was established in all the colonies after brief experimentation with corporate ownership. Other characteristics of colonial land tenure were the widespread ownership of land and the failure of efforts to transplant parts of Europe's outmoded feudal land system.

New England. Legislatures usually disposed of land in the form of township grants to groups of individuals. Villages were organized with private and public sections: grantees acquired farms and house lots; meadow, marsh, and woodland were held in common. In time the common land was distributed to newcomers or to original settlers who had performed a special service. Most holdings in New England were small, although in the eighteenth century large grants were sometimes made to individuals or to land-promotion companies.

Middle Colonies. In contrast to the New England system,

grants were usually made to individuals rather than to groups. In the proprietary colonies land tenure was subject to feudal obligations, but quitrents (rents paid in lieu of obligatory services) were not heavy burdens. The agriculture of this section necessitated somewhat larger farms than in New England, but not so large as the plantations of the South. The huge patroonships in New York were an exception to the rule.

Southern Colonies. All grants were made to individuals, frequently with light quitrent obligations. There were some small holdings—primarily in upland regions of the interior—but large plantations were the general rule. Great estates were procured in several ways: grants made by the crown and colonial legislatures; the headright system, by which anyone transporting a settler to America was entitled to a grant of land (usually 50 acres a head); and by outright purchase. The English custom of primogeniture and entail tended to perpetuate the great estates.

CAPITAL INVESTMENT

The greatest amount of investment was in agriculture, real estate, and British government securities. Manufacturing was less attractive than other types of capital investment. Gradually, however, those with surplus capital saw the possibilities of profit in such enterprises as iron works, lumber and flour mills, potash and pearlash works, and breweries.

Capital for colonial enterprise came from both English and American sources, with the latter becoming increasingly more important. The American capitalist class consisted mainly of merchants, landed proprietors, and prominent officeholders. In general there was a shortage of capital (especially for investment in manufacturing) which tended to restrict productive enterprise and to cause high interest rates.

AGRICULTURE

Agriculture was the chief occupation of about 90 per cent of the colonists throughout the colonial period, and it was the most important source of wealth. The limitation of trade, especially in the early period, made the production of a food supply essential; to the extent that trade with other regions was possible, Americans found it profitable to specialize in agricultural exports. This was true because the abundance and cheapness of good soil gave the colonists their greatest relative economic advantage. Colonial farming, like the contemporary European agriculture, was very primitive: tools were crude, and methods were unscientific. The unfortunate results were "land-butchery" and the exhaustion of much land.

New England. Because the soil and climate in New England did not permit the production of great agricultural staples for export, farming was of the subsistence variety. Crops raised included Indian corn, wheat, barley, oats, many kinds of vegetables, apples, and pears. Native nuts and berries of all types were plentiful. The settlers raised cattle, horses, hogs, and sheep, and exported some pork to the West Indies.

The New England farms were almost completely self-sufficient, but were not remunerative. Frequently the farmer engaged in other activities to supplement his small income. Although New England soil was less fertile than that in other areas, it provided an adequate living for the great majority of the colonial population.

The Middle Colonies. The region from New York to Maryland was the most advantageous for general farming: all types of farms existed, from small subsistence farms to huge plantations. The climate was milder and the soil was generally much better than in New England; the valleys of the Hudson, Susquehanna, and Delaware rivers were very fertile and productive of surpluses for export, especially wheat, corn, rye, barley, and buckwheat. There was also an abundance of fruits and vegetables. Livestock was more plentiful and of much better quality than in New England.

The Southern Colonies. Although there was diversified farming in the interior upland regions and on the poor lands of North Carolina, the production of staple crops dominated the agriculture of the southern colonies, and made farming in this region more like a capitalistic enterprise than elsewhere in English America. Staple planters raised specialized export crops on large plantations worked first by indentured servants and later by Negro slaves. The southern economy was greatly affected by external forces: much depended upon the world prices of staples; the South relied upon outside shipping interests for the marketing of exports; the planters became increasingly dependent upon English creditors who financed the purchase of new lands and slaves and helped to support the South's relatively high standard of living. In Maryland and Virginia, tobacco was the all-important staple; farther south, rice and indigo were raised. The production of staples to the neglect of other crops, and wasteful methods of cultivation, resulted in soil exhaustion.

OTHER EXTRACTIVE INDUSTRIES

Activities in nonagricultural extractive industries were the fur trade, various occupations based on forest resources, and fishing and whaling. Although they involved only a small minority of the population, these activities proved to be a significant source of wealth for the settlers and had a profound influence upon the expansion of the colonial economy.

The Fur Trade. The fur trade depended mainly on two factors: European demand and trade with Indians.

European Demand. The abundance of fur-bearing animals in America and the insatiable demand for pelts in Europe encouraged the development of a lucrative colonial fur trade. Furs, which were considered a mark of distinction, had been obtained previously in northern and eastern Europe, but this source of supply had been exhausted. French, Dutch, and English traders eagerly competed for control of the American fur trade, and London, Amsterdam, and Paris supplanted older eastern centers of this business. The value of the colonial fur trade increased rapidly, reaching an estimated £180,000 annually in the region north of the Potomac and Ohio rivers in the 1760's.

Trade with Indians. Colonies having access to the interior developed an Indian trade, exchanging blankets, kettles, knives, guns, liquor, trinkets, and other items for furs. Albany, New York, became one important center for this trade. The English took over the Dutch trade and extended operations westward to the eastern Great Lakes region. Some eastern Indians acted as middlemen in the trade between western Indians and the

English. In the South, Charleston and, later, Augusta were centers where traders brought large numbers of deerskins.

Forest Resources. The abundance of forest resources made possible the development of industries such as lumbering, the manufacture of naval stores, and shipbuilding.

LUMBERING. In addition to the great local demand for lumber, there was a profitable export market. Sawmills were erected at the fall lines of the streams: e.g., c. 1635 at Portsmouth, New Hampshire, and in 1652 in Virginia. Exported lumber products included masts, hoops, staves, barrels, shingles, clapboards, and sawn lumber. The British encouraged export to England, but it was more profitable to ship lumber to southern Europe and the West Indies.

NAVAL STORES. Because of England's dependence upon Scandinavia for supplies of tar, pitch, resin, and turpentine, the production of these naval stores in the American colonies was encouraged. In 1705 bounties were granted, and in 1706 it was decreed that naval stores could be exported only to England. Although naval stores were a staple of New England, the greatest colonial producer was South Carolina.

SHIPBUILDING. With the necessary materials readily available, and with a great demand for ships both at home and abroad, shipbuilding was stimulated. This industry began in New England very early, and the colonists were soon able to compete with English builders. In the eighteenth century the industry became important in Virginia and the Carolinas.

Fishing and Whaling. Europeans had been attracted to the North American fishing banks long before settlement began. Some fish was consumed locally, but codfish became the most valuable export staple of New England.

Spermaceti, oil, whalebone, and ambergris were in demand, and whales were numerous in the North Atlantic. In the eighteenth century Nantucket, Provincetown, New Bedford, and Marblehead were important whaling centers. Newport led in the manufacture of spermaceti candles.

COLONIAL MANUFACTURING

Agriculture was the leading occupation of colonial America, but there was some primitive industry. Industrial progress was slow, however, because of capital and labor shortages and British restrictions. The British encouraged the production of raw materials and primary manufactures, but they discouraged the manufacture of finished products.

Household Production. Members of the family made a great many things, and colonial farms were largely self-sufficient. Typical household activities were spinning and weaving, curing and salting meat, making wooden tools, furniture, and casks, leather-working, and making shoes, gloves, and clothes. Sometimes items for outside use and export were made in the home or on the farm: nails, casks, barrel staves, and shingles. Another phase of household industry was the putting-out system that had developed by the time of the Revolution. By this method capitalist entrepreneurs supplied stock and sometimes implements to individual workers, and later collected and sold the finished product. This system of production was most important in the production of thread, cloth, and shoes.

Mills and Factories. Some plants, independent of the household, were established very early when machinery and power were necessary. Oftentimes sawmills, gristmills, and fulling mills were built and supported by towns. Other mills included iron works, glass shops, breweries, shipyards, and small textile plants. These industries were most numerous in the northern and middle colonies, but smaller works were established on many southern plantations.

COLONIAL LABOR

Conditions in colonial America favored the rapid growth of population: wealthy resources, abundantly available, provided great opportunities for the common man; there was a scarcity of labor. These factors were an inducement to immigration and a high birth rate. The growth of population was approximately as follows.

POPULATION OF THE UNITED STATES, 1640-1775

Year	Population	Year	Population
1640	28,000	1720	500,000
1660	85,000	1740	900,000
1700	275,000	1775	2,500,000

Because of the difficulties of travel and transport, colonists settled on the coast and along navigable rivers. By 1775 the population had not moved far beyond the fall line of the eastern rivers; only a few frontiersmen had ventured beyond the Appalachian Mountains. The population of the leading cities in 1775 is estimated as follows: Philadelphia, 40,000; New York, 28,000; Boston, 20,000; Newport, 12,000; Charleston, 12,000.

Labor and the Colonial Economy. The scarcity of labor affected colonial economy seriously: production was somewhat restricted despite the fact that wages were from 30 to 100 per cent higher than in England. Free workmen were not numerous enough to meet the demand for labor in America for several reasons. (1) Although emigration to the colonies was encouraged by the English government in the early period, Parliament later took steps to prevent the emigration of skilled workers. (2) The problem of transportation across the Atlantic was a large one. (3) It was easy to obtain land in America, and settlers found independence attractive. Because of the comparative absence of a free workingmen's class, family and co-operative work was common, and unfree labor was imported.

Indentured Servants. In the seventeenth century a large portion of the laboring population outside of New England consisted of white indentured servants. It is estimated that about one-half of all white immigrants in the colonial period were of this type, and that perhaps three-fourths of the population of Pennsylvania, Maryland, and Virginia in 1775 came of this stock.

By 1750 the number of immigrant servants had decreased sharply, and by the Revolution this type of immigration had almost ceased.

VOLUNTARY SERVANTS. Many who were eager to come to America agreed to contracts binding them to labor for a period ranging from three to seven years in return for passage to America.

INVOLUNTARY SERVANTS. This category included debtors, vagrants, criminals, and kidnapped persons. Imprisonment for indebtedness and vagrancy was common in England at this time, and shipment of these undesirables to America seemed more humane and less expensive. Although the colonists objected to the practice, many of the servants brought to Maryland and Virginia were of this class. Additional laborers were obtained from unscrupulous ship captains who kidnapped thousands of children and adults and, despite Parliamentary legislation forbidding this traffic, sold them into servitude in America.

Conditions of Servitude. Indentured servants had certain rights: masters were obliged to provide food, clothing, shelter, and medical and spiritual care; and indentured servants had access to courts in cases of maltreatment. Servants sometimes enjoyed privileges such as the suffrage and the right to own property. Treatment of white servants was not severe at first, but it became more harsh owing to the influence of Negro slave codes. At the end of the period of indenture servants were free, and no stigma was attached to them because of their servitude. Former servants became wealthy, and in some cases they held political office.

Negro Slavery. The Dutch first introduced Negro slavery to the English colonies in 1619. Slaves were not numerous in the seventeenth century, however. It was only when white servants and free workers failed to meet the demand for labor in the southern colonies that Negro slavery became important. During the eighteenth century Negroes were used in increasing numbers on tobacco plantations and in the unhealthful rice fields of South Carolina and Georgia. In the North there was no great economic need for slaves; the few brought in generally were domestic servants. The number of Negro slaves is estimated to have increased as follows.

NUMBER OF SLAVES, 1714-1790

Year	Number of Slaves	Year	Number of Slaves
1714	60,000	1775	500,000
1754	300,000	1790	697,000 (first census)

Labor Controls. Early colonial governments adopted regulations intended to meet the problem of labor shortage and relatively high wages. The efforts made included (1) the establishment of forced labor by vagrants and strangers, (2) the diligent pursuit of fugitive servants, (3) the establishment of maximum wages, and (4) the regulation of prices of basic goods. Although practically all the colonies attempted such regulations in the early period, New England made the greatest effort. These regulatory activities proved ineffective generally, and they were abandoned after a short time.

Labor Organization. Although there was some co-operation amongst licensed workmen, such as carters, porters, and bakers, workingmen's combinations were uncommon and at best temporary. In a few scattered instances craftsmen did join in protest against price and wage regulations, and later against British imperial policies. The European guild system was not generally established in America either, but there were a few examples of this institution: e.g., in 1644, shipbuildng was placed under the control of a chartered company in Massachusetts; in 1648, the shoemakers and coopers were organized with a monopolistic charter; in 1718, Philadelphia gave similar rights to shoemakers, coopers, and tailors. These institutions were short-lived because of the demand for labor and the difficulty of enforcing regulations.

ECONOMIC NATIONALISM AND COLONIAL PRODUCTION

British colonial policy was a form of economic nationalism quite common in the seventeenth and eighteenth centuries. The colonies were expected to be a source of needed supplies, and to be an outlet for British manufactured goods. The policy included measures for (1) the encouragement and protection of home manufacturing, (2) the encouragement of colonial production of raw materials and primary manufactures, and (3) the discouragement of colonial production of finished manufactures.

Colonial Advantages. Bounties encouraged the production of some colonial commodities, especially lumber, naval stores, and indigo. Colonial shipbuilding, which would have developed in any event, derived some advantage from the British policy of discouraging the use of foreign-built vessels in the English merchant marine. The prohibition of tobacco-raising in England did not have much influence on colonial production.

Colonial Disadvantages. British regulations were generally more detrimental than beneficial to colonial production. Regulations which forbade the marketing of colonial products, like tobacco, in continental Europe were a hardship. Restrictions on colonial industry had a harmful effect also: in 1699, a law prohibited the export of wool or woolens and the shipment from one colony to another; in 1732, a similar law regulated the production of hats; in 1750, an act forbade the establishment of any more slitting mills in the colonies.

Summary of Effects. The British regulations were never strictly enforced, and the Americans paid little attention to them. Nevertheless, the colonists resented the British restrictions, and this was a contributing factor to the discontent which led to the American Revolution.

REVIEW QUESTIONS

1. Indicate how private enterprise was established in colonial America.
2. Compare the systems of land tenure in various sections of colonial America.
3. What were the leading characteristics of colonial agriculture? How important was agriculture in the colonial economy?
4. Describe agricultural production in New England, the middle colonies, and the southern colonies.
5. Discuss the economic basis and the organization of the colonial fur trade.
6. What industries based upon forest resources developed in the colonies? How important was each?
7. How extensive was household production in colonial America? Mill production?
8. Explain the shortage of labor in colonial America. How important was indentured servitude? Negro slavery?

5

COLONIAL COMMERCE

In order to obtain funds for the purchase of British manufactured goods, the colonies had to find markets for their own products. It was necessary for them to develop trade and commerce, domestic and foreign. These activities were limited by the available means of transportation and communication.

TRANSPORTATION AND COMMUNICATION

The colonies were a group of separated settlements that usually knew little of one another, for travel was slow and difficult, and communication was uncertain.

Modes of Travel and Transport. Water transport was faster and easier than travel by land, for there were many good harbors and navigable rivers along the Atlantic Coast. The population lived near the waterways: the southern plantations were located on rivers; all important cities were on waterways. Ocean travel, however, remained hazardous and voyages were long. The Pilgrims spent over two months en route to America, and in the Revolutionary period a voyage to Europe still took from six to ten weeks.

Land travel was slow, dangerous, and very uncomfortable. The dirt roads usually followed Indian trails; they were dusty in the summer and muddy in the spring. By the end of the colonial period roads connected Boston and Savannah and extended west to Pittsburgh. Most travel was on foot or horseback, but some was by vehicles. The first public coach ran from Burlington to Perth Amboy, New Jersey, in 1732. By 1756 there was a through coach from New York to Philadelphia, traveling eighteen hours a day and taking three days for the trip. In 1794 the journey from Boston to New York City took one week.

Communication. In the seventeenth century communication was entirely a private matter; news traveled by mouth or through letters. The first American newspaper was the *Boston News Letter,* founded in 1704. Delivery of mail was slow and uncertain, and before 1681 there was no organized agency for carrying the mail. At first the postal service was run as a private enterprise, but in 1710 an imperial postal system was organized by act of Parliament.

DOMESTIC COMMERCE

The expansion of commerce within the colonies encouraged the development of both land and water transport and stimulated the growth of commercial centers.

Land Transport. The difficulty of land transport restricted internal commerce; because of high transportation charges few goods could be carried profitably. Along the coast and around the larger towns, where the largest markets were, land transport was considerable. By 1732 regular wagon traffic was established on part of the route between New York and Philadelphia. There were many peddlers in all of the colonies who served as indispensable distributors of small manufactured goods.

Water Transport. The rivers of the Atlantic Coast were more important lanes of commerce than land routes. The southern and middle colonies were better endowed with navigable rivers than New England. The Hudson River was a busy waterway with over 100 vessels trading between Albany and New York City in 1770. Philadelphia became the center of commerce on the Delaware and Schuylkill rivers. South of the Potomac numerous rivers were useful in trade.

Coastal Trade. The greatest part of domestic commerce consisted of coastal traffic. This trade was in part an adjunct of foreign commerce: American goods were collected in important centers for export; European products, imported by a few leading ports, were distributed to smaller centers. Some domestic goods found markets in other parts of America: New England shipped fish, rum, meat and manufactured items to the other colonies; the middle colonies sent grains, flour, and some manufactures to New England and the South; southern staples were brought to northern ports.

FOREIGN COMMERCE

Foreign commerce was a vital factor in the economy of the colonies. Notwithstanding the existence of serious obstacles to the expansion of foreign commerce, the colonies developed profitable trade.

Difficulties of Trade. In addition to the difficulty of transport, there were other factors hindering trade. Parliamentary statutes limited areas of trade and endeavored to ensure the shipment of some commodities to the mother country. Most of these restrictions, however, were evaded without much trouble. Piracy and privateering were other hazards in a period of many wars and free-booting expeditions. An additional hindrance to trade was the inadequate money supply of the colonies.

British Mercantilism. As parts of a mercantile empire, the colonies were expected to supplement the economy of the mother country, to supply needed goods, to provide an outlet for English manufactures, and to conduct much of their trade for the greatest benefit of England. A Parliamentary navigation act of 1651 reserved the trade of the empire to British and colonial vessels. An act of 1660 provided that certain "enumerated articles" could be shipped only to England. The list of goods, greatly expanded in the eighteenth century, included tobacco, sugar, indigo, naval stores, rice, furs, lumber, and molasses. Colonial imports from Europe had to be shipped by way of England in English vessels and were subject to high duties. Direct trade between Europe and the colonies was permitted in only a few instances: salt could be brought from Spain, wines from Madeira and Azores, and provisions and horses from Ireland and Scotland. The British also regulated American trade with foreign colonies, the most famous case being the molasses trade with the Spanish and French West Indies. In 1733 a duty on foreign molasses and sugar imported by the Americans, prohibitive if enforced, was levied; the

Sugar Act of 1764 reduced the duty on molasses but provided for the enforcement of the law.

The mercantile restrictions did not bear so heavily upon the colonies as it might seem. The navigation laws were constantly evaded—often with the collusion of poorly paid customs officers—and before 1760 the colonies enjoyed a great amount of economic freedom. Also some benefits in the form of bounties and preferential tariffs were accorded the Americans.

Areas of Trade. Colonial products were shipped mainly to England, southern Europe, and the West Indies. The greatest volume of trade was with the mother country, an understandable situation in view of the prevailing mercantilist theories. The accompanying tables indicate the estimated value in pounds sterling of the trade of the American colonies with different regions in 1769.

EXPORTS TO STATED AREAS

Origin	Great Britain	Southern Europe	West Indies	Africa	Total
Colonies: Pennsylvania and Northward	284,269	335,810	555,612	19,584	1,195,275
Southern Colonies: Maryland and Southward	1,247,245	216,923	192,292	690	1,657,150
All Colonies	1,531,514	552,733	747,904	20,274	2,852,425

IMPORTS FROM STATED AREAS

Destination	Great Britain	Southern Europe	West Indies	Africa	Total
Northern Colonies	504,614	54,909	594,421	877	1,154,821
Southern Colonies	1,100,367	21,770	195,326	151,120	1,468,583
All Colonies	1,604,481	76,679	789,747	151,997	2,623,404

The tables reveal that nearly three-fourths of the trade of the southern colonies was with Great Britain. The trade of the northern colonies was more evenly distributed.

The International Balance of Payments. The American colonies north of Maryland had an unfavorable balance of trade with England. This was offset in part by the fact that the northern colonies had a merchant marine and reaped the profits of the carrying trade, and in part by the favorable balance of trade with southern Europe. While the southern American colonies had a favorable balance of trade with Great Britain at times, they had to bear the expenses of shipping and marketing their staples. These costs usually more than overcame the South's favorable balance of trade with the result that these colonies suffered from chronic indebtedness.

The Trade of the Southern Colonies. The colonies south of Pennsylvania traded mainly with England, exporting tobacco, rice, indigo, and naval stores, and importing hardware, dry-goods, and furniture. Because of the direct exchange between the southern colonies and Great Britain, these colonies were valued very highly by the British. Merchant creditors found even the planters' indebtedness profitable, so heavy were the interest charges.

The Trade of the Northern Colonies. The northern colonies had a more diverse commercial history. Although they exported some naval stores, metals, furs, and lumber to England, their staples were not needed in the mother country. In fact, these colonies competed with England in some ways and were less desirable parts of the mercantile empire than the southern provinces.

Although they wanted English manufactures, the colonies north of Maryland could not pay for them directly with exports to England. Consequently, the staples—grain, foodstuffs, fish, and lumber—were shipped to the West Indies and to southern Europe. There cargoes were taken on which could be sold in England to pay for colonial imports of manufactures. Examples of triangular trades are shown in the accompanying diagrams.

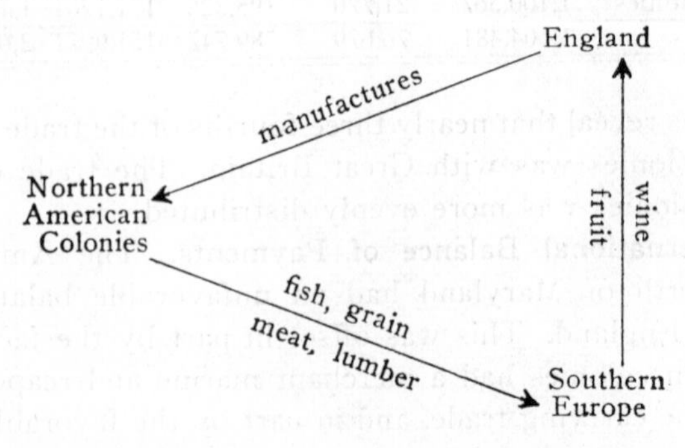

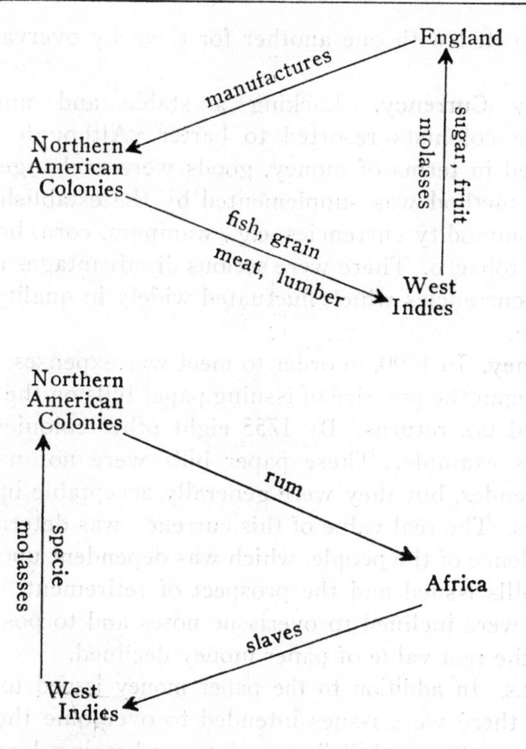

The most famous triangular trade is the last one diagrammed. Much of it was illegally carried on with the French and Spanish West Indies as the colonial merchants evaded the heavy duty on imports of foreign molasses. This trade was vital to the New England economy, and the attempt to realize a revenue from it began the opposition to British policy which culminated in the American Revolution.

COLONIAL CURRENCY

Colonial commerce was hindered by the absence of an adequate medium of exchange. It was impossible to establish a gold and silver currency because the colonists did not have supplies of these metals and could not obtain enough of them through foreign trade. Some Spanish and Portuguese coins made their way into the English colonies. The value of these coins in terms of goods or paper money varied because the colonies competed with one another for them by overvaluing this specie.

Commodity Currency. Lacking a stable and uniform currency, the colonists resorted to barter. Although value was expressed in terms of money, goods were exchanged for goods. This method was supplemented by the establishment of various commodity currencies, e.g., wampum, corn, beaver, rice, tar, and tobacco. There were serious disadvantages in the use of these currencies which fluctuated widely in quality and market value.

Paper Money. In 1690, in order to meet war expenses, Massachusetts began the practice of issuing paper bills on the basis of anticipated tax returns. By 1755 eight other colonies had followed this example. These paper bills were not usually made legal tender, but they were generally acceptable in payment of taxes. The real value of this currency was determined by the confidence of the people, which was dependent upon the number of bills issued and the prospect of retirement. Since the colonies were inclined to overissue notes and to postpone repayment, the real value of paper money declined.

LOAN BILLS. In addition to the paper money issued to meet fiscal needs, there were issues intended to overcome the currency shortage. "Loan bills" were interest-bearing loans by colonial governments to individuals on the security of land and property. These issues were generally limited in extent. South Carolina established the first public loan bank in 1712; several other colonies followed suit.

LAND BANKS. These were private organizations that issued another kind of paper money, similar in purpose and nature to the public "loan bills." They were interest-bearing notes, repayable over a period of years, issued on the security of land mortgages. Schemes of this sort were attempted in New Hampshire, Connecticut, South Carolina, and Massachusetts. The struggles between creditors and debtors caused Parliament to forbid the establishment of such "banks" in the colonies. In 1751 Parliament prohibited the further issuance of bills of credit in New England; this prohibition was extended to the rest of the colonies in 1764. Notwithstanding the soundness of these restrictions in view of colonial abuses of paper money in the past, the Americans regarded these English measures as a hardship and a violation of rights.

REVIEW QUESTIONS

1. Compare modes of travel in colonial America.
2. What were the chief difficulties of trade in the colonial period?
3. Explain the mercantile regulations as they affected colonial trade.
4. Why did the English consider the southern colonies more valuable than the northern colonies?
5. Why did the triangular trades develop?
6. Was the international balance of payments favorable or unfavorable to the northern colonies? To the southern colonies?
7. Why were commodity currencies adopted by the colonists? How satisfactory were these currencies?
8. How successful were colonial experiments with paper money? With "loan bills"? With "land banks"?

6

ECONOMIC ASPECTS OF THE REVOLUTIONARY PERIOD

The Revolution was not only a war for American independence but also a domestic struggle for political and economic control. In the latter aspect the Revolution appears as a democratic movement for greater freedom and individualism: the attainment of broader political responsibility was one phase; the elimination of economic privilege and the creation of new economic opportunities was another. The spirit of individualism and the love of freedom that characterized the Revolution hindered cooperation in the war effort and in the establishment of a new government.

IMPERIAL CONTROVERSY, 1760-1776

In the period 1760 to 1776, there developed a crisis in the British Empire, the outcomes of which were civil war and American independence. Prior to 1760 there was little British interference in colonial affairs, and there was comparatively free trade within the empire. The attempted solution of problems created by the French and Indian War ended the period of neglect and revealed a sharp conflict between English and colonial interests. The revitalization of the mercantile system, which threatened the economic security of the northern colonies, and the imposition of political controls, which menaced the virtual self-government of all the colonies, made the American Revolution inevitable.

Results of French and Indian War. The French and Indian War, concluded in 1763, was the last of a long series of wars fought by England and France for control of eastern North America. The peace of 1763 eliminated France from North America: the land between the Appalachians and the Mississippi, and Canada were ceded to England; Louisiana was ceded to Spain. At the same time Spain ceded Florida to England.

British Colonial Policy. In the middle of the eighteenth century a new colonial policy was begun. The British began to regard their empire as something more than a mercantile system: they developed a "territorial" and administrative concept of empire. The French and Indian War created new problems: a much larger geographic area had to be administered; there was a serious Indian menace; the expenses of war and defense were substantial. The Proclamation of 1763, forbidding land grants and settlement west of the Appalachian Mountains, attempted to solve the problem of the western lands, but produced a loud protest from the colonists. The British also determined to enforce the navigation laws and to collect a colonial revenue. Therefore new administrative machinery was provided, and a series of revenue laws was passed. It was unfortunate for the British that these measures were attempted during a postwar period of depression.

New Revenue Measures. The Sugar Act (1764) lowered the import duty on foreign molasses, but provided for the strict enforcement of the law. This measure also imposed duties on sugar, wines, indigo, silks and coffee. The colonists protested that the law was economically inexpedient, and in 1766 the molasses duty was modified. The Stamp Act (1765) levied taxes on legal papers, newspapers, pamphlets and other documents. Although the tax was not a heavy burden, it affected many people and produced a united colonial protest. The Townshend Acts (1767) provided new machinery for the enforcement of the navigation laws and imposed duties on certain English manufactures and tea imported by the Americans.

Colonial Opposition. Opposition to the new colonial policy proceeded from economic protests to constitutional arguments. Northern merchants, displeased with the Sugar Act and the enforcement of the navigation laws, emphasized the economic inexpedience of the new policy. They enlisted the aid of the poorer and more radical elements of society, which were eager to gain political and economic influence. When the radicals obtained control of the opposition movement, it became more violent and progressively denied the political authority of the mother country over the colonies. With this turn of events many of the merchants and upper classes deserted the revolutionary party.

British Concessions. When the colonists violently disobeyed the revenue laws and resorted to nonimportation and nonconsumption schemes, Parliament yielded and repealed the obnoxious measures—the Stamp Act in 1766 and the Townshend Acts in 1770. Under no circumstances, however, would Parliament relinquish its right to tax the colonies.

Tea Act, 1773. A period of quiet followed 1770, but colonial opposition was revived when Parliament passed the Tea Act of 1773. This law sought to save the East India Company from bankruptcy by giving it a virtual monopoly in the colonial tea trade. Americans regarded the Tea Act as an ominous measure even though it enabled them to buy tea more cheaply. The most extreme example of the widespread opposition to the act was the Boston Tea Party.

Coercion and Revolution. When the British decided to punish the Bostonians by closing the port, sending troops there, and altering the charter of Massachusetts, a Continental Congress was called to unite the colonial resistance. The Congress demanded that the colonists' grievances be redressed, and to enforce the demand it organized the "continental association," a plan of economic coercion. The opposition of Massachusetts patriots to the altered government and the military occupation of Boston led to violence in early 1775. Growing sentiment in favor of a separation from England defeated efforts at reconciliation, and the colonists declared their independence, July 4, 1776.

ECONOMIC PROBLEMS OF THE WAR

The chief economic problems of the war were: (1) procuring war supplies, (2) financing the war, and (3) supplying civilian needs. Once independence was achieved, Americans had to wrestle with many old problems and some new ones: economic dislocations followed the war; the new nation had to reconcile liberty and order, localism and central authority.

Conflicting Interests. The necessity of establishing a new political system made the solution of economic problems the more difficult. Differences in economic interests and social conditions bred intercolonial rivalries: e.g., the outlooks of the New England people and southerners differed greatly. Within some colonies and regions there were sharp sectional antagonisms: e.g., the clash of the tidewater aristocrats and the small farmers of the interior in the South; and the conflict of eastern and western people in Massachusetts, which later assumed violent form as Shays' Rebellion.

REVOLUTIONISTS. The strength of the revolutionary party was in the lower and middle classes, but some outstanding figures of the upper classes were revolutionists. The patriot party included the following important elements: (1) *Southern planters.* They disliked the domination of their trade by merchant creditors, who charged high interest rates, obtained high prices for imported manufactures, and paid poorly for staple crops. The West, a new area of investment for them, was closed by the Proclamation of 1763. The planters were strong believers in the sanctity of private property. (2) *Merchants.* They were displeased with restraints on commerce and exclusion from western land speculation. (3) *Small farmers.* The curtailment of trade meant lower prices for farm surpluses, and the Proclamation of 1763 closed the frontier. (4) *Town workers.* Unprivileged laborers were oppressed by an upper class which was generally supported by the British government. Angered by political and social discrimination against them, and made to believe that British policy was largely responsible, the laborers were ardent revolutionists.

LOYALISTS. In 1776 probably one-third of the Americans were loyal to Great Britain. Some Tories joined the British army, and many fled from their American homes to safer places. Among the loyalists were the following: (1) crown officials and friends, who were dependent upon English support for their positions; (2) Anglican clergy, who enjoyed special positions in some colonies; (3) proprietary interests in Pennsylvania and Maryland, whose wealth and privileged positions depended on the English connections; (4) a minority of southern planters, who feared the prospect of debtor laws and mob rule; (5) merchants, who dared not risk their extensive interests, and who were opposed to radicalism.

POLITICAL WEAKNESS. Fear of central authority and local patriotisms resulted in the establishment of a loose federal union under the Articles of Confederation, which seemed more like an international agreement amongst sovereign states than a workable government. The Continental Congress conducted the war in the name of all the states, but it had very little actual authority. The states were loath to give Congress the power to tax, so the central government was dependent upon requisitions and loans for support. Congress also found it impossible to maintain financial and economic regularity. Because of its deplorable impotence, the first United States government commanded little respect from other powers.

Supplies for the Army. The task of supplying the colonial armies was difficult because (1) colonial ability to produce was in itself limited, and (2) the political organization was inadequate. Arms and ammunition were not produced in sufficient quantity in the colonies, and, until 1778, nearly nine-tenths of the powder used by the Americans was obtained abroad. The colonial output of guns, gun powder, and iron products increased but was unable to meet the increased demand of wartime. Army clothing had to be imported because the colonial production of wool was insufficient. Some foodstuffs such as sugar, molasses, and tea were scarce, but other foods were plentiful. Another phase of the problem was the distribution of supplies, made difficult by poor transportation facilities and the lack of a strong central government.

Foreign Aid. Hatred of England was the most important factor causing foreign powers to aid the American revolutionists. Before the war ended, France, Holland, and Spain were at war with England: the French, eager to avenge their humiliating defeat in the French and Indian War, concluded a military alliance with the United States in 1778; the Spanish, eager to regain Gibraltar, declared war on England in 1779; the Dutch, who engaged in supplying the Americans, were so great a menace that England declared war on Holland in 1780.

French aid was the most important and vital to the success of the Revolution: France supplied not only arms, ammunition, and other war materials, but also financial help; and French military and naval aid proved a deciding factor in the outcome of the war.

Financing of the War. Although the cost of the war to the United States was only about 100 million dollars in terms of gold, the Congress had great difficulty in raising that sum. While it had authority to borrow money, Congress was not empowered to tax; soon the credit of the United States failed, and it was hard to get loans. Robert Morris, the Superintendent of Finance near the end of the war, struggled in vain to establish the credit of the government and to create a national revenue. The main ways of paying for the war were by (1) foreign loans, (2) domestic loans, (3) requisitions on states, and (4) the issuance of fiat money.

LOANS. Congress was able to borrow 7.8 million dollars in gold abroad, 6.3 million from France, the remainder from Holland and Spain. With most of this the government bought supplies in Europe, but it used some to pay the interest charged on the American debt. At home, Congress raised about 11 million dollars through loans. The scarcity of liquid capital, the doubt that the colonists could win the war, and the lack of a banking system to organize credit made domestic borrowing difficult.

REQUISITIONS AND TAXATION. Through requisitions on the states, Congress obtained only 5.7 million dollars in gold. The states either ignored the requests of Congress or met them only in part. Although the states could tax, they hesitated to do so because taxes are always distasteful and the memory of English taxation was still fresh. At first the states raised money by the sale of notes and the issue of paper money; rapid depreciation and the loss of credit resulted. From 1777 on, taxes were levied generally, but the amount obtained was small. Another means by which some states raised considerable money was through the confiscation of Tory property.

PAPER MONEY. Fiat money accounted for 41 million dollars of the central government's income in terms of gold. Between June, 1775, and November, 1779, Congress authorized the issuance of 191 million dollars in paper currency. To maintain the value of this money, Congress pledged its faith and asked the States to provide the means for redemption. This suggestion was ignored, however, and as the issues increased, the "Continentals" depreciated badly. Congress did not declare its notes legal tender, but asked the states to penalize persons who refused to accept them. Most states complied, decreeing that refusal constituted extinguishment of the debt. Despite the legal tender acts, price-fixing, and the retirement of some bills, the "Continentals" were devaluated to the extent of 500-1,000 to 1 in terms of specie in 1781.

In addition to Congressional issues of paper money, eleven states issued nearly 250 million dollars in bills of credit, the worst offender being Virginia, with 128 million. These issues depreciated sharply, also. Another factor adding to the currency confusion was the deliberate and competitive devaluation of bills by states that wanted to attract foreign specie.

ECONOMIC ACTIVITY IN WARTIME

The civilian population did not suffer from a lack of the necessities of life during the Revolution. This was true because the demands of the army on American production were not great, and the country was to a large extent self-sufficient. There was indeed an appearance of luxury and extravagance, for people anxiously exchanged depreciating paper money for goods. The chaotic currency caused hardship for some; creditors suffered through payment in depreciated money; laborers had to accept a lower standard of living because wages did not rise so quickly as prices. The same factors produced benefits for others: debtors gained by rising prices; the stimulus of war permitted great profits in some lines of agriculture, industry, and commerce.

Agriculture. There were some minor raids and depredations, but war did not greatly impede agriculture. The most serious threat was the fact that the British blockade and control of the leading seaports would interfere with the export of farm staples. Agriculture was not seriously upset, however, for the army's need for foodstuffs was great, and there were some exports despite the efforts of the British navy.

Industry. American manufacturing increased during the

Revolutionary period. Before 1775 the non-importation schemes acted as a protective tariff, and in wartime there was an unusual demand for manufactures at the very time that foreign supplies were likely to be shut off. Industries which made the most progress were those producing arms, ammunition, and textiles. There was official encouragement of the production of war materials: Rhode Island and Massachusetts offered bounties for gunpowder, Connecticut for gunlocks; and in 1778 Congress established a plant at Springfield where cannon were cast. Despite production for government needs, the manufacture of iron declined. Both household and factory textile manufacturing increased during the war, and several states granted subsidies and bounties for the production of wool. Other industries which made some progress at this time were those manufacturing salt, paper, glass, and pottery.

Commerce. With the assertion of American independence, commerce was encouraged in several ways: British mercantile restrictions were ended; colonial ports were thrown open to the world; privateering was encouraged. But war had detrimental effects, too: protection was no longer provided by the British navy; the Atlantic coast was blockaded, and from 1776 to 1779 the British seized 570 vessels.

New Trade. While commerce with British ports was forbidden, the Dutch, French, and Spanish were eager to trade in the new market. Despite the blockade, there was an adequate supply of European products by 1777. Imports included not only war supplies but also many luxury items. In return the Americans exported mainly tobacco, grain, flour, and rice.

Privateers. Perhaps 90,000 Americans were engaged in privateering, which rivalled legitimate commerce in these years. While risks were great, the prospect of profit and adventure lured men into this business. The number of seizures made is not known, but it was considerable. Constant losses at the hands of privateers caused English merchants to demand an early end to the war.

THE CRITICAL PERIOD, 1783-1789

Following the conclusion of the Treaty of Paris (1783) there began a critical period, during which the new nation struggled with the problems of postwar adjustments and reorganization.

Treaty of Paris, 1783. The treaty of peace with England assured American independence, and the United States was granted all the territory east of the Mississippi River between Canada and Florida. The British did not, however, evacuate the old northwest until 1795. The treaty gave Americans the right to navigate the Mississippi, but this question caused difficulty because Spain controlled the mouth of the river. Creditors were to meet no impediment in the collection of debts, and Congress agreed to "recommend" to the states that confiscated loyalist property be restored or payment made for it. The United States obtained fishing rights within British territorial waters in the North Atlantic, but the treaty did not include any commercial arrangement between the two states.

Effects of Peace. The return of peace brought hardship to some Americans. As the demand for goods declined, prices dropped, and debtors suffered. A flood of imports from Europe further depressed prices, and drew off whatever specie had accumulated during the war. Debtors called for the reduction or cancellation of debts and the issuance of paper money. Farmers in general suffered from falling prices, but the southern producers of staples benefited from a strong foreign demand. Some industries that had developed during the war now had difficulty: the demand for war supplies decreased; British imports competed with domestic goods.

Postwar Reorganization. Foremost among the postwar problems confronting the young republic was that of reconciling local sovereignty and central authority so as to promote general welfare and raise the prestige of the United States. It was also necessary to restrain to a certain extent the individualism and radicalism of the age in the interest of security and order. This postwar period was not so critical as historians, who overemphasized the political confusion of the time, once believed. While parts of the economy suffered a depression, other elements were active and expanding. There was a demand for capital for the organization of land, turnpike, canal, and manufacturing companies.

COMMERCE. Foreign trade underwent the most complete reorganization. Immediate losses resulted from the prohibition of trade with the British West Indies, the closing of British markets to some American exports, and the seizure of the African slave trade by others. Factors which offset these losses to some extent were direct exports to Europe, the continuance of some British bounties for American goods, the evasion of the law restricting trade with the British West Indies, the opening of the French West Indies to Americans in 1784, the beginning of trade in the Far East, and commercial treaties with Holland, Prussia, and Sweden.

FINANCIAL COLLAPSE. The unwillingness of the states to establish a source of national revenue threatened to lead the United States to bankruptcy. Requisitions on states were poorly met, and foreign loans yielded only 2.3 million dollars. The receipts of the federal government were insufficient to meet all current obligations and the arrears of interest on the debt rose from 3.1 million dollars in 1783 to 11.4 million in 1789. The weakness of the federal financial structure caused many to demand a new government.

PAPER MONEY. Seven states issued paper money, looking for an easy way to pay heavy obligations, and trying to stimulate business by raising prices. The efforts of some states to enforce the acceptance of depreciated paper money proved ineffective.

The Movement for a New Government. Political confusion and interstate rivalry gave impetus to the movement for a new government.

POLITICAL CONFUSION. Under the Articles of Confederation the United States was a loose union of virtually independent states. The impotence of Congress was deplorable. Unable to tax, Congress relied upon requisitions and loans for financial support. Another serious weakness was the lack of power to regulate domestic and foreign commerce. When England refused to conclude a commercial treaty with the United States, ten of the states retaliated with tonnage duties on British ships or tariffs on British goods. Since these regulations were not uniform, and there were still some free American ports, British goods continued to come in.

INTERSTATE RIVALRY. Each state had individual ambitions and

problems, and many disputes arose. States conducted petty commercial wars against each other, levying duties and placing embargoes on the goods of rivals.

Protection of Economic Interests. Although political weakness was not responsible for the economic conditions after the war, those persons whose economic interests were endangered by political confusion led the movement for a new constitution. The threat to property interests from debtors' demands for stay laws and for paper money produced an anxious clamor from owners of capital. To many Shays' Rebellion in Massachusetts, 1786-1787, during which farmers refused to let courts sit to judge them for indebtedness, was a very ominous event. Groups that agitated for a stronger government included (1) owners of Continental paper money, bonds, and certificates of indebtedness, (2) merchants and manufacturers, who wanted protection against foreign discrimination, (3) domestic merchants, who desired a stable currency and unrestricted interstate commerce, and (4) land speculators, who believed that the value of their holdings would be increased.

THE CONSTITUTIONAL CONVENTION. After several preliminary meetings for the purpose of amending the Articles of Confederation, the Constitutional Convention met in Philadelphia from May to September, 1787, and drew up the Constitution. Revolutionary radicals were conspicuous by their absence, and over half the delegates were either investors or speculators in public securities. Although there were some conflicting interests that had to be compromised, the delegates were largely in agreement on fundamental economic questions. The dominant purpose of the Convention was the establishment of a government that would safeguard mercantile and agrarian capitalism.

A STRONGER UNION. The completed Constitution, which went into effect in March, 1789, provided for a much stronger union than the Articles of Confederation. The Constitution was declared the "supreme law of the land," and an effective central government was established.

Economic Provisions of the Constitution. The glaring economic weaknesses of the Articles of Confederation were removed. Especially noteworthy were the powers given the central government over commerce, taxation, and currency.

COMMERCE. Congress was given authority to regulate both foreign and interstate commerce. Import duties were to be uniform throughout the United States, and no export duties were to be levied. The latter provision was intended to protect exporters of staples. The government was not to interfere with the slave trade for twenty years, and the import duty was not to exceed ten dollars per slave. To regularize and protect commerce, Congress was empowered to determine weights and measures, to establish a postal service, and to provide uniform bankruptcy laws.

TAXATION. Congress was given authority "to lay and collect Taxes, Duties, Imports, and Excises, to pay the Debts and provide for the common Defense and general Welfare." Direct taxation could be levied on the basis of population, not on property. This provision was to protect those who feared that the mass of people would try to put the burden of federal support on the landholders. The House of Representatives, more democratically elected than the Senate, was given the sole authority to originate revenue laws.

CURRENCY. Congress was given the sole authority to coin money and determine its value, and to punish counterfeiting. The states were forbidden to coin money or issue bills of credit; or to declare anything but gold and silver legal tender; or to pass laws impairing the obligation of contracts.

REVIEW QUESTIONS

1. What were the results of the French and Indian War?
2. What were the nature and purposes of British colonial policy from 1760 to 1776? Why did the colonists oppose this policy?
3. To what extent was the Revolution the result of conflict between rival economic interests?
4. What were the main economic problems of the war?
5. How did political weaknesses contribute to the problem of waging war? The problems of postwar reorganization?
6. For what economic reasons were some Americans revolutionists and others loyalists?
7. Discuss the ways in which the Revolution was financed.
8. What were the effects of paper money issues?
9. What effects did the war have on agriculture? Industry? Commerce?

10. What were the economic provisions of the Treaty of Paris, 1783?
11. What effect did peace have on the American economy?
12. What economic interests were eager to have a strong federal government? Why?
13. In what ways was the Constitution intended to promote a more stable economy?

7

PUBLIC FINANCE AND FISCAL POLICY, 1789 TO 1860

The interests that had drawn up the Constitution also dominated the new government of the United States. Measures which were adopted were intended to safeguard and promote commercial, financial, and landed interests.

FEDERALIST FINANCE

The problem of creating a national revenue was the first one approached by the new government. No issue was more pressing: credit had to be re-established, and the debt retired; current expenses had to be met. Alexander Hamilton, the first Secretary of the Treasury, proposed policies which, when adopted, put the United States on a firm financial basis.

Revenue Measures. On July 4, 1789, the first tariff was passed. Although it was mainly a revenue measure with the low average rate of 8½ per cent, it afforded some protection to American producers. The tariff was raised in 1790, 1792, and 1794. Hamilton advocated excise taxes to obtain additional income and also to display federal authority. The revenue raised was not great, and the tax on whiskey evoked complaints from western Pennsylvanians. The "Whiskey Rebellion" of 1794 was suppressed, however, and the federal authority upheld. Jefferson's administration finally repealed the whiskey tax in 1802.

Funding of the Old Debt. Hamilton's "Report on the Public Credit" (1790) analyzed the public debt outstanding in December, 1789, as follows:

Foreign debt	$11,710,379
Domestic debt	40,414,086
State debts of Revolutionary origin (estimate)	25,000,000
Total public debt	$77,124,465

Hamilton proposed (1) that the federal government assume all of this public debt, (2) that new bonds be issued in place of older issues, and (3) that provision for interest payment and retirement of the debt be made.

CONFLICTING INTERESTS. Although there was no objection to the payment of the foreign debt, there was controversy over the terms of the assumption of the old domestic debt. Some thought it unnecessary to pay the long arrearages of interest, amounting to 13 million dollars, but Hamilton argued that payment of the interest charges was necessary to secure the nation's credit. Some opposed redemption of the debt at full specie value because it was felt that speculators rather than the original creditors of the Continental and Confederation governments would benefit. Hamilton contended that the security of transfer was an important characteristic of the national debt and was essential to the establishment of public credit. The Funding Act of 1790 incorporated the Hamiltonian proposals.

ASSUMPTION OF STATE DEBTS. Hamilton proposed that the federal government assume state debts that had been incurred during the Revolution. Opposition to this proposal was based on two facts: (1) some states, whose debts were large, would be favored at the expense of others; (2) speculators, rather than the original holders of depreciated securities, would benefit. Hamilton's policy prevailed.

Federalist Debt Policy. The debt policy of the Federalists may be summarized as follows.

FOREIGN DEBT. Obligations in this category were met for the first few years through new loans from the Dutch which totaled 9.4 million dollars in the 1790's. Repayment of the new obligation was not to start until 1802. Negotiations for the settlement of the old Revolutionary debt owed France continued until 1795 when France accepted American bonds redeemable between 1807 and 1815 for the amount due.

DOMESTIC DEBT. It was expected that the debt would be steadily paid off from surplus revenue. Although new revenues were adopted, the Federalists could not balance the budget or reduce the debt. They had to resort to new loans. On January 1, 1801, the national debt was 7.5 million dollars larger than in 1791.

SHORT-TERM LOANS. Loans were obtained at first from the Bank of New York and the Bank of North America. Although repaid quickly, these loans were replaced by others. The borrowings from the Bank of the United States, chartered in 1791, reached a high of 6.2 million in 1796.

PURCHASE FUND. In order that the value of the federal stock should be maintained, the Funding Act of 1790 provided that a Purchase Fund be created and used to purchase stock if it fell below par value. This operated effectively until 1795 when it ceased to function. New issues were sold at a discount until the crisis of 1798 with France when issues were accepted readily at par.

RETIREMENT. In 1795 the Purchase Fund was transformed into a Sinking Fund which very slowly but systematically began to retire the debt. Because of the slow rate of retirement and the cessation of operation of the Purchase Fund, government issues fell off badly until 1798 when three loans were floated more successfully.

Summary of Federalist Finance. The Federalist policies were somewhat overambitious for the existing economy of the United States. In 1800 nearly one-third of the budget was devoted to interest charges on the national debt, and over one-half to defense expenditures. The cautious policies followed by the Jeffersonians in the next few years proved to be a salutary reaction to Federalist finance.

JEFFERSONIAN FINANCE

Thomas Jefferson, who became president in 1801, had views very different from those of Hamilton. He favored an agrarian society of small landowners and believed in a public policy of laissez-faire. He opposed Hamilton's ideal of a strong federal government which would foster industrialism.

Jefferson's Financial Policies. Policies which characterized the finances of the nation during the next decade were (1) economy in government, (2) tax reduction, and (3) rapid retirement of the national debt. Despite their belief in these policies, Jefferson and his followers, because of the necessities of the times, took steps which greatly strengthened the national government and encouraged industrialism.

Expenditures. Albert Gallatin, Secretary of the Treasury, set out to reduce government expenditures, primarily by cutting military expenses. Although this policy of retrenchment and extreme economy succeeded for a time, various exigencies during this period as well as new government undertakings, such as the Louisiana Purchase and internal improvements, eventually blocked the program.

Income and Debt Policy. In 1802 the entire internal revenue system developed by the Federalists was repealed. Although Gallatin feared the loss of revenue, Jefferson proposed that the government obtain its income exclusively from the tariff (increased in 1804) and the proceeds of land sales. Prosperous trade (except in 1809 and 1810) brought in a large revenue, and the income from land sales also increased sharply. As a result there were annual surpluses in the period 1801-1811 (except in the year 1809) which permitted the reduction of the public debt from 80.7 million dollars in 1801 to 45.2 million in 1811.

War of 1812. During the war tariff receipts fell off and the government was unable to meet increased expenses. Loans were floated only with difficulty and at discounts. Also, an internal revenue system, begun in 1813, proved ineffective. The result was that the public debt rose from 45.2 million dollars on January 1, 1812, to 119.6 million on September 30, 1815.

THE PERIOD FROM THE WAR OF 1812 TO THE CIVIL WAR

In 18 of the 21 years from 1815 to 1836 there were Treasury surpluses. The tariff, the main source of revenue, was raised several times, not for revenue purposes but for the protection of American industry. As a result of the protest of the South against the tariff, rates were lowered in the 1830's and customs receipts were reduced. At this time, however, revenue from land sales increased sharply from only 1.5 million dollars in 1829 to 24.9 million in 1836. Total federal receipts which were 24.8 million dollars in 1829 rose to 50.8 in 1836. In the same period the public debt was reduced from 48.6 million to 1.9 million dollars.

Panic of 1837. In 1836 Congress provided for the distribution of the Treasury surplus to the states in quarterly installments. This policy was abandoned after three payments because receipts declined sharply in 1837. In the period of depression, 1837 to 1843, there were deficits in every year except 1839, and the debt rose from 4.9 million dollars in 1837 to 27.2 million in 1843. The demand for protection as well as the need for revenue resulted in the adoption of higher tariff rates in 1842.

The Period 1843 to 1860. Following the panic of 1837 the nation enjoyed prosperity until the crisis of 1857. There were deficits in the period of the Mexican War, 1847-1849, but in the 1850's there were surpluses for eight successive years. The national debt, which had jumped from 16.8 million dollars in 1846 to 68.3 million in 1851, was reduced to 28.7 million dollars in 1857. Growing customs receipts, reaching a high point of 64.2 million dollars in 1854, were supplemented by the substantial proceeds of land sales in the middle of the decade. In 1857 there occurred a serious financial crisis and industrial depression, and there began a series of deficits which lasted until after the Civil War.

REVIEW QUESTIONS

1. Explain the measures taken by Alexander Hamilton to restore the credit of the United States.
2. Indicate how the national debt was funded by the Federalists. Why was there opposition to this program?
3. What progress did the Federalists make in retiring the national debt?
4. What steps were taken by the Federalists to maintain the value of government securities?
5. What policies characterized Jeffersonian finance?
6. How successful were the Jeffersonians in retiring the national debt?
7. What financial difficulties were encountered in the War of 1812?
8. What were the most important sources of revenue in the period after the War of 1812?
9. Indicate generally how the size of the national debt fluctuated in the period from the War of 1812 to the Civil War.

8

AGRICULTURE BEFORE 1860

During the period 1789 to 1860, agriculture continued to be the most important economic activity of the American people. Agricultural productivity greatly increased, and the area of cultivation was extended into the fertile Mississippi Valley. In these years there were many technical improvements and advances in scientific farming. The development of transportation facilities aided marketing and permitted agricultural specialization.

TECHNICAL PROGRESS AND SCIENTIFIC FARMING

Technical progress in agriculture was characterized by the development of improved implements, scientific techniques, and increased agricultural knowledge.

Improved Implements. In the period 1820-1860 there was a great deal of agricultural experimentation and many new farm machines were developed. The use of new implements, made of iron and steel instead of wood, lightened or displaced labor, and permitted greater productivity.

The Plow. Before 1820 plows were made of wood, sheathed in part with iron, and they were clumsy and inefficient. As early as 1797 Charles Newbold of New Jersey patented a one-piece cast-iron plow which performed successfully, but was not popular because of the rapid wear of the metal. In the early 1800's David Peacock developed cast-iron plows of three pieces which were more acceptable. Jethro Wood patented a plow in 1819 which was of improved shape, had a steel-tipped share, and was made of standardized, replaceable parts. In 1847 John

Deere of Illinois built the first all-steel plow, a tool far superior to all previous plows, which was an immediate success.

REAPERS. In the 1830's reapers were patented by Obed Hussey of Maryland and Cyrus McCormick of Virginia. Hussey's reapers were not perfected and so failed of adoption, but McCormick successfully developed, improved, and sold his machine. He established a plant at Chicago which made large numbers of reapers available to farmers. By 1860 about 100,000 were in operation and during the Civil War another 250,000 came into use.

THE COTTON GIN. Eli Whitney's invention in 1793 solved the problem of separating seeds from cotton fiber. It was a simple device, easily built, which at first produced about 50 pounds of cotton a day. Improvements and the introduction of horsepower greatly increased the daily output of the cotton gin. One author has commented that the cotton gin "was the first important agricultural invention produced in this country, and its significance in the development of American economic life is second to that of no other technological invention."[1]

OTHER INVENTIONS. This period also produced such implements as the thresher, the horsehay-rake, the tedder, seed drills for sowing wheat, and corn planters and cultivators.

Scientific Techniques. Because there was an abundance of land, scientific agriculture came to America slowly. After the Revolution, however, wealthy planters became interested in improved methods of farming, and in the early nineteenth century there was much experimentation with new crops and improved livestock. The interest in new crops resulted in the introduction of the mulberry plant, Chinese sorghum, alfalfa, and numerous varieties of old staples. Many of these experiments failed, but some were of economic significance. Also, in this period, methods of preserving and renewing the fertility of the soil were widely adopted: (1) crop rotation, (2) cultivation of legumes, (3) better use of fertilizers, and (4) control of erosion.

Agricultural Knowledge. The dissemination of information concerning new agricultural methods, crops, and implements

[1] Clarence H. Danhof, *The Growth of the American Economy,* ed. by H. F. Williamson (New York, 1951), p. 133.

was facilitated by the following: (1) *Agricultural societies.* (Washington and Franklin were members of the Philadelphia Society for Promoting Agriculture.) (2) *Agricultural fairs.* (3) *Farm literature.* This began importantly with the establishment of *The American Farmer* at Baltimore in 1819. (4) *Agricultural schools.* The first school devoted mainly to agricultural instruction was the Gardiner Lyceum, founded at Gardiner, Maine, in 1822. State colleges were founded in the 1850's in Michigan, Pennsylvania, and Maryland. (5) *Federal aid.* Beginning in 1839, small Congressional appropriations were made to promote agricultural investigations. In 1862 a Bureau of Agriculture was established. The Morrill Act of 1862 provided for grants of public land to states for the purpose of founding schools for instruction in agriculture, mechanical arts, and military science.

AGRICULTURAL SECTIONALISM AND SPECIALIZATION

In the first half of the nineteenth century, the American people moved into the great interior of North America, one of the most fertile regions in the world.

Westward Expansion. Improved transportation facilities gave the western farmers an outlet for their agricultural products and permitted specialization in grains and meat. The easy availability of land and the fever of land speculation discouraged scientific agriculture and resulted in soil exhaustion. Eastern farmers (faced with this competition) were forced to turn to specialized production, such as dairying, market gardening, and fruit raising.

Old Northwest. The region between the Ohio River and the Great Lakes, extending westward into the prairies beyond the Mississippi, was opened to cultivation in the first half of the nineteenth century. This area was found to be extremely fertile, free of rocks and easily cultivated. The Great Lakes and the Mississippi River system provided fine natural trade routes, which were supplemented by the Cumberland Road, the Erie Canal, the Pennsylvania Canal, and, after 1840, the railroads.

The production of grain was the most important part of western agriculture. At first, when marketing was difficult, corn was used mainly for feeding livestock or for making whiskey. With the further development of transportation, cereal production increased, and by the middle of the century there was considerable export to England.

Livestock production was also important in the old northwest. Westerners drove herds of hogs and cattle eastward annually for marketing. Primitive meat-packing began before 1820; until about 1860, Cincinnati was the foremost center of this activity.

The East. In New England, an agricultural revolution occurred during the first half of the nineteenth century as self-sufficiency gave way to specialization. Growing urban centers became a market for local farm products: root crops, corn, beef and wool. The development of railroads (and competition from western grain and meat) forced another reorganization of New England agriculture. The production of beef and pork declined while dairying, truck gardening, and tobacco raising increased. Similar developments took place in the Middle Atlantic states, even though this area was in a better position than New England to compete with western agriculture.

The South. In the colonial period, the South developed the production of rice, tobacco, indigo; after the Revolution, southern agriculture was dominated by cotton cultivation. There was little cotton grown before the Revolution because of the lack of a market, the greater profit in tobacco, and the difficulty of separating seeds from cotton fiber. Between 1790 and 1830, a revolution occurred in southern agriculture: cotton production rose from about 5.2 million to 507.2 million pounds annually. This increase is attributable to (1) technological advances, (2) the development of a market, (3) damage to the market for rice and indigo upon our separation from England, and (4) the depletion of tobacco lands.

THE SHIFTING SCENE OF COTTON CULTURE. In 1820 Georgia and South Carolina raised over one-half of the cotton produced in the United States. In 1850 the leading producers ranked as follows: Alabama, Georgia, Mississippi, South Carolina. In 1860, Mississippi, Alabama, and Louisiana raised over one-half of the total crop; the production of Texas surpassed that of South Carolina. Southern cities reflected this change: Charleston and Savannah declined while Memphis, Mobile, and New

Orleans increased in importance. By 1860 New Orleans handled about one-half of the total cotton crop.

SLAVERY. The increase in cotton production resulted in the firm establishment of slavery: the numbers of slaves rose from 698,000 in 1790 to about 4,500,000 in 1860. The South's attitude toward slavery changed from one of apology in the time of the Revolution to one of positive defense by 1830. Prices for slaves went up rapidly with the increased demand for them: before 1790, about $300; 1830, about $800; 1850-1860, from $1,200 to $2,000.

OTHER ASPECTS OF SOUTHERN AGRICULTURE. Tobacco was the leading staple of the colonial period, and in 1800 it was still the most valuable United States export. Thereafter it declined in importance until about 1840 when production increased with the introduction of a new species and an improved method of curing. In 1860 Virginia was the greatest producer of tobacco, but the total production of the Mississippi Valley states was greater than the production of the Atlantic states.

Sugar cane production was sizable in Louisiana, and in the decade, 1850-1860, the average annual production was 280,000 hogsheads. In 1860 at least 180,000 slaves were employed in this enterprise. Rice production, largely in South Carolina and Georgia, tripled between 1820 and 1850. Peculiar problems attended this type of agriculture: (1) only certain swampy lands could be used; (2) scientific farming was necessary for the maintenance of soil fertility; and (3) competition with cotton and sugar plantations for slave labor was keen. Hemp growing developed in Kentucky, Tennessee, Arkansas, and Missouri. Crops produced for home consumption included vegetables, corn, wheat, rye, barley, buckwheat, and oats.

REVIEW QUESTIONS

1. What were the major agricultural trends during the period 1789-1860?
2. What contributions to agricultural progress were made by Jethro Wood, Charles Newbold, and John Deere?
3. Explain the revolution in southern agriculture from 1790 to 1830.
4. What scientific methods were utilized to maintain or restore soil fertility before the Civil War?

5. In what ways was agricultural information disseminated before 1860?
6. What were the effects of the westward movement on American agriculture?
7. What crops besides cotton were raised in the South? How important were they?

9

POPULATION AND LABOR BEFORE THE CIVIL WAR

By 1860 the population of the United States had increased to 31.4 million, and the center of population was moving steadily westward. The rapid growth of population was due to a high birth rate and to steadily increasing immigration. By far the majority of Americans were engaged in agriculture, but the beginnings of industrialism and of organized labor could be seen.

POPULATION

The following data concerning rate of population growth, immigration, and shifts in the geographical distribution of the people need to be emphasized.

Growth. The total population increased from 3.9 million in 1790 to 9.6 million in 1820, and to 31.4 million in 1860. The rate of growth was much greater than that in western European nations; by 1860 the population of the United States exceeded that of Great Britain, and nearly equaled that of France or Germany. Of the American population in 1860 about 4.5 million were Negroes.

Immigration. Before 1825 fewer than 10,000 immigrants entered the United States annually. Thereafter the numbers increased greatly: in 1837 the figure was 79,000; in 1842, after a temporary reduction due to economic conditions following the panic of 1837, the number rose to over 100,000; agricultural distress and revolutions in Europe during the 1840's stimulated emigration to the United States; the peak figure (in the period before the Civil War) of 427,000 was reached in 1854. Most of the immigrants came from the United Kingdom and Germany. The German immigrants often settled on farms west of the Appalachians. It is estimated that at least five-sixths of the Irish remained on the Atlantic seaboard, many of them as unskilled laborers in the cities. Probably two-thirds of the English, Scotch, and Welsh remained in the Northeast, and the remainder settled in the West.

Distribution of Population. In 1790, 94 per cent of the American people lived east of the Appalachians; only 250,000 lived to the west. By 1820, the population in the West had risen to 27 per cent, and, by 1850, to 45 per cent. In 1780, 2.7 per cent of the population lived in cities (places with 8,000 or more inhabitants); by 1860, this category had reached 16.1 per cent. In 1780 only 5 towns had 8,000 inhabitants; in 1860, 141 places were at least that large. The population of leading cities in 1860 was as follows: New York, 1,175,000; Philadelphia, 566,000; Baltimore, 212,000.

LABOR

From 1790 to 1860 many changes occurred in the supply, conditions, and economic position of labor.

The Labor Supply. A general willingness to work has always characterized Americans. Until recently the work week was long, vacations were few, and retirement while one was still able to work was unheard of. The labor supply was augmented by the employment of women and children. The number of persons over 10 years of age gainfully employed increased from 2.9 million in 1820 to 10.5 million in 1860. The following percentages of the total population were engaged in particular occupations.

Occupations	1820	1860
Agriculture	71.88	59.70
Manufacturing and mechanic arts	12.15	18.35
Domestic and personal service	10.00	9.52
Professions	2.81	2.90

Although wages were relatively high in America, there were few day laborers available. There was a need for skilled workers, especially in the factories, and this retarded manufacturing to some extent. Before the Napoleonic wars, only a handful of factories used complicated machinery, but the war period stimulated manufacturing and many new machines were introduced. The need for labor was met in part by skilled immigrants, but often farmers and hand workers learned how to operate machines. Not until the 1830's did the supply of skilled labor catch up with the demand.

Laboring Conditions. About 1800 it was common to work from sunup to sunset. By 1830 skilled city artisans had obtained a 10-hour work day, but factory laborers worked 12- and 13-hour days. One author suggests that a "typical working week about 1860 was a little under 70 hours."[1]

WAGES. Generally there was an upward trend of wages in the period 1800-1860, the level of 1860 being about double that of 1800. The following table indicates the levels of wages for different workers. (Figures do not include allowances for board.)

DAILY WAGES OF AMERICAN WORKERS

Labor Group	1820	1860
Common labor	$ .75	$1.00-1.25
Farm labor	.50	1.00
Skilled artisans and mechanics	1.25-1.50	1.50-2.00

The wages of women and children in factories were considerably lower than those of common laborers.

FACTORY CONDITIONS. In addition to the long hours of work, conditions in the factories were often unsanitary and unhealthful. Frequently a sort of industrial feudalism made the lot of laborers difficult. Workers lived in company houses, bought supplies in company stores, and lived under the constant surveillance of employers. In the 1840's the depression made conditions for the factory workers worse: wages were reduced; there was considerable unemployment; employers used black lists to prevent unionization.

Child Labor. Few statistics of child labor before the Civil War are available. The number of children employed in factories varied from region to region, but the greatest number were in the cotton textile factories of southern New England.

[1] C. W. Wright, *Economic History of the United States* (New York, 1951), p. 328.

Family System of Employment. Instead of following the English method of apprenticeship and transferring children from poorhouses, American employers advertised for entire families to work. This was advantageous both to the employees and to employers because (1) families were not separated, (2) parents could discipline children, and (3) employers were less responsible for the care of employees.

Conditions of Child Labor. Most children in the labor force were between the ages of 8 and 12; very few were under 7 years of age. The period of work varied from 11 to 14 hours a day. Child labor was employed only in the lighter tasks.

Effects of System. There were evil effects upon both the minds and bodies of the young. Factories were unhealthful places; excessive brutality occurred at times; education was neglected. Early efforts to curtail the excesses of the system were ineffective.

Woman Labor. Women workers constituted 20 per cent of the total factory labor force in 1860. They were most numerous in the boot and shoe, ready-made clothing, and cotton textile industries. In the first two industries mentioned the putting-out system (with work taken out to be done at home) was used, but in the last, women worked in factories. In 1831, 80 per cent of the workers in Massachusetts textile mills were women.

The "Waltham System." Textile manufacturers deliberately sought women employees. Since English factory conditions were poor and had created an evil impression, Boston promoters sought to make the work moral and not degrading. Only persons of good character were hired, and any guilty of improper conduct were discharged. Company boarding houses, strictly supervised in the early period, were provided for women who did not have homes near by. The "Waltham System" (initiated in Waltham, Massachusetts) was established in Lowell and other areas of the industry.

Effects of Woman Labor. At first most of the women worked for only a few years, but gradually a permanent female laboring class appeared. Conditions grew worse as employers' feeling of parental responsibility declined, and women of less strict character were employed.

Changes in the Economic Position of Labor. The beginnings of the American labor movement resulted from the attempts of laborers to cope with changing economic conditions through collective action. Among these conditions were the following: (1) Specialization and the division of labor lessened the amount of skill and training needed, thereby increasing the mobility of labor and the competition among workers. (2) Although productivity increased, most of the resulting gain tended to go to consumers in the form of lower prices rather than to laborers in the form of higher wages.

The Early Organization of Labor. Organization began among the skilled workers in the trades rather than in the factories. Local unions appeared immediately after the Revolution, but the labor movement in the United States is not said to have begun until the 1820's. The labor organizations which existed before the Civil War were generally impermanent bodies, established to redress special grievances, and dissolved shortly when either successful or defeated. Not until 1842 was the right of laborers to join unions recognized by the courts.

Labor in the 1820's. In 1827 Philadelphia carpenters went on strike for a 10-hour day; they were quickly joined by painters, glaziers, and bricklayers. In Philadelphia the Mechanics' Union of Trade Associations was organized. Similar associations appeared in other cities, and there were national unions formed by some craftsmen: shoemakers, comb-makers, carpenters, hand-loom weavers, and printers. In 1834 a national convention of labor representatives was held.

The Workingmen's Party. In 1828 the Workingmen's Party was formed in Philadelphia, and in at least fifteen other states there were local labor parties. The demands of the workers included shorter hours, better working conditions, and legal status for labor unions. Results of these political efforts were local and temporary, and by 1832 the movement had largely failed. This first general effort at unionization disappeared during the panic of 1837.

Labor in the 1850's. With the return of prosperity in the late 1840's labor began to organize again. Many local unions and a few national unions were organized in the 1850's. Among the national groups were the Typographical Union, the Stone Cutters Union, and the National Union of Machinists and

Blacksmiths. The panic of 1857 retarded unionism somewhat, but did not obliterate it as the panic of 1837 had done.

Legal Status for Labor. Under English common law any workingmen's combination for the purpose of raising wages was regarded as a conspiracy against the public. Between 1806 and 1815 several conspiracy convictions against workers were obtained in America. In 1842 in the case of *Commonwealth* v. *Hunt,* laborers' right to organize for lawful purposes was recognized. The use of labor weapons was still restricted by legal action, however.

Pre-Civil War Gains of Labor. In addition to legal status labor made other gains. In 1840 government employees were given a 10-hour work day, and by 1860 this principle was spreading in private industry. Between 1800 and 1860 wages doubled, and unions were especially successful in obtaining increases in the 1850's.

REVIEW QUESTIONS

1. Indicate the extent of population growth from 1790 to 1860.
2. Discuss the extent of urbanism before the Civil War.
3. How important and extensive was immigration before 1860?
4. How extensive was child labor in the pre-Civil War period? What was meant by the family system of employment?
5. How extensive was woman labor before the Civil War? Discuss the nature and effects of the "Waltham System."
6. How successful were labor's efforts to organize in this period?

10

TRANSPORTATION DEVELOPMENTS BEFORE THE CIVIL WAR

Transportation and communication have been essential factors throughout the development of the American economy. The impossibility of rapid contact and transport retarded expansion, and contributed to disunity and localism in our early history. The development of new facilities in the early nineteenth century greatly increased geographic expansion and made possible agricultural and industrial growth.

General Factors. The population and business followed natural waterways in our early life. Although the United States is unusually well equipped with waterways, most of the rivers of the interior run from north to south. Since population moved largely from east to west, natural waterways were not always of service, and it was necessary to develop other transportation aids. Improvements in the early nineteenth century occurred mainly in three lines: (1) turnpikes and improved roads; (2) canals and improved natural waterways; (3) steam transport on land and water.

Improved Roads and Turnpikes. Improved facilities for land transport were necessary for economic progress, and in the early nineteenth century old roads were improved, and turnpikes were constructed. Local roads were built and repaired by town and county governments with some help from the states. Constitutional objections and state jealousies prevented much federal assistance for the development of highways. Roads were often poorly constructed and not suited to the needs of long-distance traffic. Many private companies built and operated turnpikes in areas where traffic was great enough to ensure financial gain.

PRIVATE COMPANIES. In the states from Pennsylvania northward turnpike construction was left largely to private companies. States relieved themselves of the responsibility of providing the needed roads by chartering corporations, operating on the profit motive, to build and operate highways. States attempted to assure the people of adequate service through charter provisions regulating rates. The Lancaster Turnpike, the first important one of its kind in America, was chartered by Pennsylvania in 1792, and a road was completed connecting Philadelphia and Lancaster (66 miles) in 1794. By 1810 there were 180 turnpike companies in New England; by 1813, 137 New York companies had built about 1,400 miles; by 1832, 86 Pennsylvania companies had built 2,200 miles.

DECLINE OF PRIVATE COMPANIES. After 1825 private turnpike companies began to disappear, and roads reverted to public control. The experience of the Lancaster Turnpike illustrates general difficulties. The cost of construction was much greater than original estimates, and the company had to make further demands on shareholders; although the stock finally reached par value in 1807, the company had not realized more than 2 per cent profit thus far. Furthermore, turnpike companies often aroused hostility. Road-building had been a public enterprise previously, and people resented the fact that private individuals were given the power to seize private property through the exercise of eminent domain, and to charge tolls.

THE GALLATIN PLAN. Nationalists and various economic interests agitated for federal aid to support internal improvements. Jeffersonians became loose constructionists of the Constitution to justify this exertion of federal authority. Secretary of the Treasury Albert Gallatin made a famous report to Congress on internal improvements in 1808. He recommended federal aid for the construction of (1) a number of canals across several peninsulas along the Atlantic Coast, (2) a north-south turnpike from Maine to Georgia, and (3) east-west roads to connect eastern rivers with the Ohio River.

THE CUMBERLAND ROAD. This highway, sometimes called the National Road, connected the Atlantic seacoast with the Ohio

Valley. Although planned as early as 1803 it was not started until 1811. The road followed Braddock's route, reaching Wheeling, West Virginia, in 1818, Columbus, Ohio, in 1833, and Vandalia, Illinois, in 1852. The Cumberland Road was 834 miles long and cost the federal government $6,821,000, but was a great national achievement. It was a convenient highway for westward migration, and it greatly reduced the time and cost of transportation. The road was of great benefit to Philadelphia and Baltimore, and it brought prosperity to the areas through which it ran. Although there were many other plans for federal aid to internal improvements, they were discouraged by President Jackson's veto of the Maysville Road Bill in 1830.

Canals. Interest in canals as an aid to land transport had existed since the time of the Revolution. Although canals were expensive and sometimes froze over or were washed out, transportation on them was easier than on land. Three common types of canals were (1) passages around some obstacle in a river, (2) connecting links between navigable rivers and lakes, and (3) east-west canals designed to draw western business to an eastern terminal. The Erie Canal was the great prototype of the last kind; many eastern cities attempted similar projects. The period of the most extensive canal construction was between the War of 1812 and the panic of 1837.

Early canals included a canal between Richmond and Westham, Virginia, projected in the 1780's, the Dismal Swamp Canal in Virginia and North Carolina, constructed in the years 1787 to 1794, and the Middlesex Canal between the Merrimac and Charles rivers in Massachusetts, built in the period 1795 to 1808.

THE ERIE CANAL. This ran from the Hudson River near Albany to Buffalo on Lake Erie, and was completed by the state of New York in 1825. It was 363 miles long, 30 feet wide, and 4 feet deep; it could accommodate 30-ton barges. The cost was about 7 million dollars, but the success of the canal was so great that within ten years the tolls collected exceeded the cost of construction. Subsidiary canals were constructed to connect with Lakes Ontario, Seneca, and Champlain.

The economic consequences of the Erie Canal were great.

(1) New York City outdistanced Philadelphia as the outlet for the produce of the Great Lake region and the Northwest. The cost of transportation between Buffalo and New York was reduced more than 75 per cent, and the time consumed was cut by almost two-thirds. (2) Western New York and the Northwest grew and expanded rapidly after the Erie was opened: agricultural produce increased greatly in value; western New York cities and Great Lake ports thrived.

THE PENNSYLVANIA CANAL. Between 1826 and 1834 Pennsylvania constructed a canal and portage railway system which connected Philadelphia and Pittsburgh. This canal, a "mechanical marvel," was 394 miles long and cost over 10 million dollars. It brought some western trade to Philadelphia, but was not so successful as the Erie Canal.

OTHER EASTERN CANALS. The Delaware and Raritan Canal extended from Bordentown on the Delaware to New Brunswick on the Raritan in New Jersey. The Morris Canal connected the Hudson at Jersey City with the Delaware at Phillipsburg. The Delaware and Chesapeake Canal, connecting the Delaware and Chesapeake Bay, was completed in 1829. Maryland built the Chesapeake and Ohio Canal with some help from the federal government. This canal was not successful because it did not cross the mountains and the competition of the Baltimore and Ohio Railroad was too strong.

CANALS IN THE NORTHWEST. Ohio was very active in canal-building, constructing over 1,000 miles by 1850. Two canals connected Lake Erie with the Ohio River. Indiana completed the Wabash and Erie Canal in 1843, connecting Lake Erie with the Ohio River. Illinois built the Illinois and Michigan Canal, reaching from Lake Michigan to the Illinois River. Wisconsin joined Lake Michigan and the Mississippi by constructing a canal between the Fox and Wisconsin rivers. In 1855 Michigan completed a canal around St. Mary's Falls between Lakes Huron and Superior.

Railroads. The beginning of American steam railroads came in the late 1820's. There had been railroads in use in the United States before this, but they employed man power, horse power, or stationary engines. The steam railroad offered obvious advantages: unlike waterways it did not freeze in the winter; it could often go through terrain where canals were impossible.

EARLY RAILROADS. Among the early railroad experiments were the following: (1) the Baltimore and Ohio Railroad completed thirteen miles of road, 1828-1830; (2) an attempt in 1829 to run an English steam locomotive on the Carbondale and Honesdale Railroad (now part of the Delaware and Hudson) failed; (3) by 1833, 136 miles of road with steam locomotives were in operation from Charleston to Hamburg, South Carolina.

RIVALRY OF EASTERN CITIES. There was a great struggle among the Atlantic seaboard cities (Boston, New York, Philadelphia, Baltimore, Charleston, Savannah) for control of traffic from the interior. By 1850 only one railroad reached into the interior, and sixteen different companies operated that road. In 1853 the disorganized New York system was consolidated into the New York Central. In the 1850's a number of other lines connecting the Atlantic Coast with the interior were completed: the New York and Erie reached Lake Erie in 1851; the Pennsylvania Railroad reached Pittsburgh in 1853; the Baltimore and Ohio reached Wheeling in 1853.

SOUTHERN RAILROADS. The Western and Atlantic Railroad of Georgia reached the Tennessee in 1850; it connected with the rail system of the Northwest in 1854, and Chattanooga became the most important rail terminal in the Southwest. The Mobile and Ohio reached Cairo, Illinois, in 1859. The New Orleans, Jackson, and Great Northern connected New Orleans and Tennessee in 1859.

LOCATION OF RAILROADS. As late as 1850 about 80 per cent of the nation's railroad mileage was to the east of the Appalachian Highland. By 1860, however, nearly one-half of the national total of 31,246 miles was in the trans-Appalachian region. Early railroads in the West followed the pattern of canals in the area (connecting the Great Lakes and the Mississippi River system), but the roads of the 1850's raced directly westward to such cities as Chicago, St. Louis, and Milwaukee. Because of its strategic location Chicago became the chief railroad center of the Middle West.

FINANCING RAILROADS. By the time of the Civil War railroads were the nation's most important corporations, and in a great many states they had the largest capitalization of all

RAILROAD MILEAGE IN THE UNITED STATES

Region	1830	1840	1850	1860
New England		517	2,508	3,660
Middle Atlantic States	30	1,566	3,105	6,354
Trans-Mississippi West		40	80	2,906
Southeast	10	522	1,717	5,351
Old Southwest		74	336	3,392
Old Northwest		111	1,276	9,583
Total	40	2,830	9,022	31,246

companies. Great difficulty was encountered in obtaining capital to construct railroads: financial insecurity in an unsettled country made prospective investors wary. However, over $1,250,000,000 was invested in railroads, 1830-1860, much of this money coming from Europe. Public aid supplemented private capital. (1) Local governments probably gave most of all. (2) A number of states aided railroads in various ways. Georgia actually built and operated a line between Atlanta and Chattanooga until 1870. (3) Federal land grants to railroads (mainly in the Northwest and Southwest) were worth 31 million dollars by 1861.

SIGNIFICANCE OF RAILROADS. The settlement and development of the West was greatly facilitated: settlers were offered better transportation, and marketing was made easier. Railroads stimulated manufacturing by widening markets and providing access to raw materials. In the 1850's the Northwest and the Northeast were linked securely by railroads, affecting significantly political as well as economic associations just prior to the Civil War.

Steamboats. In 1807 Robert Fulton made the first successful steamboat voyage in the "Clermont." Commercial use of the steamboat followed. As this new development was perfected, the cost and time of transportation were reduced. Fulton and his associates were granted a monopoly of steamboat traffic in the waters of New York and Louisiana, but in 1824 in the case of *Gibbons* v. *Ogden* the grant was forbidden on the ground that it was a violation of Congressional control of interstate commerce. Although steamboats entered the coastal trade by the 1830's, sailing craft still dominated that business in 1860. Steam transport on the internal rivers was of great importance. As early as 1821 the tonnage of steamboats putting in at New

Orleans outweighed that of barges, flatboats, etc. In 1860 over 700 steamboats were in use on western rivers. The development of this commerce was of great economic consequence: river ports such as Cincinnati, Louisville, St. Louis, and Memphis flourished; New Orleans became one of the leading commercial centers of the world. The federal government took only a small part in the development of domestic commerce: by 1860, 3 million dollars had been appropriated to improve river navigation; surveys of rivers and coasts were made; lighthouses were built; Congressional acts of 1838 and 1852 provided for safety regulations and the licensing of pilots and engineers.

REVIEW QUESTIONS

1. What were the eras of transportation development before the Civil War?
2. How were turnpikes constructed and operated?
3. Indicate the extent of federal aid to transportation development before the Civil War.
4. What was the economic significance of the Erie Canal?
5. How important were canals in the development of the Old Northwest?
6. Discuss the economic significance of railroads before the Civil War
7. How were the early railroads financed?
8. How important was steam transport in internal commerce before 1860?

11

WESTWARD EXPANSION BEFORE THE CIVIL WAR

Before the Revolution the American population had not moved far beyond the Appalachian barrier, but with the elimination of the French menace and the English restrictions, and the improvement of transportation, the movement westward was accelerated. The acquisition and conquest of wild lands in the interior and western part of the continent were an outstanding force in the growth of the American economy and the shaping of American character.

SIGNIFICANCE OF THE FRONTIER

Hunters, traders, and missionaries made the first westward advances, establishing trade routes with such posts as Pittsburgh, Chicago, and St. Louis. Next came the ranchers, who used the land for grazing livestock. Following the ranchers were the farmers, the first in small, isolated groups, eager to move on quickly, and later arrivals in more densely settled, permanent communities. Farming gave way to commerce and business in favorable areas. These stages were not always distinguishable and they frequently overlapped. Generally, however, these successive economic frontiers explain much of the westward movement.

Navigable rivers provided the easiest and the fastest routes to the interior for the frontiersmen. The French had the easiest access to the interior, proceeding from the St. Lawrence Valley to the Great Lakes and the Mississippi River system. There were several important routes inland from the Atlantic seaboard. (1) The Hudson and Mohawk river valleys provided the best road, but this was blocked for some time by the Iroquois Indians. Settlers found it possible to proceed from the Mohawk to the Allegheny and then to the Ohio River. (2) Another route went from the Potomac River to the Monongahela, and from there to the Ohio in western Pennsylvania. This route was later followed by the Cumberland or National Road. (3) The most important route for early settlers was through the Appalachian Valley, and the Cumberland Gap, or the Tennessee Valley.

THE FRONTIER IN THE REVOLUTIONARY PERIOD

The conclusion of the French and Indian War in 1763 left England in control of all of North America east of the Mississippi River. Removal of the French menace did not open the West for English settlement because the Indians feared their advance, and in 1763 and 1764 there was a general insurrection led by Pontiac, an Ottowa chief.

British Western Policy. To settle the Indian problem the English government issued the Proclamation of 1763, forbidding settlement beyond the Appalachian ridge. In a series of treaties with the Indians, however, new lands were opened to the whites. Although the Proclamation of 1763 did not retard westward expansion very much, the colonists resented the British effort to keep them east of the mountains. Land speculators, especially, felt that their interests had been damaged.

The Quebec Act of 1774 extended the boundaries of the province of Quebec to the Ohio and Mississippi rivers, threatening to exclude settlers from the eastern colonies. The Quebec Act also invalidated charter grants of land in the old northwest to the English Atlantic colonies. It further angered the Protestant colonists by granting to French Catholics freedom of worship in Quebec.

Winning the West. During the Revolution the British encouraged the Indians to attack the outlying American settlements, some of which were now on the west slopes of the Appalachians. In 1778 George Rogers Clark, with a Virginia commission, captured the English posts at Kaskaskia on the Mississippi and at Vincennes on the Wabash. Clark's victories in the old northwest were the basis of United States claims to this area. These claims were confirmed by the treaty at the end of the Revolution. The British held some of the posts in the Northwest until 1795, however.

Early Frontier Advance. The early frontier settlements included those of Tennessee, Kentucky, and the old northwest.

TENNESSEE. The first settlement was in the Watauga River Valley, founded by James Robertson and John Sevier in 1768. Control of this settlement was disputed by Virginia and North Carolina, and the Watauga community was practically independent until 1778. Then it became part of North Carolina. In 1779 Robertson led a group from Watauga to Nashboro on the Cumberland River in middle Tennessee. From 1784 to 1789 the Tennessee pioneers organized the independent state of Franklin, and sought admittance to the United States. In 1789 North Carolina reasserted her sovereignty. Tennessee's population in 1790 was 35,000, and it became a separate state in 1796.

KENTUCKY. Settlement began in 1769, but little progress was made until the Indians were defeated in Lord Dunmore's War in 1774. Boonesboro was founded in 1775 by Daniel Boone, agent of the Transylvania Company, which bought the land between the Cumberland and Kentucky rivers from the Indians. Virginia claimed jurisdiction over this region, and in 1778 the Transylvania Company's title to the land was invalidated. Louisville was founded in 1779, and by 1790 there were over 70,000 settlers in Kentucky. It became a state in 1792.

THE OLD NORTHWEST. Settlement north of the Ohio River began later than in Tennessee and Kentucky. Conflicting claims to the area, and the Indian menace, retarded expansion. The Land Ordinance of 1785, which provided for the surveying of the Northwest, and the Northwest Ordinance of 1787, which set up a territorial government, aided the opening of the region. The first settlement in Ohio was Marietta, founded by the Ohio Company of Associates. This company had secured an option to buy 2 million acres of land, payment to be made in depreciated Continental scrip. Although the company defaulted in its payments, Congress granted it title to about 1 million acres. Another land company that encouraged settlement and confused land titles was the Scioto Company. A third group led by John Cleves Symmes of New Jersey secured an option to buy 1 million acres, and settled the towns of Columbia and Cincinnati. The Census of 1790 declared the population of the northwest to be 4,280. Settlement of the eastern part was rapid in the next decade, and Ohio became a state in 1802.

The Mississippi Valley in American Diplomacy. The Mississippi River was of great significance to the trans-Appalachian settlers; navigation of the river and the right of deposit at New Orleans were necessary for the marketing of their produce. Until the United States guaranteed to westerners these privileges, they were uneasy and discontented.

RIGHT OF NAVIGATION AND DEPOSIT. The Treaty of 1783 with England had included the privilege of navigating the Mississippi, but this meant little as long as Spain controlled the mouth of the river. In 1784 Spain closed the Mississippi to American shipping. Not until 1795 in the Treaty of San Lorenzo with Spain did the United States gain the right to navigate the Mississippi and to deposit goods at New Orleans for a period of three years.

LOUISIANA PURCHASE. In 1800 Napoleon Bonaparte persuaded the Spanish government to retrocede the province of Louisiana to France. This produced anxiety in the United States, and negotiations were quickly begun for the purchase of New Orleans and the Floridas (West Florida then extended to the east bank of the Mississippi). In 1803, after the loss of a French army in Santo Domingo, Napoleon agreed to sell the entire province of Louisiana, stretching from the Mississippi to the Rocky Mountains, to the United States for 15 million dollars. President Jefferson had constitutional scruples against the acquisition of new territory, but realizing the great importance of control of the Mississippi, he urged the adoption of the purchase treaty.

LAND POLICY

Major developments in federal land policy included the Land Ordinance of 1785, the act of 1796, and the pre-emption act of 1841.

Land Ordinance of 1785. This basic measure provided for the surveying of public land in the Northwest Territory. Rectangular townships of 36 square miles were laid out, and one square mile section in each township was reserved for education. Land offices were established for the sale of public land at auction at a price of not less than $1 an acre. Half of each township was to be sold in sections of 640 acres, and half was to be sold intact.

Act of 1796. No land was to be sold until the land was surveyed and the Indian title extinguished. Alternate townships were to be sold in lots of 8 sections; intervening townships in single sections. A minimum of 640 acres could be purchased. The price was raised to $2 an acre, but a credit system, allowing a year for payment, was introduced.

Since 640 acres was too large a unit of sale for the ordinary settler, Congress gradually reduced the acreage: 1800, 320 acres; 1804, 160 acres; 1820, 80 acres. The act of 1820 reduced the price to $1.25 an acre, and abolished the credit system of purchase.

Pre-emption Act of 1841. The act permitted squatters, who had preceded government surveyors in the westward movement, to purchase land they had occupied, free from competitive bids.

Weakness of Land Policy. Although federal land policy became increasingly more liberal, the land laws favored speculators rather than settlers. The government's price was too high for poor settlers; no limit was set on the amount one might purchase; settlement and improvement of the land were not required.

MOVEMENT OF THE FRONTIER TO AND BEYOND THE MISSISSIPPI RIVER

The westward movement was accelerated during and after the War of 1812.

The Old Southwest. Settlement of the trans-Appalachian South advanced rapidly in the early nineteenth century: the population of Mississippi Territory grew from 40,000 in 1810 to 203,000 in 1820; Mississippi and Alabama became states in 1817 and 1819, respectively. Cotton cultivation was extended

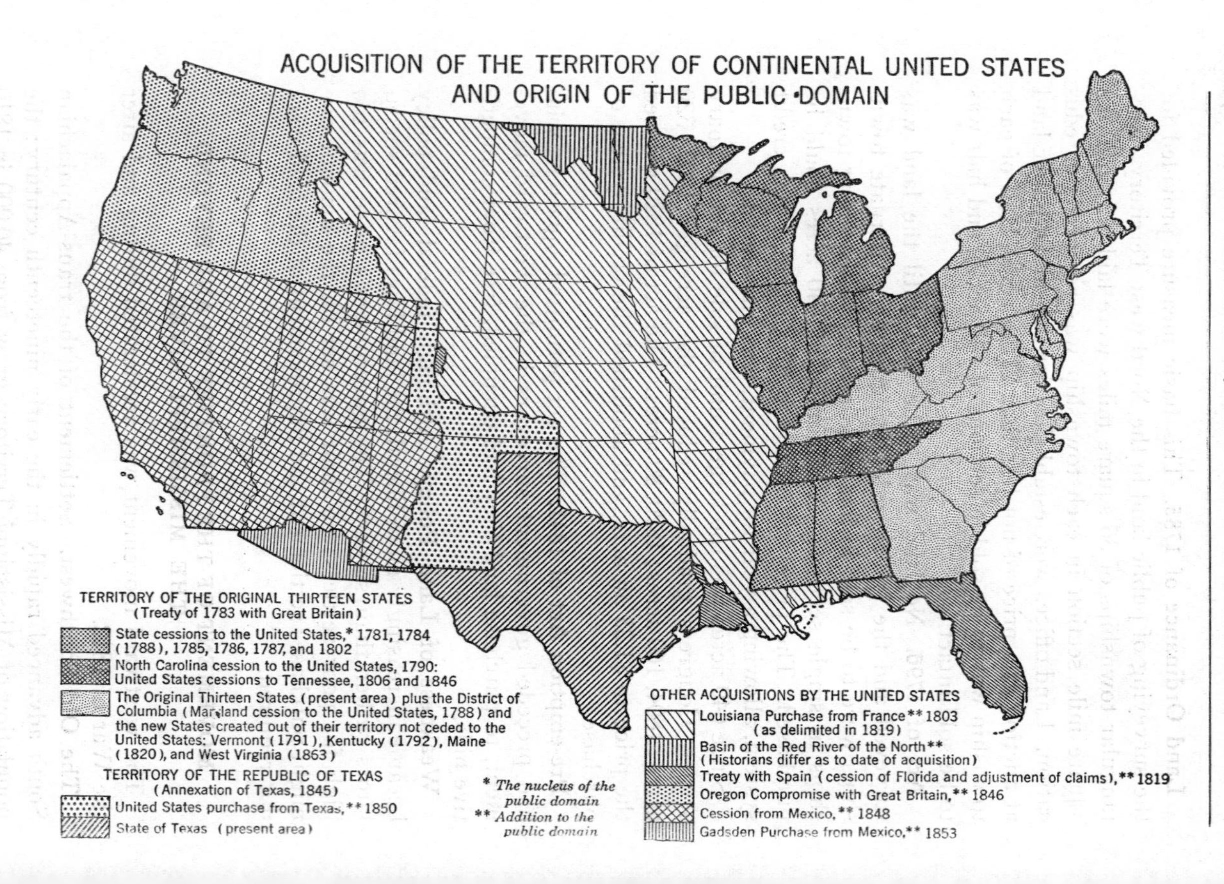
ACQUISITION OF THE TERRITORY OF CONTINENTAL UNITED STATES
AND ORIGIN OF THE PUBLIC DOMAIN
TERRITORY OF THE ORIGINAL THIRTEEN STATES
(Treaty of 1783 with Great Britain)
State cessions to the United States,* 1781, 1784 (1788), 1785, 1786, 1787, and 1802
North Carolina cession to the United States, 1790: United States cessions to Tennessee, 1806 and 1846
The Original Thirteen States (present area) plus the District of Columbia (Maryland cession to the United States, 1788) and the new States created out of their territory not ceded to the United States: Vermont (1791), Kentucky (1792), Maine (1820), and West Virginia (1863)
TERRITORY OF THE REPUBLIC OF TEXAS
(Annexation of Texas, 1845)
United States purchase from Texas,** 1850
State of Texas (present area)
* The nucleus of the public domain
** Addition to the public domain
OTHER ACQUISITIONS BY THE UNITED STATES
Louisiana Purchase from France** 1803 (as delimited in 1819)
Basin of the Red River of the North** (Historians differ as to date of acquisition)
Treaty with Spain (cession of Florida and adjustment of claims),** 1819
Oregon Compromise with Great Britain,** 1846
Cession from Mexico,** 1848
Gadsden Purchase from Mexico,** 1853

quickly into the Gulf states, and in the 1830's this area surpassed the old South in the production of cotton.

Florida. In 1819 the United States acquired this southeastern peninsula from Spain, by assuming American claims on Spain to the extent of 5 million dollars. Florida became a state in 1845.

The Trans-Mississippi Southwest. Settlement advanced quickly enough to permit the organization of the following states: Louisiana (1812), Missouri (1820), Arkansas (1836), Texas (1845).

TEXAS. The early settlers of Texas, largely from the United States, won their independence of Mexico in 1836. The republic of Texas offered itself for annexation to the United States at once, but not until 1845 was Texas annexed. War with Mexico, 1846-1848, determined the southern boundary of Texas to be the Rio Grande River. At the end of the Mexican War the United States also acquired the great southwest and California for 18 million dollars.

THE GADSDEN PURCHASE. In 1853, with a view to the construction of a transcontinental railroad, the United States purchased an additional strip of territory along the southwestern boundary from Mexico for 10 million dollars.

The Old Northwest. The settlement of the area (Ohio, Indiana, Illinois, Michigan, Wisconsin) proceeded very rapidly, especially after the War of 1812. Several factors stimulated this advance. (1) Economic distress during and after the War of 1812 caused many to go west. (2) Grants of land in this region were made to soldiers. (3) The Indian menace was removed, beginning with William H. Harrison's victory at Tippecanoe in 1811. (4) Transportation facilities were improved: the National Road led into the Ohio Valley; steam transport on the western rivers was introduced in 1811; the Erie Canal was completed in 1825. Dates for the admission of states are: Indiana, 1816; Illinois, 1818; Michigan, 1836; Wisconsin, 1848; Iowa, 1848; Minnesota, 1858. The settlers of the Northwest were: (1) pioneers from the central Atlantic states; (2) Scotch-Irish small farmers of the South, who had been displaced by large planters; (3) German immigrants. The economy of the area was dominated by small grain and livestock farms. Slavery had been forbidden by the Northwest Ordinance of 1787.

THE FAR WEST BEGINNINGS

In the years 1804 to 1806, Lewis and Clark ascended the Missouri River, crossed the Rockies, and descended the Columbia River to the Pacific Ocean. Zebulon Pike, at about the same time, followed the Arkansas River to the Rockies, and then struck south toward the Rio Grande and the Spanish colonies, eventually returning to Louisiana.

Oregon. Interest in Oregon resulted from the fur trade begun by New Englanders as early as 1788. Astoria was founded in 1811 by John Jacob Astor's American Fur Company. Two British companies, the Hudson's Bay Company and the Northwest Company, bought out the American merchants and dominated Oregon until the 1840's. During this period Oregon was held jointly by the United States and Great Britain. In the 1830's American interest in Oregon was revived by propagandists, and migration there began. In the next decade the American population of the area increased greatly and in 1846 the United States and England divided the Oregon territory. The 49th parallel became the United States border in the far northwest.

Utah. The Mormons founded a settlement at Salt Lake in Utah in 1847, and within a year there were 5,000 settlers in the colony. Led by efficient organizers, and fired with religious zeal, the Mormons built irrigation works and established a prosperous community in the desert.

California. Gold was discovered in California in 1848, and in 1850 the population exceeded 90,000. Settlers came by sea, either by way of Cape Horn or the Isthmus of Panama, and by the long overland route across the continent. The first transcontinental railroad, the Union Pacific, was not completed until 1869. A few gold-seekers "struck it rich," but the placer-mine deposits were soon exhausted and the settlers had to adjust themselves to more normal lives. In 1850 California was admitted to the Union.

REVIEW QUESTIONS

1. How influential has the frontier been in the growth of the American economy?
2. What were the chief routes from the Atlantic coast to the interior?
3. What effect did British western policy have on the American Revolution?
4. Describe the beginnings of settlement in Kentucky, Tennessee, and Ohio.
5. Discuss the importance of the Mississippi River in our early economic history. What part did the struggle for the Mississippi play in our political and diplomatic affairs?
6. Outline American land policy before 1860. What were its chief shortcomings?
7. Explain the progress of settlement in (a) the Southwest and (b) the Northwest.
8. Discuss the beginnings of (a) Oregon and (b) California.

12

BEGINNINGS OF AMERICAN INDUSTRIALISM

Between 1789 and 1860 the chief occupation of the American people was agriculture, but the beginnings of industrialism came in this period, too. Before the War of 1812 the United States was dependent upon Europe for the finer manufactured goods; thereafter the factory system became firmly established and the demand for manufactured goods was for the most part met by domestic producers. In this period, manufacturing assumed an independent economic status and ceased to be merely an auxiliary part of merchant capitalism.

MANUFACTURING FROM THE REVOLUTION TO 1815

Manufacturers had to cope with a number of problems. (1) Dependence on Europe. Following the Revolution, trade with Europe was resumed and American manufacturers found it difficult to compete with cheaper English goods. (2) Lack of capital. Capitalists were more eager to invest in tried fields of activity like trade or land speculation than in manufacturing. Inadequate banking facilities added to this difficulty. (3) Scarcity of labor. The availability of good land and the prospect of profit from agriculture tended to lessen the supply of labor available to manufacturers and to increase its cost. (4) Need for improved transportation. Before the introduction of steam power, transportation was slow and dependent upon the weather, and marketing was difficult. (5) Lack of managerial experience.

Encouraging Factors. Impetus to manufacturing came from

several sources: (1) the difficulty of importing European goods preceding and during the War of 1812; (2) the introduction of power-driven machinery in cotton manufacturing; (3) government bounties and subsidies; (4) a persistent desire to be independent of Europe.

Effects of the War of 1812. Because of the interruption of trade, capital was diverted from mercantile to industrial investments. The scarcity of imported goods encouraged the development of American manufacturing, and a surge of nationalism encouraged the growth of economic independence.

RISE OF THE FACTORY SYSTEM

The factory system was firmly established in the first half of the nineteenth century, and by the time of the Civil War household manufacturing and work by itinerant artisans had been largely eliminated. The first successful textile mill was built by Samuel Slater at Providence, Rhode Island, in 1789. Other experiments of the same period at Beverly, Massachusetts, and Philadelphia proved temporary. In 1814 Patrick Tracy Jackson and Francis Cabot Lowell established "the first modern factory" in America at Waltham, Massachusetts, for the manufacture of cotton cloth. Other entrepreneurs quickly followed their example.

Power. Water power was first used by a short-lived textile mill founded at Paterson, New Jersey in 1791. The first factory use of steam is claimed for a sawmill in New York in 1803. Although water power continued to be the main type used in America for many years, the use of steam gradually increased.

PROGRESS IN SPECIFIC INDUSTRIES

Significant developments occurred in textile manufacturing, iron and minor metal manufacturing, and the processing of foodstuffs.

Cotton Textiles. The interruption of trade before and during the War of 1812 greatly stimulated cotton manufacturing. In 1814 a factory was established at Waltham, Massachusetts, where for the first time spinning and weaving machinery was included in the same factory. With the return of peace in 1815 English competition ruined many infant industries. The tariff of 1816 offered protection, and improved machinery encouraged American manufacturers, however. The growth after 1820 was very rapid, and from 1840 to 1860 cotton manufacturing increased 150 per cent. Although 69 per cent of this industry was located in New England in 1860, there were other developments in the Hudson, Mohawk, and Delaware valleys.

Woolen Manufactures. Progress in woolens was slow, and in 1860 the United States was still importing raw wool and woolen manufactures from England. English competition in this industry was very difficult to overcome despite the impetus of the War of 1812 and the protective tariff. It was not until the 1840's that the factory system supplanted domestic production in this industry. Between 1840 and 1860 the number of woolen factories rose from 1420 to 1909, the capital invested from 15.7 to 35.5 million dollars, and the value of the product from 20.6 to 68.8 million.

Other Textiles. Linen, an important homespun product in colonial America, was largely replaced by the cheaper cotton and woolen cloth. A few factories producing linen were established, but the duty imposed on imported flax by the tariff of 1828 virtually ruined the industry. By 1860 the total value of factory-made linens was only $700,000. The manufacture of hemp for bagging and bale cloth became important in the Ohio valley. In 1860 Kentucky produced 5.7 million yards of bagging, and Missouri 3.6 million. Silk manufacture was slow in developing. The Census of 1860 revealed that the total value of silk goods was 6.5 million dollars.

Iron Manufacturing. Competition with the more advanced English manufacturers retarded American production. During and after the War of 1812, however, a number of factors encouraged the development of the iron industry. (1) Technical improvements. The use of coal and the introduction of machinery in smelting permitted large-scale operations. (2) New resources. After 1820 the iron industry expanded into western Pennsylvania and the Ohio valley. By 1860 the use of ore from the Lake Superior region had begun. (3) Demand for new products. As the nineteenth century advanced there was increased demand for such iron products as steam engines, locomotives, rails, farm machinery, textile machinery, and stoves. (4) The tariff. Between 1818 and 1828 tariffs ranging from 40 to 100 per cent were imposed on iron imports. By 1860 the total iron production of the United States was almost 1 million tons. Pennsylvania produced more than one-half of this amount; Ohio was the second largest producer. The output of steel, however, was less than 12,000 tons in 1860.

Minor Metal Manufactures. New England was the center of the industries producing small metal products. Among iron and steel goods were axes, springs, bolts, firearms, clocks, wire, and cutlery. Southern New England also led in the production of tinware, brassware, and cheap jewelry.

Processing of Foodstuffs. Steady expansion occurred in flour-milling and meat-packing, and in the liquor industry.

FLOUR-MILLING. In the late eighteenth century Oliver Evans invented labor-saving machinery which greatly increased the productivity of flour mills. As the population moved westward and grain production increased, flour-milling became an important industry. Baltimore was the early leader in flour-milling, developing a flour trade with the South, Latin America, and Europe. Other eastern centers were Richmond and Rochester. The most important western milling town was St. Louis. This city with its fine river and rail transportation facilities captured markets for flour in the South and the East.

MEAT-PACKING. Before the coming of canals and railroads cattle and hogs were driven to eastern markets. Improved transportation facilitated the establishment of slaughtering and meat-packing towns in the west. Usually meat was smoked, cured, or pickled and shipped to market. Expensive and undependable canned meat made its appearance just before the Civil War. By-products of meat-packing led to the establishment of factories for the production of soap, glue, lard, oil, and brushes. Cincinnati was the leading center for meat-packing until the mid-nineteenth century. Thereafter Chicago assumed first place.

LIQUOR INDUSTRY. Grain-distilling moved westward as flour-milling did. Due to the high cost of transportation farmers of western Pennsylvania, Maryland, and Virginia found it more profitable to market whiskey than grain. After 1810 Cincinnati became the greatest center for the production of whiskey.

THE LOCATION OF INDUSTRY

A variety of factors, including availability of raw materials, capital, labor, and transportation facilities affected the location of industry.

Northeast. In the colonial period the Northeast assumed the leadership in industry. Populous New England, with poor agricultural resources, plenty of water power, and an active commerce, was suited to manufacturing, but the area lacked raw materials. The middle Atlantic states had better resources and also had easier access to the interior, but agriculture competed with industry for capital and labor supply. There developed, however, plants producing detailed and finished manufactures in the Hudson, Mohawk, and Delaware valleys and in such centers as New York, Philadelphia, Newark, Rochester, Paterson, and Pittsburgh.

South. The establishment of some industries, such as cotton mills at Graniteville, South Carolina, and iron works at Richmond, Virginia, gave promise of industrial progress, but the overwhelming interest in agriculture prevented much industrial development before the Civil War.

Northwest. The Ohio valley established considerable manufacturing by 1860; the area in general produced flour, meat products, farm machinery, lumber, cordage, bagging, and whiskey.

MANUFACTURING BY SECTIONS, 1860

Sections	Number of Establishments	Capital Invested	Average Number of Laborers	Annual Value of Products
New England	20,671	$ 257,477,783	391,836	$ 468,599,287
Middle states	53,387	435,061,964	546,243	802,338,392
Western states	36,785	194,212,543	209,909	384,606,530
Southern states	20,631	95,975,185	110,721	155,531,281
Pacific states	8,777	23,380,334	50,204	71,229,989
Territories	282	3,747,906	2,333	3,556,197
Total	140,533	$1,009,855,715	1,311,246	$1,885,861,676

ECONOMIC ORGANIZATION OF INDUSTRY

The development of manufacturing depended in part upon the ability of entrepreneurs to attract financial support. Gradually, the growing industries earned profits to help finance expansion. The need of obtaining funds was one of the reasons for the general adoption of the corporate form of business organization.

Capital Supply. The lack of capital for manufacturing was a problem which persisted until after the Civil War. There was a natural tendency to invest in those economic activities which promised the greatest profit—land companies, turnpikes, canals, railroads. This was true of foreign as well as domestic capital. Furthermore, public funds were not made available to industry as was the case in transportation developments. Public assistance consisted of limited loans and subsidies, tax exemption for short periods, and the right to conduct lotteries. The rate of increase of capital supply available to industry varied greatly because of financial crises and wars which diverted capital to other uses.

There was a conspicuous transfer of capital from foreign commerce to manufacturing in the period of the Napoleonic wars. Domestic commerce yielded some capital to industry throughout the early nineteenth century. Gradually, however, industry itself became the most important producer of capital. Capital invested in manufacturing rose from 50 million dollars in 1820 to 500 million in 1850 and 1,000 million in 1860.

Business Organization. The most important forms of business organization until the mid-nineteenth century were the partnership and the joint-stock company, the latter being in reality an enlarged partnership. The joint-stock business form was used successfully first by groups of merchants, but gradually it became popular for small industrial ventures as well.

The corporate form of business offered the advantages of (1) broadly distributed ownership, (2) the ability to attract many investors through the sale of low-cost shares, and (3) limited liability. Despite the difficulties of securing a charter in the early period, corporations rose steadily in number. New York in 1811 provided the first general incorporation law; Massachusetts and Connecticut adopted similar measures by 1830. Liberal provisions in these early laws were modified somewhat in the period of the panic of 1837 and after. Although restrictions on corporate activity, intended to protect the public, were imposed by state laws, incorporation was still easy, and the long-run effect of the laws was to encourage the use of the corporate form of business.

EXTENT OF MANUFACTURING IN 1860

The total value of manufactures in 1860 was about 1,800 million dollars, or almost ten times the estimated value in 1810. Nearly 1.2 million workers (less than 25 per cent women) were engaged in manufacturing, and over 900 million dollars was invested in industry. The leading industries ranked as follows in the value of the product of each: cotton goods, iron, sawed lumber, boots and shoes, ready-made clothing, flour and meal, steam-engine machinery, woolen and worsted goods, and leather.

REVIEW QUESTIONS

1. What were the outstanding problems confronting American industry, 1789-1815?
2. What factors encouraged the growth of industry before 1815?
3. What were the effects of the War of 1812 on industry?
4. Name some of the outstanding entrepreneurs who helped establish the factory system in America. Describe their work.
5. What progress was made in cotton manufacturing before the Civil War? In woolens? In linen, hemp, and silk manufactures?
6. What conditions favored the development of the iron industry?
7. How important was industry in the economy of the Northeast by 1860? The South? The Northwest?

13

FOREIGN TRADE AND MARITIME INDUSTRIES, 1789-1860

From the outbreak of the American Revolution to the end of the Napoleonic wars, American shipping was confronted by abnormal conditions. Independence resulted in trade dislocation and necessitated reorganization. Until 1807 conditions were prosperous, but thereafter American commerce suffered badly from effects of the European wars and restrictions of the United States government. After 1815 more normal conditions returned, and the steady growth of shipping resulted. By mid-century came the glorious peak of the clipper-ship era, but by the time of the Civil War American commerce had entered a period of decline.

EXPANSION OF COMMERCE, 1789-1807

While the ports of the British Empire were closed to American vessels, Yankee merchants found new trade opportunities. Commerce with the Far East began shortly after the Revolution; trade with northern Europe increased; some Caribbean ports of France, Holland, Denmark, and Spain were opened to the Americans.

European War. The outbreak of war between England and France in 1793 brought commercial opportunities to Americans, the most important neutral shippers. Despite the belligerents' interference with neutral commerce, undeclared war between the United States and France (1798-1800), and war with the Tripolitan pirates (1801-1804), American trade expanded and prospered until 1807. Tonnage registered for foreign trade rose from 123,893 in 1789 to 981,017 in 1810. The percentage of United States trade handled by American vessels in the same period also increased: imports, from 17.5 to 93 per cent; exports, from 30 to 90 per cent.

COMMERCIAL DEPRESSION, 1807-1815

From 1807 to 1815 American commerce was adversely affected by European trade regulations, the restrictions of the United States government, and the outbreak of war with England in 1812.

European Trade Regulations. Both the English and the French tried to coerce the enemy through economic boycotts. The English Orders in Council declared that the coast from the Elbe to Brest was blockaded and in November, 1807, declared that no neutral could trade with France or her allies without putting in at a British port and paying duties. The French established the Continental System which tried to prevent neutrals from trading with the enemy by declaring that any vessel sailing to England was liable to seizure. These restrictions resulted in the seizure of about 1,600 American vessels. In addition there were outright attacks, such as the "Leopard's" firing on the "Chesapeake."

American Retaliation. President Jefferson resorted to economic coercion to gain respect for American neutral rights. The Embargo Act of December, 1807, prohibited American vessels from sailing for foreign ports and permitted coastal trade only under heavy bond. American exports dropped from 108.3 million dollars in 1807 to 22.4 million in 1808; imports from 138.5 million to 56.9 million. Pressure from shipping interests, especially in New England, resulted in the repeal of the embargo in March, 1809. The Non-Intercourse Act, forbidding trade with Great Britain, France, and their possessions only, was substituted. This was followed by the Macon Bill in 1810, which permitted trade with all countries, but which provided that if either belligerent withdrew the restrictions on American shipping, nonintercourse would be reimposed on the other. Deceived into believing that Napoleon had removed the French decrees, President Madison proclaimed the revival of nonintercourse against Great Britain if the Orders in Council were not repealed. The Macon Bill proved ineffectual because Napoleon continued to seize American shipping, and England ignored our demands. Notwithstanding the interference with trade in the period from 1809 to 1811, American shipping grew and prospered.

Outbreak of War. With both belligerents unmindful of American neutral rights, the United States drifted toward war in 1811. In early 1812 another embargo was established, and on June 18 the United States declared war on England. Although the ostensible causes of the war were violations of American neutrality, other factors were of more importance. Western farmers and plantation owners attributed the decline in agricultural prices to British interference with our commerce; the frontier settlers blamed the English for the Indian uprising in the northwest in 1811; and there was a strong desire to annex Florida and Canada.

Commerce and the War of 1812. The war was largely a naval one, and land operations, quite unsuccessful for the United States, were relatively unimportant. The small American navy acquitted itself well, and American privateers captured about 1,300 prizes, but the superior British navy effectively blockaded the coast of the United States and seized some 1,400 American vessels. The effect of war on commerce was great: United States exports fell from 61.3 million dollars in 1811 to 6.9 million in 1814, and imports from 53.4 million to 12.9 million. Commercial New England bitterly deplored the economic effects of this war to protect neutral shipping rights.

Peace of Ghent, 1814. American expectations of easy victories in the War of 1812 were not realized, and negotiations for peace began early. In December, 1814, peace with England was concluded with no mention of the ostensible causes of fighting. It seemed likely, however, that general peace in Europe would end the interference with American commerce.

Economic Effects of Peace. The return to peace and more normal conditions in Europe resulted in a great revival of trade. Imports flooded the American market and threatened or ruined many new businesses. Expansion in foreign trade continued until 1819, however, when there was a sharp decline. In this postwar period agreements concluded with Great

Britain, France, other European nations, and Latin American countries established reciprocal trade privileges. In 1830 England finally opened the West Indies to American shipping.

FOREIGN COMMERCE, 1820-1860

The foreign trade of the United States expanded considerably between 1820 and 1860, and there were important changes in the structure of American commerce.

VOLUME OF TRADE
(in millions of dollars)

	1821	1831	1841	1851	1860
Total imports	62	103	127	220	362
Total exports	64	81	121	218	400
Total	126	184	248	438	762

Trends. The period 1820-1830 was one of prosperity for American shipping. Tonnage in foreign trade was less in 1830 than in 1820, but a greater proportion of American trade was carried in American vessels than at any other time of our history. Registered tonnage in foreign trade increased after 1830, but the percentage of American trade carried by American vessels declined. A number of factors increased American trade: the wars between Great Britain and China, the Crimean War, the European revolutions of 1848, the California gold rush, increased immigration, and the growing cotton trade. Abnormal demand for shipping resulted in overproduction in the 1850's and the decline of the American merchant marine. The major factors contributing to the decline were as follows: (1) overproduction of vessels due to unusual demand, (2) British technological superiority in the construction of iron and steam ships, (3) the decline of various areas of trade, e.g., Far Eastern trade and West Indian trade, and (4) the panic of 1857. The Civil War period accentuated the tendency of decline that had already begun.

Balance of Payments. In only 14 out of 70 years from 1789 to 1860 did the value of United States exports exceed the value of imports. We financed our imports in several ways: (1) the shipment of goods, (2) specie exports, (3) earnings of foreign investments in America, and (4) the performance of various services. Specie shipments were not very important until after the discovery of gold in the 1840's and 1850's. Throughout the period the money earned by the American merchant marine was the largest factor in balancing payments.

Areas of Trade. The important areas with which Americans traded were Europe, Cuba, British North America, the Far East, and Spanish America.

EUROPE. Our most important trading associate was England, with which business steadily increased. Imports from England were woolen and cotton textiles, hardware, cutlery, and iron rails. Cotton became the chief American export. In the 1830's, trade with France began to grow rapidly: Americans desired silks, luxury items, and wines. Although trade with Germany also increased, the combined trade of France and Germany was not one-half of the English total. Business with Baltic and Mediterranean countries was much less important.

CUBA. The third most valuable trade of the United States was with Cuba. This trade was of more value than the total trade with the new republics of Spanish America. Cuba replaced Jamaica as our source of sugar and became an important field for American investments and a market for American products.

AREAS OF TRADE
(in millions of dollars)

Combined Imports and Exports	1821	1831	1841	1851	1860
United Kingdom	46	77	96	211	340
France	10	17	41	55	105
Cuba	11	13	17	23	46
British North America	2	4	8	18	46
Germany (Hanse)	3	5	6	16	36
Brazil	1	4	9	18	27
China	7	4	4	9	22

BRITISH NORTH AMERICA. The value of trade with British North America was only 2 million dollars in 1821, but by 1860 it had risen to 46 million (to equal the value of trade with Cuba). Tonnage cleared for this area was greater than for any other country by 1841, but the tonnage was not in proportion to the value of the trade.

FAR EAST. The trade with China and the East Indies was not so great as many glamorous accounts would seem to indicate Eastern luxuries were paid for with furs, cheap cottons, gin seng, whale products, sandalwood, tobacco, and silver dollars.

SPANISH AMERICA. The United States did a moderate amount of business with Puerto Rico, Mexico, and other Caribbean republics. After 1830, there developed a guano trade with the islands off Peru and a coffee trade with Brazil.

Commodities. The outstanding commercial development of the period after 1815 was the growth of cotton exports from a total value of 20.1 million dollars in 1821 to 191.8 million in 1860. New York City became the center for the cotton trade because of the commercial inactivity of the South and the industry of the New York merchants. The repeal of the English Corn Laws and the potato famine produced a demand for American wheat, which ranked second among exports in 1860.

FOREIGN TRADE COMMODITIES
(in millions of dollars)

Exports	1821	1830	1840	1850	1860
Cotton	20.1	29.6	63.8	71.9	191.8
Wheat and flour	4.4	6.1	11.7	7.7	19.5
Tobacco	5.6	5.5	9.8	9.9	15.9
Lumber and wood manufactures	1.5	2.0	2.9	4.8	14.6
Cotton manufactures	—	1.3	3.5	4.7	10.9
Imports					
Woolens	7.2	5.9	10.8	19.6	43.1
Cotton manufactures	7.3	7.8	6.5	20.7	33.2
Coffee	4.4	4.2	8.5	11.2	21.8
Sugar	3.5	4.6	5.5	7.5	31.0
Hides, skins, and furs	1.1	2.7	3.1	5.8	12.3

SHIPS AND SHIPBUILDING

Foreign confusion in the period 1793-1812 encouraged American shipping. The merchant marine reached a peak of 1,124,000 tons in 1810. After the War of 1812 American shipbuilding declined and did not increase substantially until the 1840's. The same factors encouraging the growth of trade in the years 1840-1860 also stimulated shipbuilding. The merchant marine reached the total of 5,539,000 tons and the value of $500,000,000 in 1861. Whereas in earlier times shipping was an outstanding area for capital investment, investments in railroads and industry were four to five times as great as those in shipping by 1860.

Packet Ships. Providing the first regular transatlantic service, packet ships sailed on specified days rather than whenever the ship was full. The beginning of packet lines came in 1818 when vessels of the Black Ball Line sailed from Liverpool and from New York. This transatlantic service was supplemented by packet lines running from New York to southern ports.

Clipper Ships. After 1845 the fast-sailing clipper ships were built. Beautiful and extremely speedy, these vessels were often able to outdistance early steamships, and they were often used in the long voyages to California and the Far East. Initial profits induced overproduction of clipper ships, and business opportunities were not sufficient to support them in the late 1850's.

Steamships. Sailing packets had established regular schedules of voyages by the time that steamships became common. Although the auxiliary steamer "Savannah" crossed the Atlantic in 1820, it was not until 1838 that regular steamship service across the Atlantic was established. Samuel Cunard established his famous line in 1840. At first Congress subsidized the development of this type of business, but after two disasters in the early 1850's this aid was discontinued. Thereafter, Atlantic liner traffic was carried on largely by foreign vessels.

WHALING AND FISHING

Whaling and fishing were fairly prosperous industries in the period before the Civil War.

Whaling. The whaling industry was retarded during the Revolution and in the Napoleonic period, but after 1815 whaling increased in significance. Early whaling was restricted to the Atlantic, but after 1835 the Pacific was a more important area for this industry. The largest whaling fleet sailed from New Bedford; Nantucket and New London ranked next in importance. The average annual production of whale products in the 25 years before the Civil War was: 118,000 barrels of sperm oil, 216,000 barrels of whale oil, and 2,324,000 pounds of whalebone. Although much of the oil was used in America, export markets for sperm oil and whalebone were found in the West Indies, South America, and Europe.

Fishing. Despite the retarding effects of the Revolution and the War of 1812, tonnage in cod-fishing increased from 25,000 in 1790 to 136,700 in 1860. The average annual value of the cod-fishing industry was about 3 million dollars. In these years tonnage engaged in mackerel-fishing grew, and there began commercial fishing for herring, halibut, and oysters. Although the fishing industry expanded, it was not relatively as important as in the colonial period. Maine and Massachusetts continued to lead in fishing.

REVIEW QUESTIONS

1. Why did the foreign trade of the United States increase during the period 1789-1807?
2. Why did United States shipping suffer in the years 1807-1815?
3. What effect did the coercive measures of the United States government have on foreign trade during the period 1807-1812?
4. Why did the United States go to war in 1812?
5. What were the effects of peace on American commerce?
6. What factors encouraged American shipping in the 1840's and 1850's?
7. What factors contributed to the decline of American shipping in the late 1850's?
8. With what nations was most of the foreign trade of the United States carried on from 1815 to 1860?
9. How important was cotton in foreign trade?
10. What was the importance of the packet ships?
11. To what extent were steamships in use by 1860?

14

MONEY AND BANKING, 1789-1860

In the period 1789-1860, a national currency was established, bimetallism was tried, and legislation was enacted to authorize the issuance of treasury notes and federal bank notes.

MONETARY HISTORY

The need for adequate money and credit became readily apparent during the first years of the national economy.

Establishment of a National Currency. The Constitution provided for the establishment of a national currency. Congress was empowered to coin money and regulate its value. No state was permitted to coin money, to issue bills of credit, or to declare anything but gold and silver legal tender.

MINT ACT OF 1792. By this measure Congress enacted Hamilton's proposals as presented in his *Report on the Mint* (April, 1791). The dollar was established as the basic unit of value, and the decimal system of reckoning was adopted. The law created a bimetallic currency standard with a mint ratio of 15 to 1. Gold coins authorized were the $10 eagle, the $5 half-eagle, and the $2.50 quarter-eagle; silver coins were the dollar, half-dollar, and quarter; in addition, there were the copper penny and the half-penny.

THE SILVER PERIOD, 1792-1834. This period was characterized by a shortage of specie. Silver predominated over gold as the circulating currency because the market ratio of silver to gold rose higher than the fixed mint ratio and, as a consequence, the overvalued silver drove gold out of circulation. The principal coin in use was the silver half-dollar; silver dollars were not minted from 1806 to 1840. Fractional coins of this period were of full weight, i.e., a dollar in change contained the same amount of silver as a silver dollar.

FOREIGN COINS. Because of the shortage of specie, foreign coins were given legal-tender status for a limited period, after which time it was assumed that currency of the United States would replace them. The expectation that foreign coins would disappear from circulation did not materialize quickly; because of the adverse balance of trade, American gold and silver tended to flow out of the country and there was a shortage of specie. In the early years of the national history, merchants found it possible to gain a premium of silver by exchanging American silver dollars for slightly heavier Spanish dollars. This obviously caused a drain on American specie, and after 1804 the United States discontinued the coinage of the silver dollar.

Bimetallism Continued—the Gold Period, 1834-1861. Despite growing opinion that bimetallism would not work, and despite pleas for monometallism, the dual standard was adjusted and continued until after the Civil War. The Coinage Act of 1834 (slightly amended in 1837) adjusted the mint ratio to 15.988 to 1 with the purpose of bringing gold back into circulation. The new ratio was very favorable to gold with the result that silver was undervalued at the mint and forced out of circulation. Discoveries of gold in California and Australia further debased gold and increased the amount of gold coin.

The Subsidiary Coinage Act of 1853 reduced the weight of subsidiary silver coins to prevent them from disappearing from circulation. Under this act a fairly adequate supply of small change was made available.

Federal Paper Money. In several periods of crisis the government issued interest-bearing treasury notes which were generally in high denominations and of short duration. During the War of 1812, Treasury notes amounting to 36.6 million dollars were issued to help meet the cost of war. Again, during the panic of 1837 eight acts authorized 47 million dollars of notes; further, at the time of the Mexican War the government issued notes in the sum of 26 million dollars.

Bank Notes. Bank issues comprised a substantial portion of currency before the Civil War. This currency included federal and local issues.

First Bank of the United States. The First Bank of the United States was authorized to issue notes which were legal tender in payment of all debts to the government. Moreover, the bank was intended to be a regulator of the currency, for it did not accept notes which state banks failed to redeem in specie.

Second Bank of the United States. Notes of the Second Bank of the United States were not to exceed 35 million dollars, the total capital, and the bank was required to maintain specie payments. This bank also was designed to act as a currency stabilizer.

State Banks. Enormous quantities of paper money were issued by local banks. There was little or no regulation of these bank issues, which often depreciated or were inconvertible in times of crisis.

Between 1812 and 1817 the total of state bank notes rose from 45 million dollars to 100 million, and the loss to the government (1814-1817) through the repudiation of notes was about 5 million. From 1820 to 1860 local bank issues rose from 16.6 million to 207 million dollars.

BANKING

From 1781 to 1860 the expanding national economy required the development of extensive banking facilities.

Early American Banks. The first American bank in the modern sense was the Bank of North America founded at Philadelphia in 1781. This institution, chartered first by the Continental Congress and then by the state of Pennsylvania, served as the fiscal agent of the government for a short time. The Bank of New York was organized in 1784 (not chartered until 1791) under articles of association written by Alexander Hamilton. The Bank of Massachusetts was chartered in 1784. By 1811 there were 88 state banks in the United States.

First Bank of the United States. Hamilton advocated the creation of a national bank. His purposes were: (1) to create a safe depository for government funds, (2) provide a fiscal agent for the government, (3) to issue paper money, and (4) to establish banking facilities for commercial operations. Strict constructionists of the Constitution declared that the Congress did not have the authority to create such a bank. Some felt that the bank would lead to a financial monopoly by Federalist capitalists. Despite strong opposition the Bank of the United States was chartered in 1791 for 20 years as a private corporation governed by 25 directors. It had a capital of 10 million dollars, 2 million of which was subscribed by the government. Notes of the bank were limited to the amount of capital stock, except upon authorization by Congress, and were receivable in taxes while redeemable at the bank in specie. The bank was forbidden to buy and sell goods except for forfeited collateral. The Secretary of the Treasury had the power to inspect the bank's affairs at any time.

SUCCESS OF THE BANK. The First Bank of the United States was a success from the start. It served as the government's depository, made loans to the government, effected transfers of money for the Treasury without charge, and assisted in establishing a sound currency by refusing to accept inconvertible bank notes. The bank also made loans to private individuals and companies, and helped to stabilize the nation's economy. During its life the bank averaged 8 per cent dividends.

END OF THE BANK. Republican political opposition, the hostility of state banks, and the West's suspicion of financial monopoly prevented the rechartering of the First Bank of the United States. At the end of the charter period in 1811, the assets of the bank were purchased by Stephen Girard of Philadelphia.

Second Bank of the United States. During the War of 1812 Treasury finances were demoralized and no central depository existed. There was great expansion of unregulated local banking and general abandonment of specie payments. As the nation's banking and currency system broke down there was growing demand for another national bank which would (1) aid the government in financing the war and (2) force the resumption of specie payments.

THE CHARTER OF 1816. In 1816 the Second Bank of the United States was chartered by Congress for 20 years with a capitalization of 35 million dollars, one-fifth of which was provided by the government. There were 25 directors, 5 of them appointed by the President. Note issues could not exceed total capital. They were receivable in all payments to the United States, and were redeemable in specie on demand. It was intended that state banks would have to resume specie payments or their notes would be driven out of circulation. Additional legislation was enacted to help promote specie resumption in general: all payments to the government after February 20, 1817, had to be made in coin, Treasury notes, United States Bank notes, or other convertible bank notes. The bank was made the depository of government funds, and also the fiscal agency of the United States.

EARLY MISMANAGEMENT. Until 1819 the bank was badly managed, and terms of the charter were flagrantly violated. The bank failed to discourage unsound banking practices and the issuance of fiat money, but made loans on easy terms and participated in the speculative schemes.

STATE HOSTILITY. Many people blamed the banks, especially the United States Bank, for the depression which began in 1819. In some states, like New York and Ohio, laws were passed to strengthen the banking system. Maryland, Tennessee, Georgia, North Carolina, Kentucky, and Ohio expressed their hatred of the United States Bank by enacting laws intended to tax branch banks out of existence. In two Supreme Court decisions, *McCulloch* v. *Maryland,* 1819, and *Osborn* v. *United States Bank,* 1824, Chief Justice John Marshall declared the state acts unconstitutional.

LATER HISTORY OF THE BANK. Under the presidency of Langdon Cheves (1819-1823) and Nicholas Biddle (1823-1836) the bank operated conservatively and soundly. The bank increased its note issues in order to provide a stable currency for the whole country, and at the same time it put pressure upon state banks to maintain specie payments, in this way checking excessive issues of paper money. Furthermore it was the most important holder of specie reserve in the country, and in times of financial strain it made loans in order to relieve pressure on other banks. In times of general stringency, as in 1828 and 1831-1832, it failed to offer relief because of its own questionable investments and the lack of a centralized banking system.

END OF THE BANK. The Second United States Bank went out

of existence in 1836 when its charter was not renewed. President Jackson, representative of the West, regarded the bank as a dangerous eastern monopoly and an undemocratic political influence. He vetoed a recharter bill in 1832, and when Biddle tried to gain support by frightening the people with a contraction of credit in 1833, public opinion turned against the bank. Not content to let the bank die a natural death in 1836, Jackson discontinued the deposit of government funds and deposited them in state banks. At the end of the federal charter Biddle obtained a charter from Pennsylvania. The reorganized bank suspended specie payment during the panic of 1837 and failed completely in 1841.

Local Banking before the Civil War. Several important factors encouraged the development of banking facilities in this period: (1) a real need for institutions which could mobilize the capital resources of an expanding nation; (2) a shortage of credit for agricultural purposes, especially in the South and West; (3) a persistent demand for cheap paper money, which was generally denied in the national currency structure; and (4) fear of a centralized money monopoly. A common conception of the time was that large supplies of money meant abundant capital, and there was great resistance to deflationary policies.

Expansion in the 1830's. Between 1829 and 1837 the number of state banks rose from 329 to 788, nominal capital from 110 million dollars to 290 million, note circulation from 48 million to 149 million, and total loans and discounts from 137 million to 525 million. This period of expansion was characterized by policies of easy credit and loose banking. Banks often engaged in speculation and made unwise loans with the result that during the panic of 1837 the abandonment of specie was general and there were many bank failures.

Recovery and Expansion. After 1843 there began an increase of banking activity, which reflected the general expansion of the economy as well as the more lenient attitude of states toward the incorporation of banks. Enthusiasm for banks was by no means universal, however. In the deep South there were fewer banks per capita in 1860 than there had been in 1840. There was antibank feeling in some western states as well.

By contrast in northern states, especially in New England, there were sharp increases in bank facilities per capita.

SUMMARY OF STATE BANKING, 1815 TO 1860
(in millions of dollars)

Year	Number	Capital	Notes in Circulation
1815	208	82.0	45.5 to 100
1820	307	102.1	40.6
1829	329	110.1	48.2
1834	506	200.0	94.8
1837	788	290.8	149.2
1840	901	358.4	107.0
1842	692	260.2	83.7
1845	707	206.0	89.6
1848	751	204.8	128.5
1850	824	217.3	131.4
1853	750	207.9	146.1
1854	1208	301.4	204.7
1857	1416	370.8	214.8
1860	1562	421.9	207.1

Banking Regulations. The right of states to regulate banks was unquestioned; states exercised controls through legislation and charters. The basic purpose was to make banks safe, that is, to make sure that they met obligations to depositors and note-holders. With varying degrees of success and failure, the states worked toward sound banking practices.

THE SUFFOLK SYSTEM. In 1818 the Suffolk Bank of Boston established a system which encouraged country banks to redeem their notes at par. In 1845 Massachusetts adopted a law forbidding banks to pay out notes except their own, which meant constant redemption and maintenance of par. Later, in 1858, Massachusetts adopted a law requiring a 15 per cent reserve for both notes and deposits.

THE SAFETY FUND SYSTEM. In 1829 New York adopted a plan for the mutual insurance of banks under which each bank paid a small percentage of capital into a safety fund. This was applied to the payment of all the liabilities (except capital stock) of failed banks after the banks' assets had been exhausted. The fund was inadequate to cope with the numerous bank failures of the panic of 1837, and more safeguards were necessary.

THE FREE BANKING SYSTEM. Before 1838 it was necessary to have a special legislative act for the establishment of a bank, and at times political favoritism and the patronage system influenced the organization of banks. In 1838 New York set up the Free Banking System, which authorized any person or association of persons to set up a bank and issue circulating notes by depositing with the state comptroller certain securities which were to be held as protection for stockholders. Even though the deposit of high-grade securities was an improvement, depreciation of bank notes still resulted. The principle of the New York system was sound, but the method of application had to be improved.

WESTERN SYSTEMS. In the West, where unsound banking practices were common, several types of regulation were attempted. The State Bank of Indiana, established in 1834 and modeled on the Bank of the United States, was well run. The State Bank of Ohio (1845-1866) adopted a sound plan of banking which provided a safety fund and a bond deposit scheme. After the panic of 1837 Louisiana established an excellent system which included the protection of deposits, regular specie settlements, and the prohibition of speculation by banks. The system proved very effective, and it influenced the establishment of the National Bank structure.

REVIEW QUESTIONS

1. What are the provisions of the Constitution concerning currency?
2. What were the provisions of the Mint Act of 1792?
3. Describe the main features of the silver period of our monetary history, 1792-1834; of the gold period, 1834-1861.
4. To what extent did the federal government issue paper money before the Civil War?
5. Indicate how the First and Second Banks of the United States were intended to serve as regulators of the currency.
6. Why was the First Bank of the United States created? How successful was it? Why was it discontinued?
7. Why was the Second Bank of the United States chartered? How well did it operate? Why was it discontinued?
8. What factors encouraged local banking during and after the War of 1812?
9. Indicate how banking grew in the 1830's, suffered during the panic of 1837, and resumed expansion.
10. Describe the main features of the following schemes of bank regulation: the Suffolk System; the Safety Fund System; the Free Banking System.

15

PERFORMANCE OF THE AMERICAN ECONOMY, 1789-1860

Prior to 1865 the two factors exerting the greatest influence upon American economic growth were the increased authority of the federal government and the geographical expansion of the nation. "Before the Revolutionary War, the separate colonies possessed their own economic and political organizations, which were tied very closely to those of the motherland. The Revolutionary War reduced somewhat economic dependence on England and strengthened considerably the interdependence of the nation's individual units. It also set up a new political and economic organization, the United States of America, which, as time went by, grew more powerful in its relations both with the individual states and with the rest of the world."[1]

ECONOMIC FLUCTUATIONS

The main economic fluctuations of the period 1789 to 1860 revolved about the Napoleonic wars and the War of 1812; postwar adjustment and expansion; speculation and growth in the 1830's; the panic of 1837; expansion in the 1850's; and the panic of 1857.

Economic Activity, 1789-1815. The American economy was variously affected by the almost continuous European war of the period and by the War of 1812. The years until 1807 were

[1] Harold M. Somers, in *Growth of the American Economy*, ed. by H. F. Williamson, p. 312.

prosperous for our essentially agricultural economy. Shipping and trade, though subjected to various interruptions, expanded and prospered. The Embargo and Nonintercourse Acts of the United States changed this trend, however; with commerce restricted, shipping and agriculture were adversely affected.

The War of 1812 affected various elements of the American economy differently. The loss of trade meant hardship for shipping and agriculture, but shortages stimulated American manufacturing. There was general inflation. The period saw a great expansion of banking and note issues because of the increase in government borrowing and spending and the end of the restraining influences of the Bank of the United States. The overextension of credit and unsound banking practices resulted in the general abandonment of specie payment.

Postwar Adjustment and Expansion. With the return of peace and the reopening of the American economy, a period of prosperity and expansion began which lasted nearly to the end of 1818. As trade was resumed the prices of imports fell quickly; the prices of domestic goods, however, remained high somewhat longer because of continued foreign demand. Adjustments were necessary for many small manufacturing companies, which had to contend with reduced profits and competition from foreign goods. The period until 1819 was characterized by the expansion of banking and credit facilities and an upward trend in business activity.

THE PANIC OF 1819. From 1819 to 1822 the nation suffered a depression. The decline of foreign demand for American foodstuffs caused farm prices to drop sharply, and there was a general contraction of English loans and credits. Many state banks failed, and specie payments were abandoned; the Bank of the United States avoided bankruptcy only by a policy of sharp contraction. Depression conditions were experienced universally: agriculture was suddenly prostrated as farm prices collapsed, land values fell ruinously, and numerous bankruptcies resulted; labor suffered seriously from unemployment and large numbers were imprisoned for indebtedness; the propertied classes were affected adversely by the decline of property values and numerous forced sales of goods.

RELIEF MEASURES. Despite the general feeling that the federal government should not assume responsibility for relief measures, the government issued two loans in 1820 and 1821, liberalized its land policy in 1820, and considered passage of a national bankruptcy law. Most of the relief work was handled by local authorities: soup kitchens were set up in New York City and other eastern cities; some western and southern states adopted appraisal and stay laws, which delayed foreclosures and protected property values in excess of a debtor's obligations; a number of states reduced or abolished imprisonment for indebtedness; and several states adopted more stringent banking laws.

Expansion in the 1830's. An increase in the supply of loanable capital and policies of easy credit encouraged speculation and business expansion. State banks were generous in making loans for many purposes, and were liberal in their requirements of collateral security. The deposit of federal government funds in favored state banks after 1832 and the distribution of three-fourths of the Treasury's surplus to the states in 1837 added to the supply of domestic capital. At the same time English and European investors bought many American securities; in 1839 estimates of British ownership of American stocks ranged from 110 million to 165 million dollars. European creditors also provided American importers with financial backing that enabled them to triple their business between 1830 and 1837.

LAND SPECULATION. From 1834 to 1837 over 42 million acres of public land were sold, the highest annual total being 20,074,-870 acres in 1836. The Specie Circular of 1836, requiring payment in specie for land, helped precipitate the panic and resulted in the reduction of land sales to 5,601,103 acres in 1837.

CANAL AND RAILROAD EXPANSION. The success of the Erie Canal encouraged the construction of additional canals and there was general enthusiasm for other internal improvements. Private as well as public funds were used to increase canal mileage from an estimated 1,270 in 1830 to 3,320 in 1840. The 1830's saw the beginning of American railroads, with somewhat less than 3,000 miles of track constructed.

STATE INDEBTEDNESS. Public investment in banks, canals, railroads, and turnpikes produced huge debts, and there was little concern for their retirement. The total debts of the states increased as follows:

1820	$ 12,790,728
1830	$ 26,470,417
1835	$ 66,472,186
1839 over	$170,000,000

The Panic of 1837. Four factors precipitated the panic of 1837. (1) President Jackson's Specie Circular, July 11, 1836, provided that only specie would be accepted in payment for public land. This measure caused a contraction of credit and created general suspicion of western bank notes. (2) On June 23, 1836, Congress provided for the distribution of the Treasury surplus on January 1, 1837, to the states. Twenty-eight million dollars was distributed, and the money was often used for construction of internal improvements. The distribution of the surplus, largely held in western banks, resulted in the contraction of the credit of the depositories. (3) A financial crisis in England decreased credit and caused a flow of specie from the United States. (4) Crop failures in 1835, 1837, and 1838 added to the distress, preventing farmers from meeting obligations. This also added to the difficulty of balancing trade and increased the demand for specie needed to meet foreign obligations.

DEPRESSION CONDITIONS. In May, 1837, New York banks discontinued specie payments, and most of the other banks soon followed suit. There was partial resumption in 1839, but then another recession set in. The United States Bank of Pennsylvania became involved in a speculative effort to maintain the price of cotton; it suspended payment in October, 1839, and failed in May, 1841. The depression saw hundreds of bank and business failures. Prices fell sharply, property value declined, wages dropped, and unemployment mounted. There was considerable unrest. Though New York, Pennsylvania, and Massachusetts were badly hurt, certain areas of the South were most severely affected. In 1841 and 1842, eight states and one territory defaulted in interest payments on their obligations.

RELIEF MEASURES. The federal government did little to alleviate the distress. Congress authorized the issuance of 10 million dollars of one-year Treasury notes. Merchants were relieved by extension of the time for payment of their customs bonds.

The last quarter of the Treasury surplus was not distributed to the states. In 1840 Congress set up an Independent Treasury to hold and disburse public money on a specie basis and to take the government out of the banking business. The Congressional Bankruptcy Act of 1841 cancelled over 450 million dollars of debts held by one million creditors. Many states adopted stay and appraisal laws to relieve debtors; in numerous cases imprisonment for debt was abandoned.

RESULTS OF THE PANIC OF 1837. The American people became decidedly cautious about internal improvements and reckless banking. States adopted constitutional amendments to prevent the use of state credit for internal improvements or the support of commercial banks. Public reactions to the business panic led to numerous reforms in state banking laws.

The Whigs repealed the Independent Treasury Act, raised the tariff in 1842 almost to the level of 1832, and tried to recharter a national bank. In 1846, with the Democrats again in power, the Independent Treasury and a lower tariff (the Walker Tariff) were restored.

Socialistic Experiments. The 1830's and 1840's produced a variety of humanitarian movements, many of them socialistic. This was due to the evils of growing industrialism and the depression, 1837-1843. A number of religious groups attempted the common ownership of property, e.g., the Pietists, Rappites, Dunkers, Shakers, and Moravians. One early experiment was that of the English socialist, Robert Owen, who established the communal town of New Harmony, Indiana, 1825-1828. Followers of Charles Fourier founded 33 settlements based on his socialistic ideas. These experiments failed because of internal difficulties, external competition, and the return of prosperity.

Expansion in the 1850's. There was rapid economic expansion in the 1850's, which was not checked until the panic of 1857. Railroad construction boomed, the value of our foreign trade reached record heights, American shipping increased importantly, and there was an accompanying expansion of banking. Owing to the prosperity of the United States, foreign investors poured large amounts of capital into the country, the bulk of it in state securities and railroad stocks and bonds. In the mid-1850's it was estimated that nearly one-fifth of all American securities, public and private, were owned abroad.

The Panic of 1857. This crisis can be traced to overinvestment and speculation, especially in western railroads. For three years before the crisis of 1857 financial conditions had been rather uncertain. Public confidence was shaken by the failure of some western banks in 1855, and people began to hoard specie. The failure of the Ohio Life Insurance and Trust Company in August, 1857, due to excessive speculation by its New York branch, precipitated the panic. The depression brought a sharp decline of commodity and stock prices, the discontinuance of specie payment, the failure of over 13,000 firms by 1860, reduced wages, and widespread unemployment. In addition to the relief work of numerous private organizations, public works were undertaken by some municipalities to provide employment. The effects of this economic crisis upon the North and the West were not fully overcome by the beginning of the Civil War.

ECONOMIC TRENDS

Major economic trends reflected the development of a national economy, changes in economic organization, and a rising standard of living.

A National Economy. In 1789 the localized colonial economy of the United States was hardly more than an undeveloped frontier of Europe. By 1860 there had developed in America a national economy, which, although still dependent upon the outside world in important respects, had established diversified production and had laid the groundwork for further growth. An important aspect of this development was the growth of the economic power of the government. As yet the policy of laissez faire was followed, and public regulations for the control of economic life were comparatively few.

Economic Organization. Until the mid-nineteenth century, merchant capitalism prevailed in the United States; that is, the economic scene was dominated by the merchant or trader. In the period after the War of 1812 the producer-entrepreneur rose in importance and gradually superseded the merchant as the dominant figure in the economy. By the time of the Civil

War the factory system had been established, great technological advances had been made, and the corporate form of business organization had become common. The United States was entering a period of industrial capitalism.

The Standard of Living. Between 1799 and 1859 the per capita real income of the country rose unevenly from about $211 to $300. This is a fair indication of the increase in per capita production in the period. The proportion of the national income derived from agriculture dropped from 39.5 per cent in 1799 to 30.8 per cent in 1859. During the same interval, income from manufacturing increased from 4.8 to 12.1 per cent. The increased real income per capita as well as the reduction of working time are indications of improvement in the standard of living.

REVIEW QUESTIONS

1. How was the American economy affected by the wars in Europe, 1789-1815?
2. What adjustments were necessary with the return of peace in 1815?
3. Describe conditions during the panic of 1819. What relief measures were undertaken?
4. What factors encouraged economic expansion in the 1830's?
5. What caused the panic of 1837?
6. Describe economic conditions during the panic of 1837. What relief measures were undertaken?
7. What economic forces led to the crisis of 1857?
8 What developments indicate a rising standard of living, 1789-1860?

16

ECONOMIC ASPECTS OF THE CIVIL WAR

The Civil War marked a turning point in American economic history. War hastened the coming of the Industrial Revolution, gave unionism its real beginning, and greatly increased agricultural productivity. For the North, ultimate victory meant the establishment of public policies favorable to the rising industrial and financial interests. For the South, final defeat meant a great social and economic revolution: the dominant planter aristocracy was overthrown and slavery was abolished. The New South was to develop a much more diversified economy than had existed before the war. The Civil War did not end sectional antagonisms, but it settled the question of secession and established the supremacy of the federal government.

ECONOMIC CAUSES OF THE CIVIL WAR

The economic causes of the Civil War were rooted in sectional differences and a struggle for the control of public policy.

Sectional Differences and Antagonisms. The Civil War resulted essentially from the growing conflict of two economic sections—the North and the South. The South was primarily an agricultural section, dominated by the cultivation of cotton. In the colonial period the South had begun a plantation economy based on the cultivation of staple crops by slave labor, and after the Revolution the great emphasis on growing cotton established the system more firmly. The North, on the other hand, was developing a more diversified and healthy economy: it raised large quantities of foodstuffs but had important commercial and industrial interests as well. In the decade before the 1860's the South became increasingly aware of its economic inferiority and fearful of the rising industrial power in the North. Conflict between these two sections was inevitable, and it focused especially on questions of public policy.

Public Policy. In the period 1830-1850 the South enjoyed sufficient political power to have its way very largely in the federal government. This dominance was due to the co-operation of the West and the Northwest with the South. In controversies about tariff and banking policies the South was victorious: from 1833 to 1861 the general trend of the tariff was downward; after 1836, when the Second Bank of the United States went out of existence, there was no central banking institution until the Civil War.

THE CRUCIAL DECADE. The decade 1850-1860 produced an accentuation of sectionalism, and political alignments were changed to coincide with the sectional lines. The southern Democrats dominated all parts of the federal government more effectively than ever before, and angered the North by their stubborn defense of slavery. The most vital issue concerned the extention of slavery into the territories of the United States.

RISE OF THE REPUBLICAN PARTY. Both major parties, the Democrats and the Whigs, which had previously been supported in both the North and the South, were now split over the question of the extension of slavery. In the middle 1850's a new party, the Republican, began to unite the northern opponents of the planter Democrats. The Republican Party took a stand in opposition to the extension of slavery and also promised the Northwest a liberal homestead law. The fact that the Northwest and the Northeast were connected more closely in the 1850's by new railroads made political co-operation between these two sections more natural. The Republican candidate in 1860, Abraham Lincoln, was elected by anti-slavery people who opposed the extension of slavery, by small farmers who wanted a homestead law, and by industrialists who demanded a protective tariff. Lincoln's election by one section exclusively, and the southern planters' loss of political power in the Northwest, seemed to indicate the end of the South's domination of the national government and to threaten the institution of slavery. The answer of the southern states to the election of Lincoln was secession from the Union and war for southern independence.

THE PLANTATION ECONOMY

The South with its plantation economy was a debtor region, dependent on slave labor and outside capital, and beset by the problems of economic inferiority to the North.

A Debtor Section. The South was a debtor section with no liquid capital and was dependent on the northern and English bankers who financed its economy. The price of cotton was determined by the world market, and most of the American crop was exported. Since the South had no merchant marine of any size, the profits of the carrying trade went to northern merchants. Manufactured items were imported by northerners who sold them in the South, reaping the profits of the middlemen. Because of the scarcity of capital and labor there was very little industry in the South. In 1860 the South produced scarcely one-tenth of the amount of cotton manufactures produced by New England. The South blamed its economic troubles on the North and believed that independence was the only solution to the difficulty. Although it is clear that the one-sided plantation economy of the South suffered in competition with the North, it is not clear that independence would have solved the South's problem.

Expansion of Slavery. One aspect of the plantation economy which attracted much attention was slavery. This labor system, begun in the colonial period, was apparently declining at the time of the Revolution, but the great expansion of cotton cultivation after 1790 resulted in the firm establishment of slavery in the South. As a result of the changing economic scene, the South's attitude toward slavery changed from one of apology at the time of the Revolution to one of positive defense by 1825.

Number of Slaves. The number of slaves increased from 750,000 in 1790 to nearly 4,000,000 in 1860. The total number of slaveowners in 1860 was 384,000. Of these 10,781 owned at least 50 slaves and 1,733 owned 100 or more. Despite the fact that the slaveowners were only a small proportion of the total population of the South, the fact that the wealth of the region was linked to the plantations gave this group disproportionate political and economic influence.

COST OF SLAVES. The increased demand for Negro slaves raised the price greatly. Prime field hands could be bought for 200 dollars in 1780, but by 1818 the cost ranged from 700 to 1,000 dollars. In 1860 the cost varied between 1,400 and 2,000 dollars. Although slave labor was inefficient, the abundance of vacant land in the West made it possible to leave exhausted soil and move westward to new and fertile land. As long as good cheap land was available, slave labor could be used to advantage by the cotton planters. This accounts in part for the great interest of the southerners in western land.

ADVANTAGES OF SLAVERY. Complete control of the slaves' time eliminated waste, and the plantation owners received the full fruit of the slave labor. In the case of rice cultivation, only slaves would work in the unhealthful fields of South Carolina. Slaveowners declared that the Negroes were better off as slaves than they would be if free. Even if economic factors were disregarded, the political and social consequences of emancipation were sufficient to convince the South of the necessity of maintaining Negro slavery.

DISADVANTAGES OF SLAVERY. Slave labor was usually reluctant, with little incentive to increase productivity. Constant supervision was necessary and overseers were expensive. Slaves were not only inefficient but usually unskilled as well. They used only the simplest tools and did not easily learn to use machinery. The methods followed by the slave labor system were disastrous in the long run, for in large areas of the South the land was ruined. It is clear that the lack of new fertile land would have eventually made slavery economically inexpedient, but in the years prior to 1860 there was no immediate danger of the exhaustion of good land.

The South's Problem. The South, with its overwhelming emphasis on cotton, was confronted by a condition of growing economic inferiority to the North. Reckless expansion in cotton cultivation, in addition to extravagant living, made the South a debtor section. It has been stated "That the South in general and particularly the lower South, was continuously a debtor region was partly due to the requirements for new capital on account of the exigencies of expansion. But the relative poverty of the South, as compared with the North, was largely the result of a system of rural economy characterized by extravagance both in production and consumption, a system which concentrated a large proportion of the money income in the hands of a relatively small proportion of the population."[1] The choices of the South in 1860 appeared to be submission to the North and destruction of the southern way of life, or secession from the Union. To many in the South the latter seemed the better choice.

NORTH AND SOUTH COMPARED

The resources of the North and the South may be compared with regard to population, armies, and economic strength.

Population. The total population of the eleven states that seceded was about 9 million, of whom 3.5 million were slaves. The population of the states remaining in the Union was over 22 million, but of this number 2.5 million lived in the border states (Delaware, Maryland, Kentucky and Missouri) which aided both sides about equally. Thus, counting only whites, the North had a 3-to-1 majority.

Armies. The greatest strength of northern armies was 1.5 million men, but throughout the war there were 2.9 million enlistments. Estimates of southern military strength vary greatly; the correct figure is probably somewhere between 450,000 and 600,000 men. Despite the numerical superiority of the North a number of factors favored the South: (a) they had interior lines of supply; (b) southern society was better fitted for militarism; (c) the South had a larger number of trained officers; (d) European governments generally sympathized with the South; (e) the South had a vital cause—the preservation of a particular form of civilization.

Economic Strength. Economically and financially, the South was badly outmatched. In 1860 the region produced only about one-fourth of the nation's wealth; two-thirds of the real property of the country was in the North. About 90 per cent of

[1] L. C. Gray, *History of Agriculture in the Southern United States* (2 vols; Washington, D.C., 1933), I, p. 460.

the nation's manufacturing and about two-thirds of the railroad mileage were also in the North.

ECONOMIC PROBLEMS OF THE NORTH

During the war the North was faced with a multitude of problems related to the expansion of production, labor conditions, and Union finances.

Expanded Production. The North and the West enjoyed prosperity during the war period after the depression of 1861. An increase in agricultural production resulted from (a) the Homestead Act, (b) immigration, (c) labor-saving machinery, and (d) an unusual demand for goods both at home and abroad. Manufacturing was also stimulated during the war. In fact, wartime requirements led to the use of production methods which hastened the Industrial Revolution in America, with the attendant danger that the developing American industries would be unable to compete with established European producers. Protection of these industries through the tariff was therefore granted by Congress. Industries which led in the subsequent expansion included those producing woolen cloth and clothes, iron, and guns and munitions.

Labor Conditions. Because of the high cost of living during the war (the average increase in prices has been estimated as high as 125 per cent) labor was at a disadvantage. Wages rose more slowly than prices, perhaps only 60 per cent above the prewar level. The war gave impetus to the American labor movement: numerous new unions appeared during the war, and in 1866 the National Labor Union was organized.

Union Finances. The Civil War produced a financial panic in 1861 in the North as banks suspended specie payments and business failures were common. Southern obligations to northern merchants totalling about 300 million dollars were almost a total loss. The federal treasury was empty; federal credit was at a low point as the government suspended specie payments. The methods used by the Union to finance the Civil War were, in order of their importance, loans, taxation, and paper money. In 1863, to aid in financing the war and to stabilize the northern economy, the national banking system was created.

LOANS. Secretary of the Treasury Chase proposed to finance the war mainly through loans, and Jay Cooke, a Philadelphia banker, floated the loans for the government. Cooke popularized bond issues, emphasizing the advantages of investment and the patriotic duty of citizens. Over 2 billion dollars was raised. Cooke received a commission of one-half of one per cent on sales up to 10 million dollars and three-eighths of one per cent on sales above that amount.

TAXATION. The North resorted to extremely heavy taxation. Excises (begun in 1862) on many goods, businesses, and services produced about 300 million dollars. Increased import duties (based on the Morrill Tariff passed in 1861, and subsequent amendments) raised about 300 million dollars. An income tax produced about 55 million dollars. A total of 667 million dollars was obtained from tax sources.

PAPER MONEY. Beginning in February, 1862, the government issued 449 million dollars in United States notes (Greenbacks). These were legal-tender bills of credit, not backed by gold or silver, but merely by the promise of the government to redeem them. The Greenback fluctuated in value in terms of gold; in 1864 it fell below 40 cents on the dollar. Not until 1875 were these paper bills made convertible into specie.

ECONOMIC PROBLEMS OF THE SOUTH

The inferior economic condition of the South made prosecution of the war difficult. Serious problems arose from inability to procure foreign assistance, numerous shortages, and confused finances.

The Importance of Cotton. The South expected cotton to be a greater force in its favor than it actually was. One reason for the lessened importance of cotton was that overproduction produced a glut on the market in 1860 and 1861. England had an ample supply and the loss of its cotton imports tended to keep up the price. (The North had some cotton on hand, but before long its production of cotton goods began to diminish.) The importance of cotton was also diminished by the fact that the English needed northern wheat and grain, for which they found it profitable to exchange arms and ammunition. Moreover, English laborers were unsympathetic toward the South (even though textile unemployment hurt them) because they were opposed to Negro slavery.

The Northern Blockade. The northern blockade had an extremely detrimental effect upon the Confederate war effort, for it prevented the export of southern produce and the import of necessary manufactures and foodstuffs. In the years 1862-1864, only one-tenth of the prewar amount of cotton was exported, and more cotton was shipped overland to the North than to Great Britain.

Scarcity of Foodstuffs and Manufactures. The South was forced to try to produce more food and to manufacture a variety of other needed commodities. Blockade-running brought tremendous profits, but supplies obtained in this way were not enough. Despite great efforts of the Confederates in manufacturing, their emphasis upon cotton placed them at a serious disadvantage. Manufacturing increased, and some essential industries were taken over by the government, but the South still had inadequate quantities of cotton cloth, whiskey, salt, guns, and gunpowder. Increased domestic manufacturing produced a considerable amount of cotton cloth and leather goods. The war brought a shift in southern agriculture, too, as cotton production decreased and food production increased. While grain production was emphasized, food was still scarce, and bread riots occurred in several large cities. The breakdown of the southern rail system and the destruction of property by Union armies further aggravated conditions of scarcity.

Confederate Finances. Confederate sources of funds included loans, taxation, and paper money.

Loans. Bond issues were floated by the Confederacy (also by individual southern states) but without much success. Bonds were often made payable in produce, and the government soon accumulated large quantities of cotton, tobacco, and other staples. Some of this was marketed and some was pledged as security for a loan floated in Europe in 1863.

Taxation. Confederate taxation was not very fruitful. The attempt to levy a direct tax through the separate states produced little; other taxes (excises, business licenses, income taxes) were disappointing. An unpopular 10 per cent levy on farm produce, payable in kind, was very helpful to the government. It is estimated that total receipts through taxation amounted to about 100 million dollars.

PAPER MONEY. The Confederacy resorted to issues of fiat money to the value of over one billion dollars and issues by state and local authorities greatly increased this figure. Depreciation of the Confederate bills exceeded that of the Greenbacks: in the summer of 1863 they were worth about 25 cents in gold per dollar; in mid-1864, 5 cents on the dollar; at the end of the war they were worthless. Northern Greenbacks that made their way into the South circulated at a premium during the war.

RESULTS OF THE CIVIL WAR

The main results of the Civil War were preservation of the Union, progress in industrialism, abolition of slavery, and the transformation of the economy of the South.

The Union Preserved. The question of secession was settled and the Union was maintained. Sectionalism was by no means ended; in some ways it was intensified. The legacy of hatred resulting from the war and reconstruction period is still a powerful factor in American history.

Industrialism Advanced. A new North emerged from the Civil War because of the stimulus to industry. Merchant capitalism was supplanted by industrial capitalism. During the war and largely through the remainder of the nineteenth century, the federal government served the growing industrial power of the North well, as indicated by tariff protection, a central banking system, large grants to railroads and generally conservative monetary policies. The agrarian West was displeased with these policies but still co-operated for the most part with the Republican Party.

Slavocracy Ended. Southern society was completely transformed: Negro slavery was ended, and the plantation system was largely eliminated. Emancipation of the Negroes was one of the greatest confiscations of property in Anglo-Saxon history. The method of emancipation was a poor one, both for the Negroes and the southern whites. The freedmen were often worse off than before—economically, socially, and morally—and were frequently the victims of frauds. The Freedmen's

Bureau, designed originally to aid the Negroes, soon degenerated into a Republican political agency. While Negroes were granted equality nominally, the South continued to place them in a position of inferiority.

The excesses of the reconstruction period aggravated the economic dislocation of the South. Carpetbaggers and scalawags saddled the South with tremendous financial burdens, and not until 1900 was southern property again worth what it was in 1860.

The New South. Share-cropping, a credit system easy to start, became the most characteristic form of agriculture. Landlords usually provided living quarters, food, tools, and seed; frequently, the return was divided into thirds allocated to land, equipment, and labor. Farmers who fell into the clutches of merchant creditors found it most difficult to escape from the system. Farm tenantry in general increased in the South, and the incomes of tenant farmers remained deplorably low.

The South developed a more diversified economy after the Civil War. By 1900 almost a billion dollars had been invested in southern industries, of which the most important were cotton textiles, iron and steel, lumbering, furniture manufacturing, and tobacco processing.

REVIEW QUESTIONS

1. Explain the growth of economic sectionalism, 1820-1860.
2. In what ways was the economy of the South subservient to that of the North?
3. What were the economic advantages and disadvantages of slavery?
4. Why did the South secede from the Union?
5. What factors aided the South in the Civil War? What factors aided the North?
6. How did the Union finance the war? How did the South do this?
7. What factors encouraged agricultural expansion during the war? Industrial expansion?
8. Discuss the importance of cotton during the war.
9. State the economic results of the war in the South and in the North.

17

PASSING OF THE FRONTIER

By the time of the Civil War the westward-moving frontier line had extended beyond the Mississippi, a number of states on the west coast had been formed, and a second frontier line was moving eastward from California and Oregon. In 1860 the great intervening area between these frontier lines contained only 1 per cent of the total population of the nation. In the latter part of the nineteenth century this barren region was largely occupied. Several transcontinental railroads facilitated the process of rapid expansion. Miners, cattlemen, and homesteaders made their way to the area, and by the turn of the century the frontier was closed.

WESTERN RAILROADS

Of major importance in the opening of the trans-Mississippi West were the transcontinental railroads. They facilitated the westward movement of settlers and the marketing of western produce.

The Union Pacific. The first of the transcontinental railroads was the Union Pacific, completed in 1869. After the beginning of settlement in California there had been increased agitation for rail connections to the Mississippi Valley. It was not until 1862, however, that the Union Pacific and Central Pacific Railroad Companies were chartered by Congress to build a railroad between California and Iowa. The federal government provided loans of 27 million dollars and made generous land grants to the roads. Unfortunately, disgraceful practices characterized the promotion and financing of the Union Pacific. The promoters of the road worked through a small Pennsylvania company, the Credit Mobilier Corporation, to which liberal construction contracts were given. Government officials, including Congressmen, were bribed by gifts of stock and money. At last, in 1872, the corrupt practices were exposed by a Congressional investigating committee. The cost of construction to the Union Pacific Railroad Company was about 94 million dollars; the actual cost to the Credit Mobilier Corporation, 44 million dollars. The huge debt with which the Union Pacific was saddled kept this company's financial status in a precarious condition for many years.

Other Western Roads. The Northern Pacific, a transcontinental railroad begun in 1864, was not completed until 1883. It ran from Minnesota to Washington. The Great Northern, which was completed in 1893 by James J. Hill and his associates, connected Minnesota and Washington. The Southern Pacific, completed in 1883, connected New Orleans with Los Angeles. In 1881 this road was linked with the Atchison, Topeka, and Santa Fé.

THE MINING FRONTIER

The discovery of gold in the West attracted a horde of settlers eager to get rich quick. California, settled by the forty-niners, became a state in 1850. When gold was discovered (in 1858) in western Utah Territory near the California border, Carson City was promptly founded. In 1859 gold was found in Colorado and overnight the Pike's Peak area was occupied. (Until recently mining continued to be the leading occupation in Colorado.) The famous Comstock lode of Nevada, discovered in 1859, produced 340 million dollars in silver in the period 1860-1890. Nevada Territory (previously a part of Utah Territory) was organized in 1861 and made a state in 1864. Although silver mining declined at the Comstock lode after 1890, new deposits of silver, gold, and copper were found in Nevada in the early twentieth century. (Copper is now the leading mineral mined in Nevada.) The discovery of gold and silver in Arizona brought miners there, and Arizona Territory (formerly a part of New Mexico Territory) was created in

1863. In the 1870's and 1880's the mining of copper began in Arizona; in the twentieth century (by 1925) this state became America's greatest producer of copper. The discovery of gold in the Northwest led to the organization of Idaho Territory in 1863. The eastern part of this region was cut off to form the territories of Montana and Wyoming in 1864 and 1868, respectively. Gold production in this area became relatively less important. Montana became a leading producer of copper.

THE DAY OF THE CATTLEMAN

For two decades after the Civil War, prior to the arrival of farmers in large numbers, ranches were operated throughout the Great Plains region stretching northward from Texas. The cattle grazed on the open range, and after the spring roundup were driven across the plains to railroad centers. Prosperity for the range cattle industry was short-lived, however; the industry declined as rapidly as it had developed.

Economic Basis of the Industry. The following factors encouraged the growth of the cattle industry: (1) the existence of the open range stretching from Texas to Montana; (2) the discovery that cattle could stand severe winters on the northern Great Plains; (3) the growth of an eastern market; (4) improved transportation; and (5) refrigeration inventions.

Cattle Towns. Cattle shipments from Abilene, Kansas, on the Kansas Pacific Railroad, reached a total of 700,000 head in 1872, only five years after the business had been started in that area. Dodge City, Kansas, on the Atchison, Topeka, and Santa Fé, was the greatest of the early cattle centers. Among other towns engaged in this industry were Wichita and Ellsworth, in Kansas, Ogallala, in Nebraska, and Miles City, in Montana. With the expansion of the range cattle industry, the meat-packing business moved westward, centering at Chicago, St. Louis, Kansas City, and Omaha.

Decline of Range Cattle Industry. After the boom period, 1875-1885, decline set in. (1) Advancing homesteaders fenced in the open range. (2) State inspection laws and legislation forbidding the driving of stock across state lines prevented the long drive. (3) Severe winters in the 1880's and a drought in

1886 greatly damaged the industry. (4) Early profits encouraged the investment of Eastern and British capital, and over-expansion resulted.

THE FARMER'S FRONTIER

Although federal land policies eventually aided the frontier farmers, they were confronted with serious problems of transportation, water scarcity, and lack of materials needed for fencing.

Federal Land Policy. The following six acts reflected the principal trends of federal land policy.

(1) The Homestead Act (1862) was the culmination of a long period of agitation for free land. A citizen, a person who had declared his intention of becoming a citizen, or the head of a family could obtain the title to 160 acres of public land merely by living on it for five years and cultivating it. Although the Homestead Act was a liberal law, its significance often has been overrated. Much of the best land had already been given away through railroad grants and educational grants, and although the measure was intended to benefit small farmers, the privilege of commuting still enabled companies to procure large tracts of land. Only 48,000,000 acres had been granted to families under the Homestead Act by 1890; thereafter, however, the act was used more often.

(2) The Morrill Act (1862) provided that any state which established a public agricultural college could receive 30,000 acres of public land for each representative that it had in Congress. Eventually every state availed itself of this opportunity.

(3) The Timber Culture Act (1873) authorized the grant of 160 acres of land to anyone who would plant and care for a certain acreage of timber. About 10 million acres were disposed of in this way, but fraudulent use of the act led to its repeal in 1891.

(4) The Desert Land Act (1877) permitted the granting of arid land at $1.25 an acre with the provision that irrigation be attempted within three years. Results were disappointing.

(5) The Timber and Stone Act (1878) authorized the sale of 160 acres of non-mineral land, valuable for timber or stone, at a minimum price of $2.50 an acre. Although the purchaser had

to swear that he would not resell the land, this provision was often violated. By 1945 some 14 million acres had been granted under this law.

(6) The Carey Act (1894) provided for the cession of a million acres of public land to states that would subsidize irrigation projects. Results were meagre.

Problems of Farming on the Great Plains. In the period 1870-1890, about 10 million new settlers appeared on the Great Plains. Farming in this region presented a number of difficult problems. (1) Transportation facilities were vital to western farmers. The railroads were of great benefit to the region, but often their practice of discrimination and exploitation made them the object of attack by the farmers. (2) The scarcity of water was an almost insuperable barrier: rainfall was usually inadequate for agriculture, and irrigation was almost impossible. Wells were sunk, sometimes as deep as 300 feet, with windmills to raise the water. This method did not, however, provide a complete solution. Irrigation projects, public and private, were attempted with little success, for only a small fraction of the area was reclaimed. More successful in combatting aridity was dry farming, a means of conserving soil moisture by special methods of cultivation. (3) The fencing problem was acute because of the lack of stone and lumber. After the Civil War, hedges of osage orange plants (still in use in some areas) were introduced. Barbed wire, invented in the 1870's, solved this problem: production of barbed wire increased from 10,000 pounds in 1874 to 80,500,000 pounds in 1880.

MEANING OF THE PASSING OF THE FRONTIER

By 1890 the frontier could be said to have disappeared. The existence of a vast unoccupied territory in the West had made American economic history somewhat different from that of western Europe, for the frontier had provided opportunities for adventursome persons and in hard times had tended to act as a safety valve. On the other hand, one should not exaggerate the importance of the passing of the frontier. Even today, land in Canada and a good deal of inferior land in the United States are still available for use. After the passing of the frontier, however, there has been more emphasis upon scientific agriculture and reclamation. Although unoccupied good land was no longer available in the West, economic decline did not follow the closing of the frontier. In the twentieth century, Americans have concentrated upon scientific and cultural frontiers.

REVIEW QUESTIONS

1. What is meant by the term "the last frontier"?
2. What forces led to the passing of the frontier?
3. Discuss the significance of railroads in the development of the West.
4. What factors permitted the rise of the range cattle industry? What forces led to its rapid decline?
5. Describe and evaluate the Homestead Act.
6. Through what measures did the federal government encourage agricultural education and irrigation in the period 1860-1900?
7. What conditions made farming on the Great Plains difficult?
8. Discuss the influence of the passing of the frontier upon American economic life.

18

CHANGING AGRICULTURE, 1860-1914

The years from the beginning of the Civil War to World War I witnessed a revolution in American agriculture. Practically all the arable land was occupied during this period, with more than 500 million acres brought under cultivation from 1860 to 1910. The expansion of the area under cultivation, increased mechanization, and greater use of scientific methods of farming contributed to productivity. Mechanized, specialized, and commercialized agriculture assumed a very significant role in the industrialization of the United States. In the years after the Civil War, however, inefficient use of the land and declining agricultural prices caused agrarian hardship and widespread political unrest.

AGRICULTURAL EXPANSION

In the period 1860 to 1910 the agricultural output of the United States was quadrupled. The acreage under cultivation

FARM STATISTICS, 1860-1945

Year	1860	1880	1900	1910	1920	1930	1945
Number of farms (in thousands)	2,044	4,009	5,737	6,362	6,448	6,289	5,859
Value of selected farm property (in millions of dollars)	7,980	12,181	20,440	41,961	80,327	58,378	63,483
Value of farm implements and machinery (in millions of dollars)	246	407	750	1,265	3,595	3,302	6,235

was doubled, the number of farms was tripled, and the value of farm property was increased five-fold.

The production of leading crops increased substantially from 1860 to 1910: as shown in the table below, corn production increased nearly 2½ times, cotton 3 times, wheat 3½ times, oats more than 4 times.

CROP STATISTICS, 1860-1945

	1860	1900	1910	1930	1945
Corn (in thousand bushels)	838,793	2,661,978	2,852,794	2,080,130	2,880,933
Cotton (in thousand bales)	3,841	10,124	11,609	13,932	9,015
Hay (in thousand tons)			75,184	74,527	108,539
Wheat (in thousand bushels)	173,105	599,315	625,476	886,522	1,108,224
Oats (in thousand bushels)	172,643	417,942	945,483	1,274,592	1,535,676*

* Figures for the year 1859.

MECHANIZATION AND SCIENTIFIC FARMING

As already noted, mechanization and scientific methods increasingly characterized American agriculture after the Civil War.

Mechanization. The unusual demand in the Civil War period and the fact that the western regions being opened up were adaptable to large-scale farming encouraged the mechanization of agriculture. Between 1860 and 1890 the value of farm machinery doubled, as old machines were more widely used and countless new inventions were introduced. Of notable importance were the Marsh harvester, patented in 1858, which cut the time of reaping in half, and the twine binder, invented in 1878, which increased eight-fold the speed of harvesting. Per capita agricultural production in the country as a whole increased from about 5.6 bushels in 1860 to 9.2 bushels in 1880.

By 1905, with the perfection of gasoline-powered implements, agriculture had been revolutionized.

The most significant results of mechanization were (1) a reduction in the manpower required for farming, (2) an increase in per capita production, (3) the cultivation of hitherto unusable land, (4) an increase in the farmer's real income, (5) greater difficulty confronting persons with little capital who wished to go into farming, and (6) the encouragement of overproduction.

Scientific Farming. A number of factors helped to popularize scientific farming. (1) Expanded markets and the development of keen competition during the post-Civil War period of declining prices encouraged the search for cheaper methods of production and the attempt to achieve high standards of quality. (2) The occupation of all readily cultivable land ended many of the wasteful practices that had characterized earlier American agriculture. (3) Agricultural education furthered scientific farming. (4) Public aid and interest were aroused in behalf of agricultural efficiency. Furthermore, in the decades after the Civil War more than 30,000 new plants were introduced on an experimental basis, including staples such as white Kaffir corn, durum wheat, oriental rice, and drought-proof alfalfa. Finally, with the aid of the federal government, diseases such as hog cholera, the hoof-and-mouth disease, and corn rot were overcome; progress was made in the control of the boll weevil, corn borer, Japanese beetle, and gypsy moth.

REGIONAL AGRICULTURE

In the post-Civil War period, significant changes occurred in the agricultural production of the four principal regions of the United States.

The Northeast. Agricultural trends in the Northeast which had begun before 1860 were accentuated during and after the Civil War. The development of transportation networks made it impossible for the northeastern farmers to compete with western farmers who specialized in growing staples such as corn and wheat. Northeastern farmers turned to dairying, raising vegetables, and growing fruits. Onions and tobacco became leading crops in the Connecticut Valley, potatoes in the

Aroostock Valley. The fertile soil of the Middle Atlantic states continued to support the production of staples, but there, too, the trend was toward specialization in dairy products, vegetables, and fruits.

The South. Although the South did not change the type of products on its plantations, methods of operation were different. With abolition the huge plantations were broken up, and sharecropping emerged as the most common system of agriculture.

The owners of the land furnished the sharecroppers with equipment and in return received from one-half to two-thirds of the crop. Tenant farming proved destructive to the soil and unsatisfactory to the tenants. Sharecropping also tended to perpetuate a one-crop system, with continued emphasis on cotton, the greatest money crop.

Other important crops included tobacco (by 1900 the pre-Civil War production had doubled) and rice. Leading states for tobacco cultivation were Kentucky, North Carolina (which became the top producer in the 1930's), South Carolina, and Tennessee. States most active in rice cultivation included South Carolina, Louisiana (which took first rank after 1890), Arkansas, Texas, and California.

The Midwest. In the great Corn Belt from Ohio to Iowa the production of corn, the foremost crop in the United States in monetary value, gave impetus to the raising of hogs, cattle and poultry. Wheat was another staple cereal grown in the interior—spring wheat in the Dakotas and westward to Washington, winter wheat from the Ohio Valley westward to Kansas and Oklahoma. In the North from Michigan into Minnesota, the farmers developed the dairy industry. In the twentieth century Wisconsin has become the leading producer of dairy products.

The Far West. Recently, California has attained a position second only to Texas in the total value of her farm products. The foremost crops are fruit and vegetables, but a substantial dairy industry also developed. Huge farms, employing migratory workers, and often controlled by banks, have become a twentieth-century manifestation of finance capitalism. In the far northwest the farming is more highly diversified, with attention divided among fruits, wheat, dairy products, and wool. To the east, in the western edge of the Cordillera region, irrigation and dry farming have made it possible to expand the production of corn, wheat, and alfalfa.

AGRICULTURE AND PUBLIC POLICY

Public policy concerning agriculture was reflected in government aid to education and to the progress of experimentation and research, and in the publication of agricultural literature.

Agricultural Education. The Morrill Act (1862) designed to help the states to establish agricultural colleges, gave impetus to agricultural education. By 1916 there were 68 land-grant colleges offering instruction in agriculture. The Smith-Lever Extension Act (1914) provided for the distribution of educational literature to persons unable to attend colleges regularly. This program was steadily expanded. The Smith-Hughes Act (1917) initiated governmental financial aid for agricultural instruction in rural public schools.

Experimentation and Research. In 1875 the first agricultural experiment station in the United States was founded at Wesleyan University, in Connecticut. The success of this station, which was supported by state appropriations as well as by private funds, led to the passage of the federal Hatch Act in 1887. This act provided for similar experiment stations in state colleges, and by 1930, 60 such stations had been established. Various government agencies (including the Bureau of Animal Industry, the Bureau of Plant Industry, the Bureau of Entomology and Plant Quarantine, and the Bureau of Agricultural Chemistry and Engineering) have carried on agricultural research and experimentation with new crops and methods.

Agricultural Literature. The United States Department of Agriculture has published and distributed numerous works helpful to farmers, such as the *Yearbook of Agriculture*, the *Farmer's Bulletin*, the *Journal of Agricultural Research*, and the *Monthly Crop Reporter*. Private agricultural organizations have published nearly 500 farm journals offering information and advice on every phase of farming.

AGRARIAN DISCONTENT

Agrarian discontent in the period 1865 to 1896 reached significant proportions. The unrest was caused by a number of forces: (1) poor methods of cultivation, soil erosion, droughts, floods, dust storms, and the ravages of pests created a serious physical problem; (2) the isolation of western farmers produced a social problem; (3) the growing strength of the industrial East made it difficult for the West to secure political redress; and (4) western farmers found themselves in a position of growing economic inferiority.

Economic Difficulties. Several adverse factors increased the economic difficulties confronting western farmers.

FALLING PRICES. In the three decades after the Civil War the farmers had to contend with declining farm prices. Thus, the price of corn fell from 75 cents per bushel in Chicago in 1869 to 28 cents in 1889; cotton, from 31 cents per pound in 1866 to 6 cents in 1894. Prices fell as a result of greatly increased productivity, notwithstanding the growth of a dependent urban population and an export market.

SCARCITY OF CREDIT. Banking facilities were not adequate for farmers' needs; the national banking system failed to provide efficiently for rural areas. Private bankers charged exorbitant interest and imposed difficult terms. Widespread agitation developed for easier credit facilities and for more and cheaper money.

THE TARIFF. The farmers bought in a protected market but sold their products in the world market. Necessary supplies frequently had tariff supports, e.g., farm machinery, barbed wire, and fertilizers. Farm prices were dependent upon the world market, and no control of them was possible.

TRANSPORTATION. The farmers were completely dependent upon railroads, which frequently disregarded their interests. Exploitation took the forms of "midnight rates" (overnight changes in rates), discrimination between shippers (and also between localities), and railroad control of elevators and warehouses. Consequently, public regulation of railroads was one of the persistent demands of the West.

Agrarian Organization. The farmers of the nation did not present a united front politically. Westerners were Republicans, supporting the party which had stood for Union in the Civil War and which had passed the Homestead Act. All the southern farmers were Democrats.

THE GRANGE. The Patrons of Husbandry (the Grange), organized in 1867, proposed to improve conditions of farmers through (1) opposition to large manufacturers, especially monopolies, (2) formation of farmers' co-operatives, and (3) efforts to provide a broader social and cultural life for farmers. Membership in the Grange reached a maximum of 1,500,000 farmers, organized into 15,000 local branches, in 1873. Grange enterprises included harvester works, plow factories, grain elevators, packing plants, insurance companies, banks, and co-operative retail stores. The Grangers were able to influence state legislatures enough to secure passage of laws regulating railroads. In 1876 the United States Supreme Court upheld the state regulation of railroad rates, but in 1886 reversed its earlier decision. Other factors also contributed to the failure of the Grange's economic program: western manufacturers became involved in long, costly patent suits; private elevators conspired with railroads to drive the Grange co-operatives out of business; the inexperience of the Grangers in business administration led to overexpansion and mismanagement.

THE FARMERS' ALLIANCES. In the 1880's two regional organizations led the agrarian crusade: the National Farmers' Alliance (the Northwestern Alliance) and the National Farmers' Alliance and Co-operative Union of America (the Southern Alliance). The two groups differed somewhat in their programs: The Southern Alliance was considered more radical than the Northern Alliance; conflicting economic interests kept the two groups separate. Although these organizations emphasized their co-operative ventures, the stress of the times brought them more and more into politics. They became closely associated with the People's Party.

THE PEOPLE'S PARTY. During the 1890's the People's Party represented the farmers' greatest demonstration of political power. In 1892 the Populists' presidential candidate, James B. Weaver, polled over a million votes. The platform of the party included: (1) governmental ownership of railroads and telegraph and telephone systems, (2) establishment of postal savings banks, (3) imposition of a graduated income tax, (4) removal of public lands from control by railroads, and (5) restoration of the free coinage of silver at a ratio of 16 to 1. In the election of 1896 the Populists joined the Democrats in supporting William Jennings Bryan; they campaigned on the issue of free silver, temporarily putting aside the other issues of the party. The defeat of Bryan by William McKinley, Republican advocate of a sound currency and the gold standard, was a serious blow to the People's Party. However, the economic position of the farmers began to improve; as a result of increased demand for farm products and currency inflation, farm prices rose. The early twentieth century was a time of agricultural expansion and prosperity, and World War I brought even better conditions for the farmers.

REVIEW QUESTIONS

1. Describe the expansion of American agriculture during the period from the Civil War to World War I.
2. What were the outstanding effects of agricultural mechanization?
3. Why was there increased interest in scientific farming after the Civil War?
4. What were the main developments in northeastern agriculture after the Civil War?
5. Why did the sharecropping system develop in the South? What were the advantages and disadvantages of this system?
6. What have been the most important farm crops of the Midwest?
7. How important was agriculture in California? In the far Northwest?
8. By what means has the federal government aided agricultural education, research, and experimentation?
9. What were the economic causes of agrarian unrest in the years 1865-1896? Why did the farmers demand monetary inflation and the regulation of railroads?
10. What were the aims of the Grange? Of the Farmers' Alliances?
11. What policies were advocated by the People's Party? Why did it fail?

19

HISTORY OF TRANSPORTATION AND COMMUNICATION TO 1914

A national system of transportation and means of rapid communication were indispensable to the industrialization of the United States. The half century after the Civil War witnessed a remarkable growth of our railroad network; in the twentieth century, transportation was further revolutionized by the development of the automobile and the airplane. In communication also, the late nineteenth and early twentieth centuries saw the significant progress of telegraphy and the introduction of telephony and wireless.

THE RAILROADS FROM 1870 TO 1910

The history of the railroads from 1870 to 1910 was marked by rapid expansion of facilities, technological improvements, consolidation, and state and federal attempts at regulation.

Expansion. The construction of railroads has been called "the country's most dramatic enterprise." With the great extension of railroads, new areas of the country (notably the West) were opened up, and improved transportation was also provided for previously settled areas. The methods of financing and promoting railroad expansion were of considerable influence upon the entire economy. Many economic activities were benefited as track mileage increased from 30,625 in 1860 to 93,261 in 1880 and to 167,191 in 1890. Construction after 1890 was slower, but advanced steadily to the highest point, 266,381, reached in 1916; thereafter, mileage decreased.

Technological Improvements. Inventions introduced during and after the Civil War made railroad transportation more efficient, safe, and comfortable. The establishment of a standard gauge aided the integration of the nation's systems. Steel rails permitted the use of far heavier and more powerful locomotives. Steel was quickly adopted for the construction of locomotives and cars. Other improvements included the automatic air brake, the safety coupler, and the friction draft gear. Pullman inventions made travelling more comfortable.

Railroad Consolidation. After an early period of keen competition, railroad operators began to expand and consolidate holdings in order to operate more efficiently and to secure greater profits. The earliest type of combination was exemplified by the railroad empire created by Cornelius Vanderbilt. He bought control of competing roads operating from New York City to Albany and from Albany to Buffalo, and organized the New York Central system. A later type of combination was the pool, or traffic association, formed to apportion business, fix rates, and thus avoid ruinous competition. Pools were based on loose agreements that proved difficult to enforce, and in 1887 the Interstate Commerce Act declared pools unconstitutional. In the 1890's and early 1900's, the process of consolidation continued as large operators secured control of smaller competing lines either through direct purchase and lease or through the holding company device. The federal government tried to prevent consolidation of railroads in the early 1900's, but accomplished little toward this end. In 1920 the passage of the Esch-Cummins bill indicated the abandonment of governmental efforts to maintain railroad competition.

By 1906 the great period of combination was over, and at that time seven huge railroad organizations owned two-thirds of the nation's railroad mileage and received about 85 per cent of the total railroad earnings. The wealthy Vanderbilt system, extending more than 22,500 miles, dominated the route from New York to the Great Lakes and Chicago. The efficient, progressive Pennsylvania Railroad and its associates controlled routes from Baltimore and Philadelphia to Pittsburgh and westward. J. P. Morgan built a system extending 18,000 miles in the Southeast with connections from Florida to the Great

Lakes and from the Atlantic to the Mississippi. In the Mississippi Valley, Jay Gould's system and the Rock Island group included nearly 32,000 miles of track. James J. Hill's Great Northern organization and its affiliates, covering some 21,000 miles, monopolized rail transport in the Northwest. The central and southern transcontinental roads were controlled by Edward H. Harriman and his associates.

Railroad Regulation. The fact that railroads were essential to the nation's economy but monopolistic and often abusive in their exercise of power necessitated public regulation.

RAILROAD ABUSES. The carriers not only charged unreasonably high rates but also sometimes changed their rates overnight. Frequently they practiced rate discrimination in favor of particular shippers, commodities, and localities. Their systematic effort to eliminate competition often worked to the detriment of the public. Western farmers were especially resentful of these railroad abuses.

STATE REGULATION. The first attempt at governmental regulation of the railroads came with the establishment of a supervisory commission in 1869. In the 1870's the states passed a number of Granger laws which regulated railroad rates and outlawed discriminative practices. In *Munn* v. *Illinois* (1876) the United States Supreme Court upheld state regulation, but in the *Wabash case* (1886) reversed its decision.

THE INTERSTATE COMMERCE ACT (1887). The Interstate Commerce Act of 1887 was the first federal attempt to regulate railroads. The main provisions of the act were: (1) railroad charges were to be just and reasonable; (2) rate discrimination between persons or localities was to be illegal; (3) pooling agreements were also outlawed; (4) notice of rate changes was to be given at least ten days in advance; (5) the Interstate Commerce Commission was authorized to hear complaints of shippers, to collect data, to make decisions, and to take cases to the federal courts if the railroads failed to obey its decisions. For one or two decades after its passage, the law proved to be quite ineffective because it was vaguely worded, the government made no serious attempt at enforcement, and the federal courts handed down a number of adverse decisions.

AMENDMENTS TO THE INTERSTATE COMMERCE ACT. The Elkins

Act (1903) imposed fines on railroads for granting rebates; not only railroad companies but also railroad officials and favored shippers involved in this practice were subject to punishment. The Hepburn Act (1906) extended the commission's authority over pipelines, express companies, and sleeping-car companies. This law also empowered the commission to fix maximum rates; by 1911 about 194,000 of the rates prevailing in 1906 had been cut in half. The Mann-Elkins Act (1910) extended the commission's authority to telephone, telegraph, cable, and wireless companies, and the commission was further empowered to suspend newly-announced rates temporarily while it determined their reasonableness. The Physical Valuation Act (1913) authorized the use of evaluations of railroad property as a basis for determining reasonable rates, but World War I postponed application of this criterion. The commission devoted about fifteen years to completion of the valuations.

In the beginning the Interstate Commerce Commission's powers were mainly supervisory, but gradually its regulatory authority over many forms of interstate business was established. Eventually it not only fixed rates but also attained complete control over the expansion and contraction of American railroad systems, including supervision over the financial administration of the roads. The original purpose of the Interstate Commerce Act to preserve competition was abandoned after World War I.

STREET RAILWAYS

Before the advent of electricity, the horse-car was the prevalent type of street railway, though there was some use of steam. The first successful electric railway was built in Kansas City in 1883; within five years there were thirteen electric systems in American cities. The inventor Frank J. Sprague, head of the Sprague Electric Railway and Motor Company, became known as the "father of the electric railway." Boston built the first subway in 1898; construction of a subway in New York City began in 1900.

After several decades of expansion a substantial decline of street railways occurred, chiefly because of the competition of gasoline power in passenger service and of steam railways in freight transportation. In the early years municipal governments encouraged the development of street railway companies, but harsh business practices subjected the railways to severe criticism and led to strict regulation or, in many instances, public ownership.

THE AUTOMOBILE

The perfection of the gasoline engine in the first half of the twentieth century revolutionized transportation. Gasoline power was first developed in Europe; in 1900 it was in the experimental stage. Intense competition developed in this field, as notable inventors, such as Charles E. Duryea, Ransom E. Olds, Henry Ford, and John D. Maxwell helped to perfect the automobile. As early as 1911, automobile production reached an annual total of 200,000 cars, though the main growth in this industry did not come until after World War I.

AVIATION

Although Wilbur and Orville Wright made their first successful airplane flight in 1903, airplanes were not used extensively before World War I. The war stimulated progress in aviation, however; in 1918 the first regular air-mail service in the world was established between New York and Washington. In 1919 a United States Navy seaplane crossed the Atlantic Ocean.

PROGRESS IN COMMUNICATION

The telegraph, invented by Samuel F. B. Morse, in 1835, was first put to practical use in 1844. The Western Union Company was organized through a combination of over fifty companies just before the Civil War; by 1880 it virtually monopolized the telegraph business. Contracts with railroads gave Western Union the right of way along tracks in return for free telegraph service. A strike in the Western Union in 1883 brought popular resentment and demand for public control of the industry; by 1900, 75 bills had been introduced in Congress to establish public operation of telegraph lines.

Shortly after Marconi perfected wireless telegraphy, early in the twentieth century, that invention was widely used in oceanic communication, and by World War I transoceanic service had been developed. After the war, major steps of progress came with the introduction of wireless telephony and radio.

In 1876 Alexander Graham Bell invented the telephone while investigating methods of teaching the deaf to talk. By 1880, 34,305 miles of telephone wires had been constructed. The early years of telephony saw a bitter struggle between the Bell Telephone Company and the Western Union Company. In 1900 the American Telephone and Telegraph Company (founded in 1896) took over the Bell Company, and in subsequent years secured control of most of the nation's telephone companies.

REVIEW QUESTIONS

1. Indicate the extent of railroad building in the period 1865 to 1914. When did the greatest amount of building occur?
2. What part did technological improvements play in railroad expansion?
3. By what methods were great railroad consolidations developed?
4. What great railroad systems were built in the East? In the Mississippi Valley? In the trans-Mississippi West?
5. What railroad abuses led to a demand for public regulations?
6. How effective was state regulation of railroads?
7. What were the provisions of the Interstate Commerce Act? Outline the important amendments to this law during the period 1887-1914.
8. Why was progress in federal regulation of interstate commerce slow?
9. Review the beginnings of automobile transportation and aviation in the United States.
10. What improvements in communication were developed in the years between the Civil War and World War I?

20

THE INDUSTRIAL REVOLUTION

Since the middle of the nineteenth century, American life has been transformed by the rise of industrialism. As a result of vastly increased industrial productivity, the national wealth has grown tremendously and the standard of living has been constantly raised. Merchant capitalism gave way to industrial capitalism, and by 1900 another form of economic organization, finance capitalism, had emerged. The consolidation of industry and the concentration of economic power which developed produced a growing demand for public regulation of economic life. In the twentieth century the United States has become the greatest industrial power in the world.

FACTORS ENCOURAGING INDUSTRIALISM

Several important advantages gave impetus to the progress of industrialization.

Natural Resources. Before the Civil War the raw materials of American manufacturing were products of forest and field rather than of mines and wells. In 1860, quantitatively speaking, wood was the chief raw material used in manufacturing. During and after the Civil War the mineral industries assumed a new role in the American economy, becoming the very foundation of the new industrial society. From 1870 to 1920 the annual value of the output of mineral industries rose from 250 million dollars to nearly 7 billion dollars. The various metals, which possessed the characteristics of durability, strength, and adaptability to precision forms, were essential to the industrial methods of the machine age.

Abundant Capital. The market for capital funds developed very slowly before 1860, but the Civil War gave impetus to the expansion of the investment market. It became necessary to provide additional facilities for the transfer of funds from the saver to the borrower as industry expanded and the government struggled to finance the war. American investors were at first unable to meet the demand for capital, and until the twentieth century foreign investors provided a large part of the capital required for the economic development of the United States. It has been estimated that a total of only 400 million dollars in American securities was owned by foreigners in 1860; the figure had risen to 1.4 billion dollars by 1869. The holdings of foreign investors in the United States continued to increase until the early years of the twentieth century, reaching a peak of 4.5 billion dollars in 1914. Meanwhile the nation was becoming self-sufficient in capital resources and by World War I was providing capital for foreign investment.

Labor Supply. The rapid increase of the native population augmented by immigration provided an adequate labor force. The number of persons with occupations rose from 10.5 million in 1860 to 29 million in 1900. In the same period the percentage of the total labor force engaged in agriculture dropped from 58.9 to 37.5; the proportion of nonagricultural labor rose from 41.1 to 62.5 per cent of the total. (See Chapter 22.)

Technology. The industrial era has been the age of the machine. Innumerable technical advances occurred in all lines of industry—from the primary extractive processes to the manufacture of finished products. These advances permitted greatly increased productivity, the improvement of quality, and the standardization of products. Before 1860 only 36,000 patents had been issued by the United States Patent Office; in the next 30 years a total of 440,000 patents were granted.

Markets. The United States became a huge free-trade market area, wherein producers were often protected against foreign competition by tariffs and other trade barriers. American manufacturers developed an increasingly important export market as well.

Transportation. The expansion of the railroad network, aiding in transporting raw materials and marketing goods, was a vital factor in the industrial growth of the nation. In the twentieth century the automobile and the airplane further revolutionized transportation.

GROWTH OF INDUSTRY

By 1890 the value of manufactures exceeded that of agricultural products; by 1900 the value of industrial goods was double that of agricultural goods. Although the United States had ranked only fourth among nations in the value of manufactures in 1860, it became the greatest industrial producer in the world by 1894. The accompanying table indicates the extent of American industrial development in seven decades after the Civil War.

AMERICAN INDUSTRIAL DEVELOPMENT, 1859-1939

Year	No. of Establishments (thousands)	No. of Wage Earners (millions)	Gross Value of Products (millions)	Value Added by Manufacture (millions)
1859	140	1.3	1,885	854
1869	252	2.0	8,385	1,395
1879	253	2.7	5,369	1,972
1889	355	4.2	9,372	4,210
1899	512	5.3	13,000	5,656
1899*	204	4.5	11,032	4,646
1909	264	6.2	19,945	8,162
1919	210	8.4	59,964	23,735
1929	206	8.3	67,994	30,591
1939	184	7.8	56,843	24,682

* Figures for this and later years exclude establishments with less than $5,000 annual value of product.

Westward Movement. The center of industry, which was only forty-one miles northwest of Harrisburg, Pennsylvania, in 1850, had moved to central Ohio by 1890. Although manufacturing shifted its geographic centers less rapidly than agriculture, it moved steadily westward toward the sources of raw materials whenever an adequate supply of labor could be found.

Location of Industry. Proximity to materials, markets, power facilities, labor supply, and capital had great influence upon the choice of locations for American industry.

THE NORTHEAST. The Northeast was the historic center of American manufacturing; the Industrial Revolution reached this region first. Factors which enabled New England and the

Middle Atlantic states to assume industrial leadership included: (1) ample water power; (2) an adequate supply of capital; (3) sufficient labor reserves; and (4) the best transportation facilities in the country. The advantages for industry in this area outweighed the lack of certain resources. Massachusetts cities and towns became leading centers for the production of boots and shoes, textiles, and electrical machinery. Southern New England specialized in manufacturing small metalware and jewelry. Major industries established in New York State included printing and publishing, textiles, foundry and machine products, meat packing, and distilling. New Jersey developed leading industries producing copper, petroleum, paints, and chemicals. Pennsylvania led the nation in iron and steel works and anthracite coal mining and also developed substantial textile manufacturing and meat-packing enterprises. In recent years that state produced more than one-fourth of America's total output of steel and nearly one-fourth of America's coal.

THE MIDDLE WEST. Because of the slowness of settlement and the scarcity of labor in the Middle West, manufacturing came to this area later than to the Northeast. During the past century, however, extensive manufacturing interests were attracted to the region by its abundant natural resources. Eventually, vast industries, such as meat packing, milling, and farm machinery manufacturing developed. The coal reserves and unequalled iron resources resulted in the establishment of a great iron and steel industry in Ohio. Michigan became the center of the huge automobile industry in the twentieth century.

THE FAR WEST. Despite increased industrial activity in the Far West during the past fifty years, progress there has not equalled that of other sections of the country. Industry in the area became closely linked to agriculture (especially in milling and meat-packing) and lumbering. In California petroleum refining eventually ranked highest in money value, and the state led all others in the production of canned fruits and vegetables.

THE SOUTH. After the Civil War the South built a more diversified economy; beginning in the 1880's manufacturing progress was substantial. Notable development took place in the production of lumber, cotton textiles, cottonseed products, petroleum, and iron and steel. Southern textile plants, for example, competed successfully with the well-established industry in New England, and Birmingham, Alabama, became one of the nation's steel centers.

The Power Revolution. An abundance of power resources aided the rapid development of American industry. From 1870 to 1950, the total power consumed in America was increased more than 2,000 per cent, while per capita consumption was increased 700 per cent. The largest proportion of utilization of the principal energy sources has come in the twentieth century: 80 per cent of all the coal mined; over 90 per cent of all the petroleum produced; and about 99 per cent of all the electricity generated.

The growth of the electric power industry was extraordinary. Production rose from 40 billion kilowatt hours in 1919 to 161 billion in 1939 and to more than 370 billion in 1951. Electricity supplied only about 3 per cent of the total power used by industry in 1899; by 1939 this source provided 59 per cent of the power consumed by industry. For household use, electricity provided efficient lighting and heating and innumerable labor-saving functions. In industry, it was flexible and easily controlled, proving to be ideal for individually-powered machines.

As the power revolution was taking place, coal continued to occupy a dominant position, but after World War I there was increasing competition from other sources of energy. The percentage of total energy consumption resulting directly from the use of coal steadily declined: in 1900 the percentage was nearly 90 per cent; in 1929, 60 per cent; in 1947, about 50 per cent. Hydro-electric power came into use in the 1890's and experienced substantial growth after 1900. This source of power regularly produced about one-third of the nation's output of electricity. (Coal continued to account for two-thirds of the nation's electric power.) After World War I, petroleum and natural gas became important in the energy pattern. In 1918, 14 per cent of the total energy consumed by the nation was produced by oil; in 1950, the percentage was 35. In the latter year, moreover, 18 per cent of the total energy used was supplied by natural gas.

PROCESSING OF FOOD PRODUCTS

Leading American industries included those for the production and processing of food. Processing of food in the home was supplanted by the use of manufactured products, which were improved in quality at the same time that prices were reduced.

In recent years, on the basis of money value, meat-packing was the leading food-processing industry, and, in fact, up to a short time ago it ranked first among all manufactures. Refrigeration, the increased use of by-products, and improved methods of canning aided the expansion of the industry. Flour milling, which held first place in value among manufactures in 1860, had fallen to third place in 1914 and to fourteenth place by 1939. Bakery products, on the other hand, rose from eleventh position in 1914 to seventh position in 1937. The canning industry, which received stimulation from the Civil War demand and from the increase of urban population, benefited from many technical advances and in the first half of the twentieth century expanded more rapidly than any other food industry. Industries with a similar record of success included brewing and distilling, the processing of dairy products, and the manufacturing of tobacco.

EXTRACTIVE INDUSTRIES

Most important among the extractive industries which developed were the coal, iron, and petroleum industries.

Coal. Coal has been the chief source of power and the leading fuel of industrial America. Until 1870 anthracite led in the industry, but thereafter bituminous production was greater. By 1914 the output of bituminous was four and one-half times as large as the production of anthracite. In 1900 America produced a total of 269,684,027 tons of coal, of which 212,316,112 tons were bituminous. In 1947, a peak year of production, 687,813,731 tons of coal, of which 630,623,722 tons were bituminous, were produced. Despite this remarkable expansion and the enormous significance of coal in our industrial society, the industry has suffered a relative decline since World War I.

Iron. The nation's output of iron ore rose from an annual average of about 10 million tons in the 1880's to nearly 70 million tons yearly during World War I. The iron industry was revolutionized by the discovery and exploitation of the Lake Superior iron mines, particularly the Mesabi mines. Extraction of iron in this region was facilitated by the development of ore-handling facilities and efficient transportation on the Great Lakes. The region contributed as much, by 1920, as 85 per cent of the nation's total iron production.

Petroleum. Progress in the petroleum industry was phenomenal. The first oil well in America was driven in 1859; by 1880 production had reached 26 million barrels annually. The figure rose to 63 million barrels in 1900 and to 1,300 million barrels in 1940, the latter representing two-thirds of the total world production. The extraordinary expansion of this industry is attributed to the early use of oil for lighting, as a fuel for internal combustion engines, and for heating.

HEAVY INDUSTRIES

Amongst the heavy industries that developed were the following: the manufacture of iron and steel products, machinery, locomotives, copper products, and shipbuilding.

Iron and Steel. Steel was essential for industrial development. In monetary value the products of steel works (excluding machinery, railroad equipment, and secondary manufactures) rank first among industrial products. Before the Civil War, steel was rare and expensive, but the introduction of the Bessemer process of smelting iron ore in 1864 led to greatly expanded production. Early in the twentieth century the Bessemer process was supplanted by the open-hearth method, which permits the use of lower-grade ores. A century of technical progress brought phenomenal expansion. Production rose in value from 207 million dollars in 1869 to nearly 804 million dollars in 1899; by 1890 the United States surpassed England in the production of pig iron, and by 1900 American steel production was greater than that of England and that of Germany combined; in 1929 the American output of steel was over fifty times the amount produced in the nation in 1869. The tendency toward large-scale production and integration culminated in the establishment in 1901 of the United States Steel Corporation, the first billion-dollar corporation in America.

GROWTH OF THE IRON AND STEEL INDUSTRY

Year	Number of Establishments	Average Number of Wage Earners	Capital	Value of Products
1869	808	77,555	$ 121,772,000	$ 207,209,000
1899	668	222,490	513,392,000	803,968,000
1909	654	278,505	1,492,316,000	1,377,152,000
1929	591	419,534	———	4,137,214,000
1937	410	359,630	———	3,330,491,000

Manufacture of Machinery. In the early years of American industrialism, machines were designed and built to order. As demand for machinery grew, companies were organized to produce specialized equipment—e.g., steam engines, locomotives, and textile machinery. After the Civil War the manufacture of machinery expanded rapidly as the growing industrial economy demanded an endless variety of machines. These included heavy equipment such as cranes, steam turbines, electric motors and dynamos, and innumerable small machines.

Locomotives. The great demand for locomotives and rolling stock provided important markets for heavy industry. In 1865 a 30-ton locomotive was considered very large; by 1950 some locomotives exceeded 130 tons in weight. The Baldwin Company dominated production in this business for many years, but in the early twentieth century the American Locomotive Company built a large number of locomotives. Old wooden cars with a capacity of 7 or 8 tons were replaced by steel cars with a capacity of 40 to 50 tons. The Pressed Steel Car Company of Pittsburgh became the leading producer of railroad cars.

Shipbuilding. The construction of iron and steel ships became one of the leading heavy industries in the late nineteenth century. Characteristics of this new industry included large capital investment, heavy and expensive equipment, and large-scale operations. The investment in iron shipbuilding, which was negligible in 1860, had risen to a value of one million dollars by 1900. Production increased from an annual average of

100,000 tons in the 1890's to 250,000 tons on the eve of World War I. War demands brought spectacular expansion.

Copper Manufactures. The most significant expansion among the nonferrous metal industries came in the copper industry. Production of copper increased from an annual average of about 8,000 tons in the 1850's to more than 900,000 tons annually during World War I. Many new uses for copper in both capital and consumer goods were found. The most important new use was in the production of electrical equipment, motors, and transmission lines. In the 1920's from one-third to nearly one-half of the copper production was consumed by the electrical and allied industries.

TEXTILE INDUSTRIES

Textile manufacturing expanded greatly in the post-Civil War period. Cotton, the chief manufacture before the war, was surpassed by woolens during the conflict and did not again attain a prominent position among textiles until the turn of the century. One feature of the period after 1880 was the rise of cotton manufacturing in the South, especially of the cheaper types of products. The number of southern cotton mills increased from 159 in 1860 to 821 in 1929, and the number of spindles from 561,000 to 18,541,000. Although cotton products remained the most valuable of the textiles, cotton declined in relative importance with increased production of silk, rayon, and new fabrics. Woolen products generally ranked next to cotton in value, but the woolen manufacturers had to compete with a variety of cheaper fabrics. Production increased but not nearly so rapidly as in the case of other textiles. During the half-century after the Civil War, the production of silk goods increased more rapidly than that of any other textile. Mechanization and tariff protection greatly aided the rise of this industry, so that the value of its production, estimated at 1.8 million dollars for 1850, had risen to 107 million dollars by 1900. Rayon, a twentieth-century development, provided severe competition for the silk industry; by 1939 the value of rayon products was nearly three times that of silks.

During the period before the Civil War, a start had been made in standardization of men's clothing and in production for the general market. After the Civil War there was great expansion in this industry; it is estimated that by 1900 about 90 per cent of the demand was supplied by ready-made clothing. The value of production had reached 500 million dollars by 1909, at which time the manufacture of shirts, collars, and similar accessories had attained a value exceeding 100 million dollars. Though progress in the manufacture of women's clothing was less rapid, by 1909 the value of the annual production had approximated 400 million dollars.

Technological advances in the carpet industry permitted large-scale production and encouraged expansion. Production increased from about 20 million square yards in 1869 to nearly 52 million square yards in 1919.

REVIEW QUESTIONS

1. What were some of the general effects of industrialization in America?
2. What factors gave impetus to industrialization?
3. Why did American industry become localized?
4. What were the chief industries of the Northeast? The Middle West? The Far West? The South?
5. Describe twentieth-century changes in the use of power in the American economy.
6. Indicate the relative importance of the leading food manufactures in American industry after 1860.
7. List the chief extractive industries of the United States.
8. Outline the growth of the iron and steel industry. What have been some of the other important heavy industries?
9. What were the chief developments in textile manufacturing after 1860? How have cottons and woolens compared in importance? What new textile industries have developed?

21

INDUSTRIAL CONSOLIDATION AND THE ANTITRUST MOVEMENT

An outstanding development in the late nineteenth and early twentieth centuries was the growth of large capitalistic combinations. These were not restricted to one economic field but were formed in manufacturing, mining, transportation, public utilities, merchandising, and even agriculture. The concentration of economic power and the frequent abuse of that power gave rise to the antitrust movement.

THE GROWTH OF HUGE COMBINATIONS

Combinations and monopolies were organized for several reasons: (1) to secure the advantages of large-scale management; (2) to eliminate competition and reap the benefits of monopoly; and (3) to regulate output and thereby stabilize prices, control production, and secure greater profits.

Devices for Establishing Large Combinations. There were half a dozen common devices utilized in the formation of monopolistic enterprises.

THE POOL. In the pool, members of an industry agreed to regulate output and to divide the marketing area among themselves. The pool was a federation of independent business units. Pooling agreements were often secret, and their effectiveness depended upon the honor of the members. The Interstate Commerce Act outlawed such agreements.

THE TRUST. The trust was an association of corporations in which the stock of the member companies was turned over to a board of trustees to effect unified management. Trust certificates were issued on the basis of the stock held in trust, and the board of trustees controlled the business policies of the combination. It was a highly centralized form of management. In 1890 New York State courts ordered the North River Sugar Refining Company's charter forfeited on the ground that the company had exceeded the powers of its charter by giving control of its stock to the sugar trust. In 1892 the pioneer trust, the Standard Oil Company, was ordered dissolved by the Ohio Supreme Court. A number of adverse court decisions and antitrust legislation, both state and federal, resulted in the abandonment of the trust as a monopolistic device.

THE HOLDING COMPANY. A holding company is one that owns a controlling share of the stock of corporations engaged in a single type of business. Controlled corporations are subsidiaries of the holding company, which may be merely a managing company (e.g., the Northern Securities Company) or an operating company (e.g., the Standard Oil Company of New Jersey). Other great holding companies were the United States Steel Corporation, the New York Central Railroad, the American Telephone and Telegraph Company, and the American Tobacco Company. In 1889 New Jersey amended its corporation law to permit the chartering of holding companies. Other states to follow New Jersey's example were Delaware, West Virginia, Maine, South Dakota, Nevada, and Florida. The holding company device was not held to be illegal in itself, but only insofar as it has been used to violate the antitrust laws.

THE MERGER. By means of the merger device, a corporation buys all the stock of its competitors prior to their dissolution. The General Electric Company, the American Sugar Refining Company, and the International Harvester Company became combinations of this type. Numerous decisions of the Supreme Court held that the merger is not illegal *per se,* but only when organized to restrain trade.

INFORMAL AGREEMENTS. Various "communities of interest" and "gentlemen's agreements" existed throughout the combination period. These were sometimes as effective as the formal combinations, and they were very difficult to control.

THE CARTEL. During the interim between the two world wars, many leading businessmen concentrated on the cartel as a means of international planning and control of business. A wide variety of cartels were established, some on an informal basis, others by means of formal compacts. Some cartels were approved and supported by national governments, some functioned on an extensive international scale without governmental sanction, and some operated in violation of national laws.

Extent of Consolidation. As the industrialization of America progressed, the leaders of industry became more and more dependent upon investment bankers for funds. With this development the control of industry passed more and more into the hands of a few financial magnates. The resulting new system of business organization became known as finance capitalism.

The early consolidation of industry (in the 1870's and 1880's) was but a feeble beginning compared to developments in the next two decades. In 1893 the twelve largest corporations had a total capital of less than a billion dollars. In 1904, 318 industrial combinations had a total capital of 7.25 billion. Morgan and Rockefeller controlled six huge railroad combinations with a total capitalization of almost 10 billion.

A Congressional committee reported in 1912 (in the *Pujo Report*) that the new oligarchy was dominated by three New York banking firms: J. P. Morgan and Company, the First National Bank (headed by George F. Baker), and the National City Bank (headed by James Stillman). These three organizations controlled about 2 billion dollars of investment funds, and were represented by some 340 directors in 112 corporations whose total resources exceeded 22 billion dollars.

The Temporary National Economic Committee, established by Congress in 1938, made some startling discoveries about the concentration of economic power in the United States. The five largest life insurance companies were found to interlock with 780 corporations, including 145 banks and 100 other insurance companies. In 1938 the Rockefeller group was in control of 5 of the 18 major oil-producing companies. In 1935 the House of Morgan had decisive influence in 13 industrial corporations, including the United States Steel Corporation, 12 utility corporations, including the American Telephone and Telegraph Company, and 11 of the nation's major railroad systems. In the investment banking business, 5 per cent of the houses controlled 91 per cent of the business, and the Morgan company alone managed 23 per cent of the total business.

PUBLIC OPINION AND INDUSTRIAL CONSOLIDATION

The English philosopher, Herbert Spencer, developed a philosophy which helped businessmen to explain and justify the industrial revolution. Spencer applied Darwin's biological theory to explain economic change, envisaging an era of broad social evolution and human progress. Free competition and laissez-faire were the great aims of Spencer's American disciples, such as E. L. Youmans, William G. Sumner, and John B. Clark, who denounced governmental intervention in the operation of the economy and upheld industrial capitalism as a system in which each contributing group received a just reward.

To many the growing concentration of economic power seemed a definite threat to American democracy. Early America had seen no such extremes of poverty and wealth, and the conspicuous waste and extravagant taste of the new aristocracy were condemned by social critics. An alarming ethical confusion emphasized the social cleavage in industrial America and produced a demand for public regulation of the new giants. The new industrial society developed its own code of ethics very slowly, and reformers were shocked by prevailing economic conditions, such as inadequate inspection and regulation of banks, insurance, railroad, and trust companies, the employment of children in mills and mines, the use of woman labor in sweat shops, and the control of politics by business.

By 1900 the problem of preserving American political and economic liberties was quite different from what it had been in the early days of the republic. The heirs of Jefferson's philosophy in the industrial age desired governmental regulation of the nation's economy; the industrialists demanded laissez-faire. Early advocates of reform were Henry D. Lloyd, Charles F. Adams, Henry George, and Edward Bellamy. Other leading writers who criticized industrial America were Richard T. Ely, Thorstein Veblen, Richard Croly, Ida Tarbell, and Louis Brandeis.

During the first half of this century there developed a growing sense of public responsibility for the preservation of traditional economic and political liberties, coupled with concern for the welfare of individuals. Public agencies exercised increasing power over economic affairs.

THE ANTITRUST MOVEMENT

The regulation of corporate combinations by the federal government began with the Sherman Act in 1890. This act provided that (1) every combination in restraint of interstate commerce was illegal; (2) persons conspiring to interfere with or to monopolize interstate commerce in any type of business were committing a crime; (3) property owned under a contract involving a conspiracy to restrain interstate commerce might be confiscated; (4) the word *person* was to apply to corporations as well as to individuals.

Little use was made of the Sherman Act during the first ten years after its passage. There were several reasons for this inactivity. (1) A prolonged depression in the 1890's diverted attention from the trusts. (2) Decisions of the United States Supreme Court impeded government regulation. For example, in 1895 the federal government charged that the American Sugar Refining Company monopolized the manufacture and sale of sugar. The Supreme Court declared that although the company controlled about 98 per cent of this industry the government had failed to prove any direct interference with interstate commerce. This decision gave great impetus to combination. (3) The federal government itself often seemed lukewarm or actually hostile to the idea of public regulation of business.

Prosecutions under the Sherman Act increased in number during the administrations of Theodore Roosevelt (44 cases), William Howard Taft (80 cases), and Woodrow Wilson (90 cases). In 1904, a holding company (the Northern Securities Company) was broken up; in 1911 the Standard Oil Company of New Jersey, convicted of restraint of interstate commerce, was dissolved.

In 1914 President Wilson secured the passage of two measures dealing with the trust problem. (1) The Clayton Antitrust Act prohibited certain corporate practices when they had the effect of lessening competition and creating monopoly —e.g., price discrimination, exclusive selling or leasing of contracts, and the purchase by one corporation of the stock of a competitor. The measure also tried to prevent interlocking directorates. (2) The Federal Trade Commission Act established a commission empowered to investigate corporate practices in interstate commerce and to issue "cease and desist" orders to corporations believed to be engaged in unfair practices.

With the outbreak of World War I the antitrust crusade lost its appeal. In the cases against the United Shoe Machinery Company (1908) and the United States Steel Corporation (1920), the United States Supreme Court declared that mere size is not a violation of the antitrust laws. These companies remained intact. In the 1920's, with a return to laissez-faire, the antitrust crusade was virtually abandoned by the government.

REVIEW QUESTIONS

1. What factors were mainly responsible for the formation of large industrial combinations?
2. How did the various devices for establishing large-scale combinations operate?
3. What is meant by *finance capitalism?*
4. Summarize the findings of the Pujo Committee and those of the Temporary National Economic Committee.
5. What are the main tenets of the philosophy of industrial progress? Who were some of its leading proponents?
6. Why did a demand for public regulation of industry arise? What outstanding writers criticized industrial and finance capitalism?
7. What were the provisions of the Sherman Antitrust Act? Why was the act ineffective for some time after its passage?
8. Describe the results of the antitrust movement of the early twentieth century. What were the important amendments to the Sherman Act?

22

THE LABOR MOVEMENT, 1860-1914

One result of the Industrial Revolution in the United States was the rise of organized labor. Pre-Civil War beginnings of unionism were meagre, but with the rapid growth of industry during and after the war, labor felt the necessity of organizing to secure better conditions. The labor movement was retarded by an unfriendly public opinion and the hostility of industry and the government. Toward the middle of the twentieth century, however, labor attained a position of great influence in the economy.

FACTORS INFLUENCING THE LABOR MOVEMENT

Four principal factors were favorable to the organization of labor unions. (1) The development of huge impersonal business units seemed to many workers to place them at the mercy of employers. (2) Labor generally felt that it had not received a fair share of the benefits of industrialism, and that it deserved higher wages and better working conditions. (3) Skilled workers were encouraged to organize in order to prevent loss of employment because of mechanization. (4) The concentration of labor in urban centers aided organization.

Several factors tended to impede the progress of labor organization. (1) The growing size and influence of business units restricted labor's bargaining power. Managers of industry had tremendous advantages in wealth, legal resources, and influence with the government in their opposition to labor organizations, and they used all these advantages in efforts to hamper the growth of unions. (2) Large-scale immigration generally lowered the scale of wages. Poorly-paid immigrant laborers, consisting mainly of unskilled workers, were difficult to organize. To some extent they made it possible for native Americans to take better positions and lessened the shock of depressions. (3) American public opinion was on the whole unfavorable to labor. Unions were often regarded as conspiracies against the public welfare. Americans respected successful industrialists, but regarded labor leaders as troublesome agitators. Moreover, the government and the courts seemed to feel that it was their patriotic duty to aid business but that to aid labor was a step toward socialism.

THE KNIGHTS OF LABOR

The greatest of the early labor unions was the Knights of Labor, an industrial union organized at Philadelphia in 1869 by a group of garment cutters led by Uriah S. Stephens. At first it operated as a secret society because of unfriendly public opinion. It refused to enter politics as a labor party, and its leaders tried to avoid industrial warfare. In 1879, when the practice of secrecy was abandoned, the organization had only 9,287 members. Its greatest growth came in the 1880's, reaching a peak of 729,000 members in 1886. Thereafter, a rapid decline set in, however, and by 1893 the union had only 74,000 members. The Knights of Labor lost influence rapidly due to a number of facts. The union leaders, especially the president, Terence V. Powderly, were not aggressive enough, for they generally compromised with employers in an effort to avoid industrial strife. Finally, association with the Haymarket Riot of 1886 brought public disapproval of the Knights of Labor.

THE AMERICAN FEDERATION OF LABOR

The American Federation of Labor was established in 1881, though the union did not officially adopt this name until 1886. Samuel Gompers, who became president in 1886, served as head of the union continuously (except for a single year) until his death in 1924. As a federation of craft unions, the organization made no effort for many years to enroll unskilled labor. In view of the tendency in mass production methods to use less and less skilled labor, this was a serious weakness. It had a membership of only 50,000 in 1884; by 1890 the total had reached 190,000; it rose to 550,000 in 1900, to 2 million in 1914, and to 5 million in 1920.

Under Gompers' conservative leadership the AFL carefully avoided radicalism and adopted a policy of political neutrality. It sought general support of the following union objectives: (1) legal incorporation of unions, (2) prohibition of child labor under 14 years, (3) compulsory education for children, (4) uniform apprenticeship laws, (5) an eight-hour work day, (6) the maintenance of the protective tariff, and (7) exemption of unions from the Sherman Antitrust Act.

EARLY INDUSTRIAL WARFARE

Periodically in the 1880's and 1890's a number of major strikes occurred—especially in the steel industry and on the railroads. During the first decade of this century the coal mines became the center of industrial strife.

May Day Strikes, 1886. Hard times beginning in 1884 resulted in labor unrest. The Knights of Labor sponsored many strikes early in 1886, seeking the adoption of the eight-hour work day. In May, 1886, an explosion during a strikers' meeting in Haymarket Square, Chicago, killed a policeman, fatally wounded 7 other persons, and injured 50 more. Since anarchists were generally held responsible for this violence, the Knights of Labor, which was associated in the public mind with radicalism, lost a great deal of its prestige.

Homestead Strike, 1892. A strike broke out in the Carnegie steel plant at Homestead, Pennsylvania, after failure to agree on a new wage scale. The company hired detectives to guard the plant; subsequent violence resulted in ten deaths. When the detectives surrendered to the strikers, the Pennsylvania National Guard was called out to keep order. An attack on Henry C. Frick, head of the company, by an anarchist alienated all sections of public opinion and the strike failed. Fewer than one-fifth of the employees were restored to their jobs, and the striking union, the Amalgamated Association of Iron and Steel Workers, went out of existence.

Pullman Strike, 1894. A reduction in wages by the Pullman Parlor Car Company, of Illinois, provoked a strike which the

American Railway Union offered to submit to mediation, but to no avail; the union then boycotted Pullman cars. A general railroad strike was called when managers of the railroads refused to detach Pullman cars, and a good deal of railroad property in Chicago was destroyed. The federal government intervened on the ground that passage of the mails was being impeded; an injunction under the Sherman Antitrust Act was issued against the American Railway Union, ordering the union to cease obstructing the mails and damaging railway property. Against the wishes of the governor of Illinois (John P. Altgeld), federal troops were sent to Chicago and the strike was broken. Eugene V. Debs, president of the American Railway Union, and other union leaders were cited for contempt of court for not obeying the injunction; Debs was sentenced to six months in prison.

Coal Strikes. In 1900 a general strike was called by the United Mine Workers, but a truce was patched up by Republican leaders who feared the effects upon their party in the national election of that year. Another strike broke out in 1902 as the United Mine Workers demanded union recognition, a nine-hour day, and a 20-per-cent wage increase. Both management and the miners were obdurate and work was not resumed until after President Theodore Roosevelt had threatened to use troops to operate the mines. Thereupon the mine operators asked the president to appoint a commission to mediate the dispute. The miners won a 10-per-cent increase in wages and a nine-hour day, but not union recognition.

INDUSTRIAL UNIONISM AND THE I.W.W.

Although the craft unions assumed and retained for many years their leadership of the labor movement, industrial unionism developed in some industries. The United Mine Workers of America and the International Longshoreman's Association were industrial unions.

The Industrial Workers of the World, the I.W.W., organized in 1906, advocated a "universal working-class movement" and urged the formation of "one great industrial union." This radical organization believed in class conflict and resorted to violent means, such as general strikes, boycotts, and sabotage, to achieve victory. The I.W.W. organized aggressively until World War I despite growing public hostility to its methods. At the peak of its activity, it probably had no more than 75,000 members.

THE PROGRESS OF LABOR TO WORLD WAR I

In the period 1860 to 1914 American labor gradually made definite progress in the improvement of working conditions.

Wages and Hours. Between 1865 and 1890 real wages rose more than 100 per cent, but from 1890 to 1914 there was only a slight rise: wages rose between 1897 and 1914, but so did prices; labor's gains were negligible. Hours of work remained long in many industries; only the organized industries had accepted the eight-hour day in general practice by 1920. Impetus in this direction was provided by a Congressional law of 1892 establishing an eight-hour day for government employees.

Child Labor and Woman Labor. Organized labor fought persistently against the exploitation of children and women. Although the actual number of child workers increased in the period before World War I, there was a decline in the percentage of child labor in the total labor force. Legislation in a number of states set minimum ages for employment, limited the working hours of children, and made elementary education compulsory. Laws of Congress to restrict child labor, however, were adjudged unconstitutional. The number of women employed in manufacturing had reached a total of 1,500,000 by 1914. Gradually the country adopted the principle that women workers, too, should have public protection. State legislation was designed to provide adequate wages and safe working conditions for women. Massachusetts enacted the first minimum wage law in 1912.

Federal Labor Legislation. In 1913 a labor department of separate cabinet rank was established. The next year the Clayton Antitrust Act exempted unions from the antitrust laws. In 1915 came the LaFollette Seamen's Act, which led to improved conditions in the merchant marine; then the Adamson Act of 1916 established an eight-hour work day for employees in interstate commerce. Laws of Congress in 1916 and

1918 to limit child labor, however, were declared unconstitutional by the United States Supreme Court.

REVIEW QUESTIONS

1. What forces retarded the growth of the American labor movement? What factors facilitated its growth?
2. Describe the organization and rapid decline of the Knights of Labor.
3. Outline the history of the American Federation of Labor.
4. Of what importance was the Haymarket Riot in the history of American labor?
5. Why did the Homestead Strike of 1892 fail? What was its significance?
6. What conditions provoked the Pullman Strike? Analyze the attitude and action of the federal government in this matter.
7. List the main steps of progress achieved by the labor movement from 1860 to 1914.

23

DOMESTIC AND FOREIGN COMMERCE

Although historical developments in general favored simultaneous progress in both domestic and foreign commerce, it is necessary to consider the special factors which influenced only one of these areas of business activity.

DOMESTIC COMMERCE

The progress of domestic commerce was affected particularly by the development of certain trade routes, state barriers to trade, and swift changes in methods of marketing.

Trade Routes. The main routes of American commerce were those from east to west because of transportation facilities, which generally followed population movements. This trend was modified, however, by sectional needs and by the development of economic specialization. Certain localities where goods were stored, wholesaled, and distributed developed as centers of commerce. The cities in which the government established the twelve Federal Reserve Banks were not only the financial but also the commercial centers of their regions.

Trade Barriers. Although the federal constitution supposedly guaranteed the free passage of interstate commerce, the states, for reasons of their own, sometimes found ways of evading the law. Some states discovered that they needed but could not obtain sufficient protection against the spread of diseases or insect pests from neighboring states; certain states interfered with trade in order to prevent any evasion of their taxes; other states tried to protect business against competition from the products of neighboring states. Notwithstanding these shortcomings and restrictions, however, the United States remained on the whole one of the few large free-trade areas of the world.

Trends in Marketing. Urbanization led to increasing specialization in wholesaling and retailing. In 1900, for example, retail selling was still largely done by the general country store or by the urban department store, which was really a glorified country store. The business of the country store (and rural peddling) began to decline after the introduction of rural free delivery, the founding of the mail-order houses (Montgomery, Ward, and Company, 1872; Sears, Roebuck, and Company, 1895), and the coming of the automobile. The automobile made it necessary for the mail-order houses to establish retail outlets in urban centers. In the cities, too, the number of chain stores multiplied, including especially those of the Atlantic and Pacific Tea Company, F. W. Woolworth and Company, the United Cigar stores, and the Kresge stores—founded in 1858, 1879, 1892, and 1897, respectively.

FOREIGN COMMERCE

Factors promoting expansion in foreign commerce included the following: (1) the settlement of new areas of the United States resulted in the expansion of agricultural production and the exploitation of mineral resources, enlarging surpluses for export; (2) industrialization also contributed to the production of a surplus of manufactures for export; (3) improved methods of transportation and communication facilitated the handling of a greater volume of trade; and (4) improved banking and credit facilities made the financing of foreign trade easier.

Growth of Foreign Commerce. The value of agricultural exports exceeded that of manufactured exports until the early years of the twentieth century, but even before then abundant natural resources of the United States and the rapid development of mass production had provided industrial surpluses for export to supplement shipments of foodstuffs. Imports as well as exports increased after the Civil War, but the increasing exports far exceeded the increasing imports. American imports consisted of goods not produced domestically (e.g., coffee and rubber) and of luxury items. The excess of exports over imports (in terms of money value) was partly balanced by (1) dividends and interest paid to foreign owners of American securities, (2) insurance and freight charges paid to Europeans, (3) money sent home by immigrants, and (4) money spent by American travellers abroad.

EXPORTS AND IMPORTS, 1860-1939

Year	Exports of Merchandise and Specie	Imports of Merchandise and Specie	Excess of Total Exports	Excess of Total Imports
1860	400,122,000	362,166,000	37,956,000	———
1900	1,499,462,000	929,771,000	569,691,000	———
1920	8,663,723,000	5,783,609,000	2,880,114,000	———
1929	5,440,985,000	4,754,950,000	686,035,000	———
1932	2,434,394,000	1,705,739,000	728,655,000	———
1939	3,192,314,000	5,978,047,000	———	2,785,733,000

The American Merchant Marine. In 1860 about 66 per cent of the total ocean-borne commerce of the United States was handled by American ships; this figure had dropped to 10 per cent by 1914. Gross tonnage in foreign trade fell from 2.5 million tons in 1860 to slightly more than 1 million tons in 1914. During this same period there was an increase of nearly 250 per cent in the tonnage of domestic coastwise, lake, and river commerce. The American shipbuilding industry found it difficult to compete with foreign builders who had developed various technical inprovements and who also benefited from low costs. American investors generally preferred to invest their capital in coastwise shipping or in foreign vessels instead of the national merchant marine. The urgent requirements of World War I, which greatly increased American tonnage in foreign commerce (from 1 million tons in 1914 to 11 million tons in 1921) greatly stimulated the domestic shipbuilding industry. American vessels, which had transported only 9 per cent of American imports and exports in 1913, handled 43 per cent of this foreign trade in 1920.

Federal Policy Concerning Foreign Commerce. Although the federal government generally adhered to a laissez-faire policy, it provided a variety of types of aid for importers and exporters, particularly after 1913, when it established a separate Department of Commerce with cabinet rank. The government built and improved harbors—a project managed by the Corps of Engineers of the United States Army—and promoted safety in navigation—a task entrusted to several agencies, such as the Bureau of Lighthouses, the Coast and Geodetic Survey, the Bureau of Marine Inspection and Navigation, and the Weather Bureau. Since early in our history the federal government has been active in granting preferential treatment to American vessels and in securing advantageous conditions for American commerce abroad. In 1912 the Bureau of Foreign and Domestic Commerce in the Department of Commerce was created to collect and make available essential information concerning foreign as well as domestic commerce.

Commodities in Foreign Trade. Examination of American exports since 1851 reveals a sharp drop in crude materials and foodstuffs and a great increase in manufactured commodities.

PERCENTAGE DISTRIBUTION OF UNITED STATES EXPORTS BY ECONOMIC CLASSES, 1851-1940

Yearly Average	Crude Materials	Crude Food-stuffs	Manu-factured Food-stuffs	Semi-manu-factures	Finished Manu-factures
1851-60	61.67	6.61	15.39	4.01	12.32
1891-95	33.67	17.21	27.22	6.32	15.57
1911-15	30.74	8.83	14.32	15.41	30.70
1916-20	18.22	9.16	17.66	15.39	39.58
1921-25	27.54	9.74	13.93	12.45	36.33
1931-35	30.23	3.85	8.83	14.51	42.57
1936-40	19.05	3.77	5.52	19.29	52.36

SOURCE: *Statistical Abstract of the United States, 1941*, p. 533.

After the Civil War the importation of raw materials increased tremendously, as did that of unprocessed foodstuffs and semi-manufactures, though less rapidly, but the importation of finished manufactured goods declined from a value of 50 per cent of total American imports in the 1850's to 20 per cent in the 1930's.

Geographic Distribution of Foreign Trade. In 1860 the major part of the foreign trade of the United States (61.2 per cent of the imports and 74.8 per cent of the exports) was with European nations. Nevertheless, as shown in the accompanying table, for the period 1860-1940 trade with Asia increased more rapidly than trade with any other region. By the 1930's American imports from Asia exceeded those from Europe.

PERCENTAGE DISTRIBUTION OF UNITED STATES IMPORTS BY ECONOMIC CLASSES, 1851-1940

Yearly Average	Crude Materials	Crude Food-stuffs	Manu-factured Food-stuffs	Semi-manu-factures	Finished Manu-factures
1851-60	9.63	11.70	15.43	12.50	50.74
1896-1900	29.47	15.08	15.93	13.35	26.17
1911-15	34.91	12.80	12.56	17.37	22.36
1915-20	40.13	12.15	16.21	17.10	14.40
1926-30	36.80	12.56	9.88	18.89	21.88
1936-40	36.39	14.26	15.42	22.81	20.39

SOURCE: *Statistical Abstract of the United States, 1941*, p. 533.

DISTRIBUTION OF UNITED STATES FOREIGN COMMERCE, 1860-1940
(percentage of total exports and imports)

Yearly Average	Northern North America		Southern North America		South America		Europe		Asia	
	Imp.	Exp.	Imp.	Exp.	Imp.	Exp.	Imp.	Exp.	Imp.	Exp.
1860	6.7	6.9	12.5	8.8	9.9	4.7	61.3	74.8	8.3	2.4
1896-1900	5.0	6.9	10.3	5.6	13.2	3.1	52.6	76.7	14.6	3.9
1911-1915	7.7	14.2	14.5	7.7	12.8	5.2	46.6	64.0	15.8	5.6
1915-1920	12.7	12.0	17.5	7.7	17.6	5.5	20.3	63.2	27.1	8.6
1936-1940	14.9	16.2	10.0	9.0	13.6	9.8	25.3	41.4	31.6	16.6

SOURCE: *Statistical Abstract of the United States, 1941*, p. 542.

TARIFF HISTORY, 1860-1914

The Morrill Tariff of 1861 initiated the system of high protective tariffs in the United States. Earlier tariffs had been kept at a low level; in fact, just before the Civil War the tendency had been to reduce tariff schedules. Duties on imports were raised during the war in order to meet the fiscal needs of the government. Periodic increases followed, and there were no significant reductions until 1913.

The Tariff Prior to 1890. Tariff legislation in 1864 raised duties to an average of 47 per cent ad valorem. The government acceded to virtually all requests for protection. In 1872 the rates were reduced 10 per cent, but they were raised again during the panic of 1873. In the 1880's both the Republican President Chester A. Arthur and the Democratic President Grover Cleveland unsuccessfully advocated the lowering of the tariff.

The McKinley Tariff, 1890. The tariff was the main issue of the election of 1888, and victory for the Republican candidate, Benjamin Harrison, led to passage of the McKinley Tariff of 1890. This measure increased the duties an average rate of 49.5 per cent, imposing very high duties on many textiles, iron, steel, glass, and tin plate. Tariffs were also placed on some farm products. Although sugar was put on the free list, domestic sugar producers were granted a bounty of two cents a pound.

Wilson-Gorman Tariff, 1894. The Wilson-Gorman Tariff, which became law without President Cleveland's signature, reduced the average rate to 39.9 per cent and placed wool, copper, and lumber on the free list. This act also levied an income tax (to make up for the revenue lost through the tariff reduction), which was declared unconstitutional.

Dingley Tariff, 1897. Although there was no demand for tariff revision during his administration, the protectionist President William McKinley called a special session of Congress which passed the Dingley Tariff. The rates fixed in this law were higher than those set in the McKinley Tariff of 1890; average rates were raised to 57 per cent, and high tariffs were imposed on raw and manufactured wool, and duties on hides were restored.

Payne-Aldrich Tariff, 1908. President William Howard Taft, interpreting a Republican campaign pledge as a promise to reduce the tariff, urged Congress to enact legislation to this end. Accordingly, the House of Representatives passed the Payne Bill, which was drastically amended in the Senate (in response to pressure from vested interests) so that the final measure, the Payne-Aldrich Tariff, retained far-reaching protection for domestic industries. The intense struggle over this legislation contributed to the defeat of the Republicans in the Congressional election of 1910 and to the victory of Woodrow Wilson in the presidential election of 1912.

Underwood Tariff, 1913. President Wilson's administration obtained passage of the Underwood-Simmons Tariff, which brought the first substantial reduction in tariff rates since 1860. This bill reduced the average of existing duties from 36.86 to 26.67 per cent, and many important commodities, including wool, lumber, coal, iron ore, pig iron, steel ingots, wire, rails, boots, shoes, wheat, flour, cattle, meat, eggs, milk, and cream were added to the free list. The duty on sugar was reduced, and its elimination was scheduled for May 1, 1916. World War I rendered the Underwood Tariff inoperative, however; American goods caused inflation, and war conditions prevented European producers from competing in the American market. After the war the Republican administrations restored a high protective tariff.

The Search for a Scientific Tariff. During most of the past century, tariff laws reflected the points of view of pressure groups and sectional interests. Reformers advocated that the tariff be "taken out of politics," and that a commission be appointed to aid Congress in preparing "scientific" tariffs. A "scientific" tariff is one that equalizes the cost of production at home and abroad. A Tariff Board, operating from 1909 to 1912, investigated tariff problems. In 1916 the United States Tariff Commission was established as a bi-partisan agency to study and recommend desirable modifications in tariff schedules. A high tariff was advocated by some as essential to the development of domestic industries, and by others as necessary for the protection of labor against competition by cheap foreign-made products, but critics charged that such a tariff merely benefited certain producers at the expense of the nation as a whole.

REVIEW QUESTIONS

1. Why was it necessary to outlaw barriers to interstate commerce?
2. Summarize the significant recent trends in domestic marketing.
3. What factors promoted the growth of foreign commerce?
4. Describe the growth of American exports during the period 1860-1939. What factors helped to offset the excess of American exports over imports?
5. Why did the American merchant marine decline after the Civil War?
6. In what ways did the federal government encourage commerce?
7. Analyze the geographic distribution of foreign trade in the years 1860-1914.
8. List the main events in the tariff history of the United States during the period 1860-1914.

24

FINANCIAL HISTORY, 1865-1914

The lessened need for revenue after the war permitted early discontinuance of excises, of the inheritance tax, and of the income tax, but only minor reductions in customs duties, the chief source of revenue, were effected.

PUBLIC FINANCE AND FISCAL POLICY

Treasury Surpluses. In the 1880's Treasury surpluses averaged over 100 million dollars annually. The government eliminated some excise taxes and proposed to reduce the tariff, but a strong demand for protection prevented a downward revision. The Treasury surpluses became an important political issue in the late 1880's, with both major parties promising reductions in government revenue. The Republicans, victorious in the election of 1888, revised the tariff in 1890 to provide increased protection for many domestic producers and to reduce government income. This measure, coupled with a general contraction in world trade, did reduce government income. At the same time federal expenditures for internal improvements, pensions, and naval construction increased. The panic of 1893 and the ensuing depression resulted in the first Treasury deficit since the Civil War and necessitated government borrowing.

The Increased Costs of Government. The expansion of governmental activities during the early years of this century required heavy expenditures; the budget had to provide for increased costs of military defense, of numerous public works, of an enlarged postal service, and of more pensions. New government agencies were established and old ones were expanded. Federal expenditures approximately doubled from the mid-1890's to the eve of World War I.

Sources of Revenue. Public revenue also increased in the early part of the twentieth century, the main sources being customs duties and excise levies. The tariff revision of 1909 resulted in the loss of revenue. With a decline in government income after 1907, there was an obvious need for new sources of revenue. In 1913 a constitutional amendment authorized Congress to levy income taxes, thus assuring the government of a new and unequalled source of income in later years.

MONETARY PROBLEMS

During the Civil War the government issued United States Notes or greenbacks amounting to nearly 450 million dollars. This was legal-tender paper money, not redeemable in gold and silver, which fluctuated in value and contributed to the inflation of the period. Wide fluctuations in the value of the greenbacks resulted from varying degrees of confidence in the government's ability to redeem the notes and from manipulations by speculators. For ten years after the war a controversy over redemption or retirement of the greenbacks raged, and not until 1875 did specie resumption take place.

Constitutionality of Greenbacks. In 1870 the United States Supreme Court decided that the greenbacks were legal tender only in payment of debts incurred since the first issue of notes, but in 1871 the greenbacks were approved as legal tender in all cases.

Retirement of Greenbacks. Inflationists urged that the amount of greenbacks in circulation be expanded, while contractionists advocated retirement. Some of the bills were retired during the years 1866 to 1868, but then retirement was stopped. In the election campaign of 1868 the Democrats advocated adoption of the "Ohio Plan," which provided for payment of both principal and interest of Civil War bonds in greenbacks. The Republicans won the election, however, and continued payment of the debt in gold. Efforts to increase the amount of paper notes in circulation failed. In 1875 the Specie Resumption Act ordered the retirement of all greenbacks in excess of 300 million dollars. In 1878, however, the Bland-

Allison bill discontinued this process of contraction, leaving 346 million dollars of greenbacks in circulation.

Specie Resumption. The Specie Resumption Act of 1875 also provided that on January 1, 1879, paper notes would be interchangeable with gold and silver. With this assurance of specie resumption, the value of greenbacks rose, reaching par in December, 1878.

National Bank Notes. On deposit of federal bonds with the federal government, national banks could issue notes to the value of 90 per cent of the deposited bonds. The total amount of notes was originally limited to 300 million dollars. National bank notes were legal tender for all obligations to the government except import duties, and could be used for all payments by the government except for payment of the principal and interest of the national debt. To eliminate currency confusion, Congress in 1865 imposed a 10-per-cent tax on state bank notes, thus forcing many of them out of circulation.

Free Silver. A demand for the free coinage of silver arose in the 1870's and continued for the remainder of the century. This demand resulted from several factors. (1) In the period after 1860 the world's output of gold slowly declined, and silver production increased greatly. (2) The value of silver, in terms of gold, declined. The market ratio of silver to gold, which had been about 15½ to 1 for many years, rose to over 16 to 1 in 1874. The mint ratio, established in 1837 by the federal government, was still about 16 to 1. (3) In 1873 the silver dollar was dropped from the list of coins to be minted. Since the mint ratio undervalued silver at that time, there was little objection to the demonetization of silver. In 1874, however, when the commercial ratio of silver to gold rose above 16 to 1, it would have been profitable to coin silver dollars at the mint ratio. The act of 1873 demonetizing silver was called the "crime of '73," and there was a clamor for free silver. Agitation was most vehement among the western farmers, who were adversely affected by the declining prices.

Bland-Allison Act, 1878. Inflationists gained a partial victory in 1878 when the Bland-Allison Act was passed over President Rutherford B. Hayes' veto. This bill provided for the monthly purchase of 2 to 4 million dollars' worth of silver to be coined into silver dollars. Silver certificates were to be issued upon deposit of the bulky silver dollars in the Treasury. During the twelve years that the Bland-Allison Act was in force, the government coined 378 million silver dollars.

Sherman Silver Purchase Act, 1890. For political reasons the Republicans agreed to passage of the Sherman Silver Purchase Act. This measure required the Treasury to buy 4,500,-000 ounces of silver monthly and to issue in payment legal-tender Treasury notes. The paper money was redeemable in gold or silver at the discretion of the Secretary of the Treasury. Under this act the government purchased almost all of the domestic output of silver and almost double the amount required by the Bland-Allison Act. During the three years of operation of the Sherman Silver Act, the government bought nearly 156 million dollars' worth of silver. These purchases endangered the gold standard, for gold was forced out of circulation by the operation of Gresham's Law. During the panic of 1893 and the subsequent depression, the Treasury was faced with a deficit. President Grover Cleveland called a special session of Congress which repealed the Sherman Silver Purchase Act in 1893. In this crisis of 1894-1896, the government maintained the gold standard through the purchase of over 200 million dollars in gold, paid for with 4-per-cent and 5-per-cent bonds.

Election of 1896. In the election of 1896 the Democrats, led by William Jennings Bryan, advocated the free coinage of silver at the ratio of 16 to 1. For some time the western farmers had demanded inflation of the currency to raise prices. The Republicans nominated William McKinley and adopted a platform calling for maintenance of the gold standard. McKinley was elected primarily because the condition of the farmers had improved in 1896 and many voters distrusted Bryan's financial policies. The agitation for free silver continued for a while, but it never again became so important an issue as in 1896.

Gold Standard Act, 1900. Gold advocates secured passage of the Currency Act of 1900, which required the Treasury to keep other forms of currency on a parity with gold and established a gold reserve of 150 million dollars.

Federal Reserve Notes. To obtain greater elasticity in the currency, the Federal Reserve Act of 1913 included a provision for Federal Reserve notes. These notes were to be backed by at least a 40-per-cent gold reserve (gold certificates after 1933); the remainder of the backing was to be in government bonds and commercial paper. Federal Reserve notes were received mainly in payment for commercial paper as it matured. In this way the new currency met the needs of business more adequately than the bank notes of the National Bank system: when money was needed, the volume of Federal Reserve notes was expanded; when demand declined, the volume of notes was reduced.

THE NATIONAL BANKING SYSTEM

The National Bank Act of 1864 established the National Bank system to counteract the effects of chaotic local banking systems, to provide a national paper currency, and to help finance the Union war effort.

Organization of the Banking System. Upon investigation and approval by the Comptroller of the Currency, national banks received charters from the federal government, capitalization being dependent upon the size of the city in which each bank was located. The earliest charters were limited to a period of twenty years; those granted in the twentieth century have had no definite limits. National banks were required to purchase a minimum amount of United States bonds. Shareholders were liable up to an amount equal to the par value of their stock (double liability). Federal bonds had to be deposited as backing for note issues, and reserves were required in order to protect depositors.

Growth of National Banks. The National Bank system provided the country with a nation-wide banking and banknote structure, and again brought the government and banks into close relationship. In order to force state banks to join the system, Congress, as already mentioned, in 1865 imposed a 10-per-cent tax on state bank notes. Most of the state banks joined the system. The number of state banks dropped from 1,562 in 1860 to 247 in 1868. In the 1870's, when it was found that banks could operate profitably without issuing notes, the number of state banks began to increase, and by 1895 they outnumbered the national banks. The number of national banks rose from 1,295 in 1865 to 7,473 in 1913. The annual total of note issues increased from 171 million dollars in 1865 to 715 million in 1913. In the same period the capital resources of national banks rose from 380 million dollars to 11,037 million.

Defects of the System. The national banking system was subject to two major shortcomings. (1) The dependence upon government bonds for note issuance caused credit stringency. Although amendments to the original act liberalized the requirements for issuance of notes, the arrangement remained inadequate. (2) Rural areas were not well served by the system, for the minimum capitalization requirement of $50,000 for places under 6,000 population was too high. Consequently, bankers preferred to serve industrial centers and to neglect agricultural regions.

MOVEMENT FOR BANKING REFORM

The panic of 1907 revealed clearly the inadequacies of the National Bank system. Insufficient currency and inelastic credit facilities intensified the emergency. In 1908 Congress passed the Aldrich-Vreeland Act, providing for the issuance of bank notes backed by commercial paper and the securities of state and local governments. The act also set up the National Monetary Commission which was to investigate banking conditions and report to Congress. The Commission report in 1912 recommended the "Aldrich Plan" for the reform of the nation's banking system. The proposal did not receive the approval of either the Republicans or the Democrats and was never formally considered by Congress.

THE FEDERAL RESERVE SYSTEM

President Woodrow Wilson urged Congress to institute drastic banking reforms, and Congress passed the Federal Reserve Act in 1913.

Federal Reserve Districts. The nation was divided into 12 economic districts and a Federal Reserve bank was established in the chief financial center of each district. Federal Reserve banks were organized in Boston, New York, Philadelphia,

Cleveland, Richmond, Atlanta, Chicago, St. Louis, Minneapolis, Kansas City, Dallas, and San Francisco. National banks were required (and other banks were encouraged) to join the Federal Reserve system by subscribing 6 per cent of their capital stock and surplus to the district Federal Reserve bank.

Control of the System. A Federal Reserve Board, consisting of eight members (the Secretary of the Treasury, the Comptroller of Currency, and six members appointed by the President), was established to govern the system. A Federal Advisory Council, consisting of representatives of the twelve Federal Reserve banks, was provided to help formulate and carry out policies. Each Federal Reserve bank had a board of nine directors, six of them selected by member banks and the three others appointed by the Federal Reserve Board.

Banking Functions. The Federal Reserve banks have served as fiscal agents of the government and as bankers' banks. Among their functions have been (1) rediscounting member banks' commercial paper, (2) buying and selling bills of exchange, and (3) making loans backed by government securities to member banks.

REVIEW QUESTIONS

1. Why were the greenbacks an unstable element in American currency? To what extent were they retired? How was their value finally stabilized?
2. Why was there a demand for free silver? State the provisions and effects of the Bland-Allison Act and the Sherman Silver Purchase Act.
3. Why did the demand for free silver die out? What is the importance of the Gold Standard Act of 1900?
4. In what ways did Federal Reserve notes meet the needs of the business world?
5. How was the National Banking system organized? What were its outstanding defects?
6. Indicate how the Federal Reserve system was organized and governed. What have been the most important banking functions of the system?

25

THE PERFORMANCE OF THE AMERICAN ECONOMY, 1865-1914

The American economy after 1865 was characterized by the dominant influence of manufacturing, the declining influence of the agricultural South, and the development of a nearly self-sufficient economic system. Despite violent economic fluctuations, the standard of living was raised.

ECONOMIC FLUCTUATIONS, 1865-1914

During and after the Civil War the northern states enjoyed unprecedented prosperity. The period was characterized by an inflated currency, widespread speculation, and agricultural and industrial expansion. Railroad mileage rose from 35,085 miles in 1865 to 70,651 miles in 1873; construction of railroads in the West was far in excess of the needs of the population. Wartime demands and improved transportation aided the growth of manufacturing; the provisions of the Homestead Act, the development of a foreign market, and the improvement of transportation facilities stimulated agriculture.

The Panic of 1873. Economic activity in general was not too greatly disrupted by the readjustments after the war. Prices dropped sharply in 1865 and continued to fall, but less rapidly, until 1871. Prices were still about 35 per cent above the prewar level. The country as a whole enjoyed prosperity for nearly a decade after the Civil War. Then the failure of Jay Cooke and Company, a huge banking firm with heavy investments in the Northern Pacific Railroad, precipitated the panic of 1873. Many banks failed, and in September, 1873, panic struck the stock market, causing sharp deflation. A depression, lasting 5 years, followed the panic as prices fell, wages declined, unemployment rose, and agrarian unrest and labor agitation developed. In 1878 recovery began for virtually all economic groups excepting the western farmers.

Period of Recovery and Expansion. Late in 1878 and in 1879 the bumper American harvests, at a time of crop failures in Europe, produced agricultural prosperity and encouraged expansion. The increase in food exports brought added imports of gold and encouraged specie resumption. By 1880 the nation had entered another period of prosperity. Despite a brief financial crisis in 1884 (attributed to speculative railroad financing and related business failures) the onward march of business continued, both in agriculture and in manufacturing.

The Panic of 1893. In the 1890's the nation suffered another financial crisis, brought on by monetary uncertainty and excessive speculation in railroads. The panic of 1893 was partially a result of the election of 1892, for many businessmen feared that the victorious Democrats would lower the tariff and abandon the gold standard. The Sherman Silver Purchase policy drove gold out of circulation simultaneously with a crisis in England which caused a flow of gold from the United States. Furthermore, the extravagant policies of the Republican administration of Benjamin Harrison had greatly reduced the Treasury surplus. In 1893 Cleveland secured the repeal of the Sherman Silver Purchase Act and began the purchase of gold which saved the gold standard. The election of 1896 settled the issue of free silver, as improved conditions for agriculture and business resulted in triumph for the conservative financial interests of the East.

The Panic of 1907. From 1896 to 1914 the price level in the United States rose about 40 per cent, and agricultural prosperity virtually ended the demand for inflation. There was a mild financial crisis in 1903 which resulted from speculation in the securities market. Business activity, except in the steel industry, was not seriously upset. A number of adverse influences had been developing, however, during the long period of prosperity. These influences stemmed from an extremely rapid growth of industry which was accompanied by world-wide speculation in new securities and overextended bank credits. These influences culminated in another financial crisis in 1907. In efforts to meet the crisis the government deposited 35 million dollars with national banks for loan to trust companies, and the bankers organized a money pool to bolster the stock market. Although the panic ended early in 1908, uncertainty in the financial market continued until the outbreak of World War I. For the nation as a whole, however, the effects of the panic of 1907 were not widespread or permanent.

ECONOMIC TRENDS

The increased relative importance of industry in the American economy can be seen in the larger proportion of the total national income derived from manufacturing. The proportion for manufacturing rose from 12.1 per cent in 1859 to 30.3 per cent in 1937, whereas that for agriculture in the same period fell from 30.8 per cent to 12.3 per cent.

Economic Concentration. The phenomenal expansion of industry after the Civil War was accompanied by a growing concentration in the control of business activity. In many lines of enterprise, individual companies were enlarged or combinations were organized to dominate their field. Increasingly the public became concerned with the problem of trusts and monopoly, as state and federal governments initiated attempts to regulate "big business."

The Standard of Living. During the period 1865 to 1914, economic progress was reflected in the fact that per capita real income rose appreciably while the length of the work day was reduced. Per capita real income rose from $233 in 1869 to a prewar high of $557 in 1913 and again to a wartime peak of $599 in 1918. The average working week in 1860 was probably about 70 hours, whereas on the eve of World War I over three-fourths of factory laborers worked 54 to 60 hours a week. These facts indicate that there had been a significant improvement in the standard of living.

REVIEW QUESTIONS

1. Describe the principal effects of the Civil War on the American economy.

2. What caused the panic of 1873?
3. What factors promoted recovery and expansion in the late 1870's and 1880's?
4. Indicate how the gold standard was threatened in the 1890's. How was it maintained?
5. What factors indicated a rising standard of living in the years 1865-1914?

26

ECONOMIC IMPERIALISM

An outstanding result of the industrial revolution was the appearance of a "new imperialism" after 1870. Essentially this term meant a struggle for control of markets, raw materials, and new investment opportunities. Noneconomic purposes of the new imperialism included the attainment of national security, power, prestige, and the spreading of Christianity. European nations, where industrialism developed first, led in the movement. Until the 1890's the United States, preoccupied with national development and having no surplus capital for investment abroad, was little interested in foreign affairs. Near the end of the nineteenth century, however, conditions changed, and the United States began to engage in imperialist activity.

EARLY AMERICAN IMPERIALISM

The early stages of American imperialism developed in the Pacific and Caribbean regions.

Pacific Interests. The United States became a Pacific power in the mid-nineteenth century with the annexation of California and the purchase of Alaska. American interest in the Far East had already developed from trading ventures in the Pacific. American merchants sold Hawaiian sandalwood in China. American whalers used Hawaiian ports. A reciprocity treaty with Hawaii in 1875 admitted sugar from the islands duty free, and by 1890 the export of sugar had risen from 18 million to 260 million pounds. In 1890 American investments in Hawaiian sugar corporations totalled 18 million dollars; in

Hawaiian railroad and shipping companies, 2 million dollars. The McKinley Tariff of 1890 placed sugar on the free list and gave a bounty of 2 cents a pound to American producers. Subsequently, competition from Cuban sugar in the United States market produced a depression among Hawaiian sugar interests. In 1893 unrest in Hawaii resulted in the overthrow of the native monarchy and the establishment of a provisional government which sought the annexation of the islands by the United States. Since President Cleveland suspected that the revolution had been instigated by Americans, annexation was delayed until 1898.

Caribbean Interests. The United States has always been interested in Cuba. The southern states were eager to extend slavery to that country; many Americans, too, as a precautionary defense measure, wanted the nation to acquire Cuba. By 1898 American investments in sugar and mining in Cuba had reached a total of 50 million dollars and the average annual trade of the United States with the island exceeded 100 million dollars. When a Cuban revolt against Spanish rule broke out in 1895, barbarous activities ensued and there was considerable destruction of property. Agitation developed in favor of intervention by the United States both for the protection of American interests and for humanitarian purposes. American businessmen, excepting those concerned with Cuban sugar, generally opposed war with Spain because they feared that it would retard recovery from the panic of 1893. Nevertheless, the United States went to war in April, 1898, to gain independence for Cuba.

Results of the Spanish-American War. The short and successful war freed Cuba from Spanish rule, but left the island an American protectorate. The Platt Amendment of 1902, incorporated in the constitution of Cuba, provided that the United States could intervene for the preservation of Cuban independence and the maintenance of order. Territories annexed outright after the war were Puerto Rico, Guam, and the Philippine Islands. Annexation of the Philippines involved a major decision in foreign policy: imperialists and anti-imperialists debated whether it was consistent with American tradition to subjugate an alien people in a distant area; whether annexation would bring competition for American interests and an influx of cheap labor; whether the Philippines would facilitate the growth of American commerce in the Far East; and whether the United States could forego the opportunity to assume "the white man's burden" and bring civilization to this backward region. Altruistic motives combined with considerations of trade and empire led to the annexation of the Philippine Islands in 1898.

UNITED STATES AND THE FAR EAST

In the early years of the twentieth century, when the partition of China was threatened by imperialist powers, the United States with the support of Great Britain endeavored to keep China open to world commerce. Secretary of State John Hay sent notes to Far Eastern powers in September, 1899, proposing the open door policy.

Principles of the Open Door Policy. The open door policy consisted of three main principles. (1) No power should interfere with any treaty port or vested interest within its sphere of influence in China. (2) The Chinese tariff should apply within the foreign powers' spheres of influence, and duties should be collected by the Chinese government. (3) No power should discriminate against foreigners in determining harbor and railroad charges in its sphere of influence. The United States further declared in July, 1900, that its policy was to "preserve Chinese territory and administrative entity" and to "safeguard for the world the principle of equal and impartial trade with all parts of the Chinese Empire." Although Hay received evasive answers from the interested powers, he announced that the open door policy was "final and definitive."

The Open Door Policy in Action. The open door policy was threatened by the Russo-Japanese War (1904-1905) and again during World War I. The principle was reaffirmed in the Washington Conference (1921-1922), but with Japan's invasion of Manchuria in 1931 it collapsed. Economic hopes based on the policy were not realized. American exports to China rose from 16.7 million dollars in 1900 to 138.4 million in 1920, but fell to 55 million in 1936. These figures represented only a small part of our total trade. The United States tried to encourage the economic penetration of China in the early years of this century, demanding that American bankers be allowed to join on equal terms in all foreign loans floated in China and that the railroads of Manchuria be neutralized. In 1910 an international banking group (including Americans) was organized to promote Chinese loans on this basis, but President Wilson withdrew American support of the proposed arrangement. By 1930 American investments in China amounted to only 240 million dollars.

The Philippine Islands. The American administration of the Philippines was efficient, liberal, and dedicated generally to the improvement of the islands. In fact, the Philippines were more of a burden than an asset to the United States, for heavy expenditures were necessary; the trade that developed was not wholly beneficial to America; and the islands failed to attract much investment capital. An act of 1902 provided for a 25-percent reduction of the American tariff on Philippine goods. In 1909 Philippine exports were admitted free (except for quotas on sugar and tobacco), and in 1913 completely free trade was established. During the years 1901-1939, American exports rose from 4 million to 83.4 million dollars, and imports from 10 million to 92 million dollars. On the other hand, certain American interests (producers of sugar, tobacco, and coconut products) objected to the competition of Philippine goods. Furthermore, American investments in the Philippines did not increase as much as had been expected—in 1935 the total was only about 250 million dollars. In the 1930's agitation for Philippine independence resulted in the Tydings-McDuffie Act of 1934, which provided for self-government to begin after a ten-year interval.

PENETRATION OF LATIN AMERICA

The penetration of Latin America by the United States was motivated by reasons of national security and by the desire to expand commerce and investments.

Cuba. To safeguard law and order and to protect American investments in the protectorate of Cuba, the United States intervened in 1906, 1912, and 1917. The Platt Amendment was abrogated in 1934, however, in accordance with the good neighbor policy of mutual respect and equality. By 1930 American investments in Cuba had grown to large proportions—amounting to 1.5 billion dollars, with 600 million dollars invested in sugar.

Puerto Rico. The American administration of Puerto Rico improved living conditions somewhat as transportation facilities were developed and public works were initiated. Nevertheless, economic conditions remained highly unsatisfactory, mainly because of overpopulation, absentee ownership of the American companies in the territory and the landless status of the natives. Free trade between Puerto Rico and the United States was established in 1902. The sugar industry expanded considerably in the twentieth century, but foreign interests (chiefly American) continued to control at least 60 per cent of the economic life of the island.

Panama. The strategic value to the United States of an Isthmian canal had long been known, but not until the late nineteenth century did that project receive serious consideration. The Hay-Pauncefote Treaty with Great Britain (1901) allowed the United States to build, operate, and defend the canal singlehanded. Negotiations were carried on for the purchase of the holdings of the New Panama Canal Company, which had begun construction of a canal. It was necessary to obtain a lease from Colombia, the sovereign power on the Isthmus of Panama. In 1903 after American efforts in this direction met with delays, the New Panama Canal Company, with the knowledge and consent of President Theodore Roosevelt, instigated a revolution which resulted in formation of a new government. The Republic of Panama was quickly recognized by the United States and the Hay-Bunau-Varilla Treaty was drawn whereby the United States guaranteed the independence of Panama and agreed to pay the new republic 10 million dollars immediately and annual sums of $250,000 after a nine-year interval. Construction of the canal was begun in 1906 and the work was completed in 1914.

The Roosevelt Corollary. The chronic unrest and excessive indebtedness of Latin American nations led Theodore Roosevelt to formulate a new principle of foreign policy. This principle, known as the Roosevelt Corollary of the Monroe

Doctrine, declared the intention of the United States to intervene in Latin America whenever necessary to prevent chronic wrong-doing and to exercise an international police force in this hemisphere.

Santo Domingo. When Santo Domingo became bankrupt in 1904, the United States intervened and took over the administration of the customs, applying 45 per cent of the income to current expenses and 55 per cent to debt retirement. In 1908 New York bankers refunded the Santo Domingo debt of 20 million dollars under a treaty stipulating that (1) the United States was to collect the customs duties until the debt had been fully paid and (2) the debt was not to be increased without the consent of the American government. In 1914 American troops landed in Santo Domingo to preserve order and protect the interests of the United States, and American marines occupied the country from 1916 to 1924. At that time another convention, which extended the financial arrangement and United States authority to intervene in Santo Domingo, was signed. During the period of occupation, Americans had secured control of about one-third of the sugar industry of the island.

Haiti. Occupation of Haiti by United States forces in 1915 resulted in a financial arrangement similar to that imposed on Santo Domingo. American marines remained on the island until 1934. Control of the principal resources and trade of the island followed financial supervision.

Nicaragua. The United States intervened in Nicaragua in 1911 when American supervision of customs was established. During two periods (1912-1925 and 1928-1933) American troops occupied this country. A treaty in 1916 granted the United States various concessions, including an option on a Nicaraguan canal route. Nicaragua paid the United States the sum of 3 million dollars to be used to settle the claims of American bankers.

Mexico. A period of relative stability in Mexican politics ended in 1913, and there followed a period of disorder and civil war. Americans with investments in Mexico worth about 1.5 billion dollars demanded protection of their interests, but President Wilson followed a policy of "watchful waiting." The United States intervened twice with troops (1914 and

1917) but soon withdrew. In 1917 Mexico's new constitution reserved the soil and subsoil to the Mexican people and forbade foreign ownership of land and water rights within certain limits of the border and the coast. These provisions were not retroactive, but American interests resented them. In 1925 a Mexican petroleum law and alien land act aimed at the expropriation of foreign holdings, but Ambassador Dwight Morrow secured respect for holdings prior to 1917. In 1938 foreign oil concessions were expropriated and since then we have been concerned with obtaining proper indemnification.

AMERICA'S FOREIGN INVESTMENTS BEFORE WORLD WAR I

During the period 1897-1914 American investments abroad rose from a total of 684.5 million to 3,696.8 million dollars.

AMOUNTS OF AMERICAN INVESTMENTS ABROAD IN SELECTED YEARS
(in millions of dollars)

Type of Investments	1897	1908	1914
Direct investments	634.5	1,638.5	2,652.3
Portfolio investments	50.0	1,069.3	1,044.5
Total	684.5	2,707.8	3,696.8

SOURCE: C. Lewis, *America's Stake in International Investments,* pp. 605-6.

The following table shows the geographic areas of American investments in the years 1897 and 1914.

AMERICAN FOREIGN INVESTMENTS IN 1897 AND 1914 BY GEOGRAPHIC AREAS
(in millions of dollars)

Year	Europe	Canada and Newfoundland	Cuba and Other West Indies	Mexico	Central America	South America	Asia
1897	151.0	189.7	49.0	200.2	21.2	37.9	23.0
1914	691.8	867.2	225.5	853.5	93.2	365.7	245.9

SOURCE: C. Lewis, *America's Stake in International Investments,* pp. 605-6.

REVIEW QUESTIONS

1. What is meant by the "new imperialism"?
2. Trace the development of American interests in Hawaii. What effect did the McKinley Tariff have on Hawaii?
3. What were the main causes of the Spanish-American War?
4. Why did the United States become an imperialist power in the 1890's? What were the results of the Spanish-American War?
5. What were the principles and purposes of the open door policy? How effective was this policy?
6. Why did the United States annex the Philippine Islands? What improvements resulted under American rule? How valuable were the Philippines to the United States?
7. How extensive are American interests in Cuba?
8. Describe the economic progress of Puerto Rico under United States rule. What have been the outstanding problems in Puerto Rico?
9. How did the United States acquire control of the Panama Canal?
10. What was the principle of the Roosevelt Corollary? How was it applied to Latin American countries?
11. Summarize the growth of American foreign investments during the period 1897 to 1914, indicating the geographic distributions of the investments.

27

WORLD WAR I AND THE AMERICAN ECONOMY

The outbreak of war in Europe in 1914 had certain immediate effects upon the economy of the United States. (1) A financial crisis impended as a result of the closing of the London Stock Exchange and the liquidation of European investments in the United States. Stock exchanges in leading centers suspended operations for several months. Heavy demands on banks for cash forced the New York banks to issue clearinghouse certificates and the national government to issue almost 68 million dollars in paper money under the Aldrich-Vreeland Act of 1908. (2) Trade and industry were seriously upset. Export markets for cotton, wheat, metals, and steel manufactures temporarily contracted. American industry was deprived of foreign ships previously available for American trade. Wartime conditions made commerce hazardous and difficult. American business prospects in 1914 and early 1915 were very uncertain.

AMERICAN INTERESTS IN WORLD WAR I

The United States, the leading nonbelligerent, found it difficult to maintain a neutral position in the years 1914 to 1917. The European belligerents, fighting for their lives, tried to restrict the enemy's imports from the United States and repeatedly violated the rights of American traders. The English blockaded German ports, redefined the term "contraband," and seized many cargoes en route to Germany or Austria. Germany, intent on starving the British into submission, resorted to submarine warfare and caused the loss of American lives and property.

A number of factors led the United States to go to war against Germany in April, 1917. By that time the American economy was linked to the Allied cause: huge shipments of supplies were being sent to England and France; private loans to the Allies amounted to 2.5 billion dollars, those to Germany only 35 million dollars. Cultural ties with England and France created sympathy for their cause. Fundamentally, however, the threat to national security and to the American way of life was the decisive consideration that led the United States to enter the war on the side of the Allies.

MOBILIZATION OF ECONOMIC RESOURCES

In the late nineteenth and early twentieth centuries the time-honored American policy of laissez-faire had suffered a decline. Business regulation by municipal, state, and federal governments was intended to eliminate abuses and to restore to citizens some of the opportunities of which they had been deprived. The trend toward increased government regulation of private industry was intensified during World War I as the government carefully supervised the production and distribution of goods.

War Industries Board. In August, 1916, Congress authorized the establishment of a Council of National Defense, consisting of six cabinet heads. This Council, with the aid of an Advisory Commission of experts representing major segments of the economy, was intended to integrate the work of economic mobilization, but it proved too unwieldy and for the most part the task was entrusted to its subdivision, the War Industries Board. The board was given increased authority in early 1918, enabling it to determine priorities of production and distribution, build new plants, adapt industries to new uses, regulate the production of civilian goods, and fix the prices of raw materials.

Industrial Expansion. Urgent need for war supplies encouraged the expansion of American industry. Moreover, certain manufactures usually imported from Europe were no longer available and these now had to be produced in the United States.

Metals and Minerals. The production of metals and minerals during the war years 1914-1917 increased as follows: iron ore, from 41.4 to 75.2 million long tons; bituminous coal, from 422.7 to 551.7 million short tons; copper, from 1,150 to 1,886 million pounds; and petroleum, from 265.7 to 335.3 million barrels.

Iron and Steel. War brought unprecedented prosperity to the iron and steel industry. The year 1914 was one of depression for the industry, but rapid expansion followed in the period 1915-1917. Exports of iron and steel products rose from 251.4 million dollars in 1915 to 1,133 million dollars in 1917. The earnings of 112 companies in 1915 totalled 203 million dollars, a profit of 7 per cent on sales; the earnings of 131 companies in 1917 amounted to 1,034 million dollars, a profit of 28 per cent on sales.

Chemicals. War brought tremendous growth to the chemical industries. There were only seven dye-manufacturing companies in the country in 1914; in 1917, there were 118 companies, and a total production valued at 104 million dollars. The value of American exports of chemicals, dyes, and drugs increased from 21.9 million dollars in 1914 to 181 million dollars in 1917. Exports of explosives rose from a value of 6.7 million dollars in 1914 to 802.7 million dollars in 1917.

Fuel Administration. A Fuel Administration was established in 1917 to stimulate production, supervise distribution, and reduce waste. The public was urged to conserve fuel. There were heatless days as well as shutdowns for some factories, stores, and amusement places. A serious problem was that of securing adequate facilities for the transportation of fuel.

Food Administration. The Food Production Act of 1917 authorized measures to stimulate agricultural production. The Food and Fuel Control Act of the same year gave the government strict control over the production, conservation, and distribution of farm products. The latter act authorized the government to purchase, store, and sell foodstuffs. There was a National Food Administration, headed by Herbert C. Hoover, which increased production and at the same time urged consumers to eat less food. Its extensive purchases enabled the

Food Administration to control the prices of farm products.

Transportation During the War. In April, 1917, the Emergency Fleet Corporation was organized to construct merchant vessels. Existing shipyards were expanded and new ones were built. Ships with a total of nearly three million tons were built during the war, and American tonnage in foreign trade increased from 2.1 million tons in 1916 to 11.0 million tons in 1921.

The inability of the nation's railroads to meet war needs under private management made it necessary for the government to take over the operation of the railroads in December, 1917. The Railroad Control Act of March, 1918, provided that government-operated roads should receive annual payments not exceeding their average net operating incomes for the three years ending June 30, 1917; that a revolving fund of 500 million dollars be established to finance the operation; and that the roads be returned to private owners within one year and nine months after ratification of the peace treaty. Under government management, railroad operations were co-ordinated so that they could provide effectively for wartime requirements.

Labor During the War. A decline in immigration, the removal of over 4 million men from the labor force into the armed services, and the rapidly expanding economy of the war period contributed to a severe shortage of labor. Despite the employment of about a million women in industry, the problem of a labor shortage persisted throughout the war. In this situation it was natural for wages to rise, though less rapidly than prices. General effects of the war were a decline in real wages and a relative decline in labor's economic position. Despite a substantial increase in union membership, radical elements were weakened or eliminated because of conservative public opinion. Labor was represented on the Council of National Defense in an effort to avoid disputes and loss of production. The War Labor Board, a judicial body created to arbitrate industrial conflicts, adjudicated about 1,500 disputes. There were 6,000 strikes during the war, but most of them were brief and insignificant.

Expansion of Foreign Trade. American exports rose in value from 2,329.7 million dollars in 1914 to 6,227.2 million dollars in 1917. In the same period the excess of exports over imports increased from 435.8 million dollars to 3,567.8 million dollars. The expansion of foreign trade (in addition to increased American investments abroad and the withdrawal of European capital invested in this country) contributed to making the United States for the first time in its history a creditor nation.

UNITED STATES FOREIGN TRADE, 1914-1921
(in millions of dollars)

Year	Exports of Domestic Merchandise	Excess of Exports Over Imports	Percentage of Agricultural Exports	Percentage of Manufactured Exports
1914	2,329.7	$ 35.8	48	47
1915	2,716.2	1,042.0	54	43
1916	4,272.2	2,074.3	36	62
1917	6,227.2	3,567.8	32	66
1918	5,838.7	2,893.0	39	58
1919	7,749.8	3,845.4	53	45
1920	8,080.5	2,802.0	43	52
1921	4,378.9	1,869.8	48	46

SOURCE: *Statistical Abstract of the United States, 1921,* pp. 840, 847, 849.

METHODS OF FINANCING WORLD WAR I

The total cost of World War I to the United States was about 35 billion dollars, including 9.4 billion dollars loaned to the Allies after April, 1917. The national debt rose from about a billion dollars before the war to over 26.5 billion dollars in 1919. This financial obligation was met in part (about one-third) by taxation and in part (about two-thirds) by loans.

Taxation. During the war, increased tax rates and the imposition of new taxes brought in much more revenue than in prewar years.

ANNUAL TAX INCOME, 1914-1919

Fiscal Year (ending June 30)	Total Tax Income (in millions of dollars)
1914	735
1915	692
1916	779
1917	1,118
1918	4,174
1919	4,648

The income tax, which was increased in 1916 and again in 1917, produced about two-thirds of the total tax income. The Act of October 3, 1917, imposed an excess profits tax, and increased the taxes (or imposed new taxes) on liquors, tobacco, luxuries, and amusements.

Loans. By means of five bond issues the United States raised almost 22.5 billion dollars. The bonds, in units of at least 50 dollars, paid interest ranging from 3½ to 4¼ per cent. Four of the loans (the *Liberty Loans*) were floated during the war; a fifth (the *Victory Liberty Loan*) was floated shortly after the Armistice. The bonds were purchased by an estimated total of 66,000,000 Americans.

Inflation in the War Period. The wartime demand for commodities resulted in shortages and steady price increases. The government's liberal credit policies also contributed to inflation. The cost of living rose during 1918 about 75 per cent and during 1920 nearly 110 per cent above the 1913 level. Despite the inflation, the large quantities of gold which flowed into the country made it unnecessary to suspend specie payments.

REVIEW QUESTIONS

1. What effect did the outbreak of war in Europe in 1914 have on the American economy?
2. Why was it difficult for the United States to maintain neutrality? Why did America finally go to war?
3. Describe the work of the War Industries Board.
4. What industries were affected most by the war?
5. What part did the Food Administration play in our mobilization? The Fuel Administration?
6. What effect did the war have upon American shipping?
7. For what reasons and under what conditions did the government operate the nation's railroads in the war period?
8. How did the war affect labor?
9. What tendencies in foreign trade developed during the war?
10. What was done about taxation and financing the World War? What use was made of government loans?

28

THE PROSPEROUS TWENTIES

After World War I the basic desire of the American people was to return to "normalcy"—meaning prewar conditions. Almost at once after the Armistice was signed, the government began to remove economic controls and to cancel war contracts. Military demobilization and industrial reconversion, though not planned systematically, were carried through quickly without serious dislocations. Surplus materials were disposed of in bargain sales at home and abroad, war contracts were adjusted, and 4,000,000 veterans were absorbed in civilian employment. The Merchant Marine Act of 1920 permitted the Shipping Board to sell about 40 per cent of the American merchant marine. In 1920 the Railroad Transportation Act returned the nation's railroads to private management.

POSTWAR ECONOMIC CONDITIONS

Despite problems of reconversion, the United States experienced prosperity until the middle of 1921. Continued government spending, heavy exports, and expansion in the housing and automobile industries stimulated the economy. A sharp decline in war production was offset by substantial increases in civilian goods. The gross national product of goods and services remained at a high level. Prices rose in 1919 and 1920; in the two years, the index of wholesale prices (using 1913 as a base of 100) reached 203.4 and 227.9, respectively.

Business began to decline in 1920, and in 1921 prices crashed. The index of wholesale prices fell to 150.6. The gross national product, calculated in terms of 1914 prices, declined from 40.1 billion dollars in 1920 to 37.6 billion dollars in 1921. It is estimated that in 1921 there were 4,754,000 unemployed and 100,000 business firms were thrown into bankruptcy.

INDUSTRIAL EXPANSION, 1923-1929

While most of the world was still feeling the effects of the postwar recession, the United States enjoyed a period of prosperity. The depression of 1921 was short-lived. Purchasing power was bolstered in 1921 because prices fell more rapidly than wages, merchants quickly sold their inventories, and lower costs of raw materials encouraged industry to produce. In the period 1923 to 1929 the national income rose from 71.6 billion to 87.2 billion dollars, the per capita real income (in terms of 1929 prices) from 634 to 716 dollars, and industrial production increased 25 per cent. New scientific inventions and management in industry and the development of mass production methods brought a high level of productivity. In the 1920's 20 billion dollars was added to the national wealth.

The Automobile Industry. The automobile industry expanded rapidly in the 1920's, and stimulated many other industries in the process. The production of cars and trucks rose from 2.2 million in 1920 to 5.3 million in 1929; registrations of automobiles increased from 8.2 to 23.1 million in the same period. In 1929 the value of the total product of the industry approached 3.5 billion dollars. (About 90 per cent of the business was done by six companies.) In the 1920's about 10 billion dollars was spent on improving the nation's highways.

The Electrical Industry. The expansion of the electrical business was a considerable factor in the prosperity of the 1920's. The production of electricity rose from 43 billion kilowatt-hours in 1920 to 97 billion in 1929; capital investment in the industry from about 12 billion dollars in 1920 to about 23 billion in 1930. There was a great increase in domestic lighting and in the use of electrical appliances—toasters, irons, fans, washing machines, and vacuum cleaners. The utilization of electrical power in industry increased tremendously during and after World War I. In the 1920's the concentration of control in the electrical business developed; in 1929 about 76 per cent of all electricity generated in the country was controlled by 12 systems.

The Construction Business. There was a boom in the construction of homes and commercial buildings. In the peak year of 1925 the value of the total product of the construction industry exceeded 6 billion dollars.

Industrial Combinations. The 1920's saw a revival of the combination movement. From 1919 to 1928 there were 1,268 new combinations in mining and manufacturing, resulting from the merger of 4,135 companies and the elimination of 5,591 companies. By the end of the decade the growing concentration of control in certain industries was apparent: two companies controlled 50 per cent of the nation's steel production; three companies dominated the automobile industry; a single firm monopolized aluminum manufacturing; and four electric light-and-power systems controlled to a large extent the nation's production of electric power.

Governmental Policy Regarding Combinations. Industrial combination, stimulated by the prosperity and confidence of the 1920's, was aided by a favorable governmental attitude and policy. The government's sympathetic point of view was reflected in (1) high protective tariffs, (2) aid in the expansion of foreign trade, (3) abandonment of trustbusting campaigns, (4) promotion of trade associations to eliminate waste and inefficiency, and (5) a decision of the Supreme Court that mere bigness is not a violation of the antitrust laws.

TRANSPORTATION IN THE 1920's

After consideration of various plans for the peacetime management of the nation's railroads, Congress passed the Esch-Cummins Act (the Railway Transportation Act of 1920). This measure provided for (1) a guaranteed net return for six months after March 1, 1920, equal to one-half the rental paid during the government's operation of the roads, (2) division of the nation into rate districts in which rates that would give a "fair return upon the aggregate value of the railroad property" were to be prescribed, (3) a "fair return" of 5½ per cent for two years to railroads pending evaluation of railroad property, (4) payment by the carriers of half of the income in excess of 6 per cent into a revolving fund to be made available for loans to needy roads, (5) consolidation of the nation's railroads, under the Interstate Commerce Commission's direction, into 20 to 35 systems, (6) strict regulation of railroad finances by the Interstate Commerce Commission, (7) establishment of minimum and maximum rates by the Commission, and (8) creation of a Railroad Labor Board to prevent strikes.

The Esch-Cummins Act did not prove very successful, for the Labor Board's decisions were not binding, the enforcement of the recapture clause proved difficult, and the railroads failed to agree on plans for consolidation. Competition from motor transport weakened the railroads in the 1920's. Although investments in railroads rose about 33 per cent and freight revenue increased slightly, passenger revenue declined about 33 per cent and taxes rose 114 million dollars from 1920 to 1929.

World War I aided progress in aviation, but interest in this field declined after the war. Not until the end of the 1920's did aviation assume commercial significance. In 1920 airplanes carried only 8.5 million pounds of mail, 417,000 passengers, and 468,571 pounds of express and freight shipments.

FARM PROBLEMS IN THE 1920's

As already mentioned, the unusual foreign and domestic demand for foodstuffs during World War I encouraged agricultural expansion, which, in addition to scientific and technological progress, resulted in greatly increased productivity. In 1921 a decline of 50 per cent in agricultural prices initiated a farm depression which outlasted the decade.

Farm Conditions, 1920-1930. During the period 1920-1930 the number of farms decreased by nearly 170,000, but the cultivated area increased about 31,000,000 acres. While the value of farm land fell from 66 billion dollars in 1920 to less than 48 billion dollars in 1930, the mortgage indebtedness of farmers rose more than 1.6 billion dollars and the proportion of tenant farmers increased from 38.1 per cent to 42.4 per cent.

Farm Relief. Farm organizations and the "farm bloc" in Congress demanded and obtained government aid for agriculture.

TARIFFS. The emergency tariff of 1921, the Fordney-McCumber

tariff of 1922, and the Smoot-Hawley tariff of 1930 were designed to help protect agriculture from foreign competition. The tariff generally was detrimental, instead of being helpful to exporters, inasmuch as it restricted the export markets for the nation's agricultural surplus.

CREDIT. Several measures were adopted to provide more credit for farmers. The War Finance Corporation was revived in 1921 to finance farm exports. The Agricultural Credits Act of 1923 and the Agricultural Marketing Act of 1929 extended credit to farmers.

MCNARY-HAUGEN BILLS. The "farm bloc" demanded legislation to help the farmers to dispose of surpluses and to raise the prices of farm products. The McNary-Haugen Bill, passed by Congress in 1927 and 1928 but twice vetoed by President Calvin Coolidge, provided for the purchase by the government of certain agricultural surpluses and the sale of these products abroad. Any loss incurred in foreign sales was to be met by an equalization fee assessed against the sales of all the producers.

AGRICULTURAL MARKETING ACT, 1929. The Agricultural Marketing Act of 1929 was designed to encourage the formation of farm co-operatives and to aid them in marketing. A Federal Farm Board was established with a revolving fund of 500 million dollars for loans to co-operatives. Grain and cotton stabilization corporations were organized to purchase the large surpluses, in an effort to maintain prices, but this attempt met with little success.

LABOR IN THE 1920's

Organized labor lost considerable strength in the 1920's. In the postwar return to "normalcy," employers reduced some of labor's previous gains, and the unions found it difficult to compete with the organized opposition of business. The American Federation of Labor lost over a million members in the decade, and efforts to unionize new industries proved unsuccessful.

Causes of Decline. There were two main causes of the decline of union prestige. (1) Capital organized an attack on unionism, popularizing the open shop and organizing company unions. Laissez-faire was advocated as the "American" public policy; organized labor was blamed for rising prices. (2) The attitude of the government was unsympathetic to labor: government opposition helped to break strikes in the coal and steel industries in 1919, and conservative court decisions hampered labor throughout the 1920's.

Labor and "Welfare Capitalism." Many employers initiated steps to improve the workers' status. Both humanitarian sentiments and the possibility of retarding unionization motivated them to provide such services as group insurance, pension systems, educational programs, profit-sharing plans, paid vacations, and recreation facilities.

REVIEW QUESTIONS

1. What were the chief problems of demobilization after World War I?
2. What factors were responsible for continued prosperity during the years 1918-1920?
3. Describe and explain agricultural expansion in the 1920's.
4. Indicate the extent of growth of the automobile industry after World War I. What effect did this have on the rest of the economy?
5. Describe the expansion of the electrical business after World War I.
6. Why was there a revival of industrial combination after World War I?
7. What were the provisions of the Transportation Act of 1920? What were the effects of this act?
8. What were the causes of the farm problem in the 1920's?
9. What measures of farm relief were attempted? How successful were they?
10. Why did organized labor suffer a decline in influence in the postwar decade?

29

THE GREAT DEPRESSION

The expansive twenties reached a climax in 1928 and 1929 as the economy approached a dangerous condition of overproduction, but the confident American people continued to speculate in eager anticipation of quick profits. The apparent prosperity of the postwar decade came to an end abruptly in a stock-market crash in October, 1929, which marked the beginning of the worst depression in the nation's history. The effects of the depression on American life were profound, for the economic upheaval shattered widespread complacency and traditional overconfidence and induced recourse to social planning to solve economic problems.

CAUSES OF THE DEPRESSION

There were a number of basic causes of the depression, all of which were interrelated, and each of which was the culmination of long-continued developments. Important factors relating to the depression included overproduction, distribution of income, agricultural maladjustments, the overextension of credit, and the insecurity of foreign trade.

Overproduction. America's capacity to produce had run ahead of purchasing power. Although the nation was consuming more goods in the 1920's, the rate of increase in consumption fell behind the rate of growth in production.

Distribution of Income. Purchasing power was limited by the fact that a large proportion of the national income went to capital claimants, that is, to owners or creditors in payment of rents, profits, royalties, and interest. The disproportionate share of these claimants induced further expansion and contributed to overproduction. Although wages and salaries increased in the 1920's, the proportion of the national income allocated to wages decreased.

Agricultural Maladjustments. The agricultural depression of the 1920's limited the purchasing power of a large segment of the population. From 1929 to 1932 average farm prices fell 64 per cent.

Overextension of Credit. By 1929 credit transactions had raised the indebtedness of the American people to a total somewhere between 100 and 150 billion dollars. Reflecting the reckless speculation of the public in securities, the bank borrowings of stock brokers rose from 3.5 billion dollars in 1927 to 8.5 billion in 1929. It is estimated that in 1929 over a million persons held stock on margin.

Insecurity of Foreign Trade. The United States, though it had become a creditor power, failed to adopt policies consistent with its new position. The surge of nationalism after World War I induced the imposition of tariffs and other trade barriers, both by the United States and by other nations, which impeded commerce with foreign countries. When world trade began to contract in 1929, many European and Latin-American debtors were unable to export enough goods to obtain the funds they needed for payment of interest charges on their American loans. Importers of American products were compelled to reduce their purchases.

CONDITIONS DURING THE DEPRESSION

On October 24, 1929, over 12 million shares were traded on the stock exchanges. Five days later, 16.4 million shares changed hands as the average price of fifty leading stocks fell 40 points. The crash was followed by repeated declines in stock prices throughout the period 1929 to 1932; thus, the average value of fifty industrials fell from 252 to 61 dollars per share, that of twenty railroads from 167 to 33 dollars per share, and that of twenty public utilities from 353 to 99 dollars per share. Millions of investors lost their savings and many were forced into bankruptcy.

Business Decline. It is estimated that by 1933 the volume of American business was only about 50 per cent of what it had been in 1929. During the period 1929-1932 the average of wholesale prices declined 33 per cent. Commercial failures rose from 24,000 in 1928 to 32,000 in 1932. In the years 1929 to 1932, over 5,000 banks were closed. The total national income declined from an estimated total of 85 billion dollars in 1929 to 37 billion dollars in 1932.

Labor. In the fall of 1930 there were about 4.5 million unemployed; in early 1933 the number was variously estimated at 12 million to 15 million. At the same time wage rates were cut sharply; by 1933 total wage payments amounted to less than 50 per cent of the 1929 total. In 1934 about 17 million people were on public relief rolls.

Agriculture. Gross farm income declined 57 per cent in the years 1929-1932, and the value of farm property was reduced by one-third. The average prices of farm products in this period fell 64 per cent; for eight primary products the decline amounted to 70 per cent.

Trade. The value of American foreign trade was reduced from 9.6 billion dollars in 1929 to 2.9 billion dollars in 1932. This decline was caused by several factors. (1) Americans stopped making loans to foreign merchants; (2) the high exchange value of the dollar discouraged the purchase of American goods; and (3) the United States and various European governments imposed trade restrictions on imports.

THE HOOVER POLICIES

In the early stages of the depression, President Herbert Hoover followed the traditional policy of laissez-faire. Gradually, however, he began to make use of governmental powers and influence to relieve economic distress. Unfortunately, his policies came too late and did not go far enough.

Industry. In November, 1929, leading representatives of business and labor met with President Hoover and agreed to continue production and to distribute work as widely as possible. This policy continued with good results for two years. In 1930 the Smoot-Hawley Tariff was passed, raising import duties an average of 20 per cent, to the highest point in our history. In 1932 Congress established the Reconstruction Finance Corporation, with a capital of 500 million dollars, to make loans to businesses in distress. By March, 1933, the RFC had advanced over 2 billion dollars to business and had made loans to state and city governments for relief activity.

Agriculture. The Agricultural Marketing Act of 1929 failed to provide relief for the farmers. In 1932 Congress increased the capital stock of the Federal Land Banks in order to make more credit available to them. This program, too, was of little value in dealing with the chronic farm problem.

Relief Measures. President Hoover advocated the expansion of public works to relieve unemployment. Expenditures for public works rose from an annual average of about 250 million dollars in the 1920's to more than 700 million for the year ending June 30, 1933. In order to co-ordinate the activities of various relief agencies, Hoover organized the President's Committee for Unemployment Relief in October, 1930.

The World Situation. In June, 1931, President Hoover proposed a moratorium for one year on all intergovernmental payments. Foreign powers accepted this proposal after some delay. Debtors found it impossible to pay debts, so the moratorium was only a recognition of reality. Shortly all of the debtors except Finland defaulted.

POLITICAL EFFECTS OF THE DEPRESSION

As the depression continued and deepened in spite of President Hoover's efforts and assurances, public opinion grew increasingly critical of the administration. In Congress during the first two years of Hoover's term, the conservative Republicans controlled the House, but in the Senate progressive Republicans held the balance of power and they sometimes opposed the administration. In the Congressional elections of 1930 the Democrats won control of the House, and in the Senate the administration had only a precarious majority based upon the support of the progressive Republicans. The political outlook for the Republicans in 1932 was very black, and in the presidential election of that year the Democratic candidate, Franklin D. Roosevelt, defeated Hoover with an electoral vote of 472 to 59. At the same time the Democrats won heavy majorities in both houses of Congress. It was evident that the

Republican party had suffered a tremendous loss of prestige and that the people were eager to turn to a party and a candidate that promised dynamic leadership.

REVIEW QUESTIONS

1. What were the fundamental causes of the depression of 1929?
2. Describe the extent and importance of the stock-market crash of 1929.
3. Summarize the effects of the depression upon industry, labor, agriculture, and commerce.
4. What measures were taken by President Hoover to cope with the depression? How successful were they?
5. Describe the political effects of the depression.

30

THE NEW DEAL

When Franklin D. Roosevelt became president in March, 1933, the nation was threatened by complete economic collapse: industry was operating at half speed, enormous numbers were unemployed, the farmers were in desperate need of relief, prices were at the lowest point of the depression, and the country's banking structure was on the verge of disintegration. On March 5 Congress was called into special session and the President proclaimed a banking holiday. Congress passed an Emergency Banking Act providing for the inspection of banks and the reopening of sound banks under license. The special session of Congress in 1933 passed many important measures during "the hundred days" before it adjourned.

BASIC TENETS OF THE NEW DEAL

Although laissez-faire was abandoned and drastic changes were introduced during the depression, there were antecedents of New Deal policies in the American past. The New Deal appeared to be more revolutionary than it was because of the conservatism of the 1920's.

Industry and Agriculture. Supporters of the New Deal believed that the capital plant had overexpanded, as far as normal requirements were concerned, both in industry and in agriculture. In order to alleviate this situation the Roosevelt administration considered governmental regulation necessary. In agriculture this meant limitation of production; in industry it meant the rigorous control of business activity, including close supervision of expansion. The government might at times be compelled to invest in business in order to supplement or even to compete with private enterprise. President Roosevelt also planned an extensive attack on monopoly.

Finance. Leaders of the New Deal believed that banking and credit agencies had become too vital to be completely private, that banking should be a semipublic service, and that governmental control of banking would aid in controlling and minimizing business fluctuations.

Labor. President Roosevelt believed that labor received an inadequate share of the national income. He proposed to encourage collective bargaining, to secure legal recognition of trade unions, and to provide for minimum wages and maximum hours.

Commerce. The New Deal advocated freer international trade. It was felt that factors hampering the natural flow of goods should be eliminated. This would encourage the absorption of American surpluses abroad and would create a healthier international economy.

Social Security. President Roosevelt and his associates felt that social problems arising from such conditions as unemployment, old age, invalidism, and child dependency should be the concern of the state, that the government should provide a reasonable degree of social security, and should attempt to alleviate economic injustices.

RELIEF AND SOCIAL SECURITY MEASURES

One broad category of New Deal activity involved relief and social security measures.

Civilian Conservation Corps (April, 1933). The Civilian Conservation Corps was established to provide work for young men on public works projects, and over 300,000 were employed in the first year of operation. The CCC was continued until 1942.

Federal Emergency Relief Administration (May, 1933). The Federal Emergency Relief Administration was empowered to provide emergency relief to the states; by 1935 it had provided 3 billion dollars for the unemployed.

Public Works Administration (June, 1933). The Public

Works Administration was set up with an initial appropriation of 3.3 billion dollars for construction projects. The PWA spent over 7 billion dollars but failed to solve the unemployment problem.

Civil Works Administration (1933-1934). The Civil Works Administration provided temporary employment for 4 million men and women in the winter of 1933-1934.

Works Progress Administration (April, 1935). The Works Progress Administration was created to expand and co-ordinate the public works program. The WPA lasted until 1942, during which time it employed about 8.5 million people and spent over 13 billion dollars provided by the federal and local governments. Its accomplishments included the construction of 122,000 public buildings, 664,000 miles of new roads, and many sewers, airports, bridges, parks, and reservoirs. In addition to this record of construction, WPA employees repaired thousands of existing public works. Through the Federal Arts Project and the National Youth Administration, the WPA gave employment to white-collar workers and aided students in furthering their education.

Housing. The problems of low-cost housing and slum clearance were approached in several ways. Under the WPA and various agricultural agencies some progress was made. The United States Housing Authority, an agency established by the Wagner-Steagall Housing Act of 1937, made loans and grants for construction purposes. Within three years the USHA had concluded contracts for the construction of about 510,000 homes.

Social Security. The Social Security Act of 1935 (amended in 1939 and 1950) provided for federal pensions for needy persons over 65 years of age. This program was to be financed by an income tax on employees and a payroll tax on employers. The monthly pensions were expected to range from 10 dollars to 85 dollars, depending upon the length of time a worker participated in the plan. At the present time nearly 50 million Americans are under this social security system. Since the enactment of the federal law in 1935, other forms of social security have been undertaken by the federal government as well as by all the states.

CURRENCY AND FINANCE

The New Deal administration wanted inflation in order to aid debtors and planned to achieve it through manipulation of the currency and expansion of credit. The fact that about nine-tenths of the nation's business is transacted on a credit basis limited the government's effort to produce inflation by means of currency manipulation.

Monetary Program. The United States abandoned the gold standard in April, 1933. By executive decrees the export of gold (except under Treasury license) was forbidden and the hoarding of gold and gold certificates was prohibited. The Gold Repeal Joint Resolution (June 5, 1933) cancelled gold clauses in all contracts.

The First Agricultural Adjustment Act (May, 1933) gave the president the authority (1) to issue a maximum of 3 billion dollars of legal-tender United States notes based only on the credit of the United States; (2) to reduce the gold content of the dollar up to 50 per cent; and (3) to coin an unlimited amount of silver at any ratio to gold that might be decided upon. In January, 1934, the government began to purchase gold at the inflated price of $20.67 per ounce. In February, 1934, the government reduced the gold content of the dollar by 40.94 per cent under the provisions of the Gold Reserve Act (January, 1934). Nevertheless, prices did not rise so rapidly as the administration wished.

In December, 1933, the government began to purchase American-mined silver at a premium price. The Silver Purchase Act (June, 1934) provided for the purchase of domestic and foreign silver until the monetary value of the government's supply of silver should be one-fourth of the combined value of the government's supply of both silver and gold, or until the price of silver rose above the monetary value of $1.293 per ounce. The result of this policy was to compel the Treasury to buy all of the domestic silver produced and much foreign silver at a high price.

Credit Measures. The New Deal's planned inflation included measures for the extension, expansion, and increased government control of business credit. The Emergency Banking Act

(March, 1933) extended the power of the Reconstruction Finance Corporation to make loans. The Loans-to-Industry Act (1934) authorized direct loans to industry up to a maximum of 580 million dollars. The Home Owners Loan Act (1933) set up the Home Owners Loan Corporation to refinance home mortgages to prevent foreclosures. The HOLC, during the three years of its operation, loaned more than 3 billion dollars to more than a million home owners. In 1936 its activities were taken over by the Federal Housing Administration, which also insured loans made by private lending agencies for new construction and repair purposes. (Measures which extended agricultural credit are considered under The New Deal and Agriculture, p. 216.)

Banking Reform. The Glass-Steagall Act (June, 1933) authorized the Federal Reserve banks to restrict speculative expansion of credit by member banks. The latter were required to give up their security affiliates and to abstain from investment banking activities. A Federal Deposit Insurance Corporation was created to guarantee deposits up to $2,500, a limit increased to $5,000 by an amendment in 1945. The Banking Act (1935) directed the reorganization of the Federal Reserve Board to make it less subject to political influence. The Board's powers were enlarged to include authority to vary its reserve requirements within limits, to examine Reserve Bank rates periodically, and to approve appointments of officers in Reserve Banks. The Federal Open Market Committee (created in 1933) was given stricter control over the credit policies of members banks of the Federal Reserve system.

Securities Regulation. The Truth-in-Securities Act (1933) prohibited the public sale of securities in interstate commerce or through the mails unless detailed information concerning the securities had been filed with the Federal Trade Commission. The Securities Exchange Act (1934) established the Securities and Exchange Commission with which information about securities had to be registered. The Commission could prohibit the sale of securities if insufficient or false information had been filed. Anyone suffering loss through false information could sue for civil damages.

THE NEW DEAL AND INDUSTRY

The New Deal attempted to eliminate wasteful competition, stimulate production, and guard against overproduction by broad social planning.

National Industrial Recovery Act (June, 1933). Recovery was to be hastened by restricting production, raising prices, increasing wages, and reducing working hours. Self-regulation of business was to be attempted, and industrial codes of fair competition to prevent price-cutting were authorized. The law designated maximum hours and minimum wages and sanctioned collective bargaining. A National Recovery Administration was established to administer the program.

The majority of industrial laborers eventually worked under the nearly 600 basic and 189 supplementary NRA codes which were drawn up. The program did not function smoothly, nor did it bring immediate recovery. Capital's influence in setting up the codes was displeasing to labor. Employers disliked the rights granted to labor unions. Small business complained that the NRA fostered monopoly. Violations of the codes were common. Finally in May, 1935, the United States Supreme Court declared the NIRA unconstitutional on the grounds that the act (1) delegated legislative power to the President without sufficient standards to direct him in the use of it and (2) provided for federal regulation of wages and hours in wholly intrastate business.

Legislation for the Coal Industry. The Guffey-Snyder Bituminous Coal Stabilization Act (1935) set up the National Bituminous Coal Commission. A code for the industry was drawn up, minimum prices were set, and maximum hours and minimum wages were established. In 1936 this law was declared unconstitutional. The Guffey-Vinson Act (1937), which re-enacted the Guffey-Snyder Act without the mandatory labor provisions, was upheld by the United States Supreme Court in 1940.

Government Regulation of Business. In the early years of the New Deal, particularly during the operation of the NRA, the antitrust laws were practically suspended. Later the attitude of the government toward monopoly began to change. The Temporary National Economic Committee (1938) investigated the concentration of economic power, and its report seemed to indicate that monopoly had been encouraged by New Deal policies. The government intensified its antitrust campaign in 1939 and 1940, but preparations for World War II thereafter made increased concentration of economic power unavoidable.

ROBINSON-PATMAN ACT (1936). The Robinson-Patman Act, aimed at chain stores, prohibited price discrimination intended to destroy competition. Most states legalized contracts by which manufacturers bound each retailer not to sell their products at less than a prescribed price. The Miller-Tydings Act (1937) exempted these price contracts from the operation of the Sherman Antitrust Act.

REGULATION OF THE ELECTRIC POWER INDUSTRY. There was a growing demand for federal regulation of the electric power industry because of the concentration of control (and the abuse of power) in this business. Federal regulation of the industry had begun in 1920 with the creation of the Federal Power Commission. The Public Utilities Holding Company Act (1935) enabled the commission to regulate rates and business practices of companies engaged in interstate commerce and prohibited holding companies beyond the second degree. Approval of the issuance of securities by the Securities and Exchange Commission was required. These purposes of the act were not realized, however, before the end of World War II.

The question of federal operation of hydroelectric plants was debated throughout the 1920's. Presidents Coolidge and Hoover vetoed bills authorizing the government to operate plants at Muscle Shoals on the Tennessee River. The Muscle Shoals-Tennessee Valley Development Act (May, 1933) established the Tennessee Valley Authority, which was authorized to erect hydroelectric plants and dams, to improve navigation on the Tennessee River, to promote flood control, to prevent soil erosion, and to engage in reforestation. The TVA was opposed by private companies because it was empowered to sell electricity in competition with private industry. After ten years of operation the agency was selling power to 83 municipalities, 45 co-operative associations, and many industrial plants. The success of the TVA in developing the Tennessee Valley stimulated interest in similar regional programs in other parts of the country.

THE NEW DEAL AND AGRICULTURE

The basic program of New Deal legislation in behalf of the farmers was as follows: (1) The establishment of parity prices, that is, the restoration of the farmer's purchasing power to the level of the period August, 1909, to July, 1914, was a primary goal. (2) The establishment of parity income later replaced the previous objective. This meant the restoration to agriculture of the same relative income in relation to the total national income that the farmer enjoyed before World War I. (3) The New Deal proposed to adjust farm production to meet market requirements. It was hoped that keeping surpluses off the market would maintain the prices of farm products. (4) Federal leadership was to be provided in soil conservation, improved land use, debt reduction, efforts to achieve security against foreclosures, rural relief, and rehabilitation for submarginal farmers and tenants.

Agricultural Adjustment Act (May, 1933). The Agricultural Adjustment Act was intended to reduce the farm surplus and raise farm income by means of (1) cotton options (cotton growers reduced acreage and in return received options to buy cotton up to a limit equal to the amount of their cut in production, but they were permitted to sell options if cotton prices rose); (2) government "rental" payments for reductions in cultivated acreage; and (3) more efficient marketing.

The Agricultural Adjustment Administration reduced the production of cotton, wheat, corn, tobacco, hogs, cattle, peanuts, rye, barley, flax, grain sorghums, sugar beets, and sugar cane. In 1934 and 1935 over 60 million acres were withdrawn from cultivation. Opposition to the AAA was based on several factors: (1) it fostered an economy of scarcity in a time of great need; (2) the increased burden produced by rising prices resulted in consumer resistance; (3) it was not clear that the program was achieving its purposes, for in 1933 crops were not much smaller than they had been in 1932 and the production of uncontrolled crops increased. Some improvement in the economic status of the farmers was noted, but, in January,

1936, the Agricultural Adjustment Act was declared unconstitutional because it violated the principle of states' rights and imposed discriminatory taxes.

Soil Conservation and Domestic Allotment Act (1936). The Soil Conservation and Domestic Allotment Act provided direct federal subsidies for producers who substituted soil-conserving crops for commercial staples.

The Agricultural Adjustment Act (1938). The second AAA represented another attempt to maintain "parity prices." The government established production quotas for each commodity, with provision for reasonable surpluses to meet emergency needs. "Parity prices" were designated. If the market price were less than the "parity price," the farmer would be given partial compensation.

Agricultural Credit. Steps were taken to extend credit to farmers and to provide security against foreclosures. (1) The Agricultural Adjustment Act (1933) empowered the Federal Land Bank to refinance farm mortgages. (2) The Farm Mortgage Refinancing Act (1934), which set up the Federal Farm Mortgage Corporation, provided similar aid. (3) The Farm Mortgage Foreclosure Act (1934) authorized the Land Bank Commissioner to make loans for the redemption of farm property. (4) The Frazier-Lemke Bankruptcy Act (1934) allowed bankrupt farmers to request an appraisal of their property and permitted them to buy it back on the installment plan over a six-year period at an interest rate of 1 per cent. If a creditor refused to accept such a settlement, bankruptcy proceedings were halted and the farmer could retain his property for five years at a fair rental. This act was found unconstitutional in 1935, but a similar measure was upheld in 1936. Under these laws the Farm Credit Administration made loans exceeding 2 billion dollars within a single year and the number of foreclosures of farm mortgages was greatly reduced.

Farm Securities Administration. The Farm Securities Administration was set up in 1937 to aid tenants, sharecroppers, farm laborers, and submarginal farmers. The FSA continued resettlement work already begun, encouraging farmers to leave submarginal lands and to move to resettlement communities. Under the terms of the Bankhead Jones Act (1937), the FSA loaned money to selected tenants and laborers for the purchase of farms. In some cases outright grants were made. The FSA also made many short-term loans to individuals and to co-operative associations for the purchase of farm equipment, the refinancing of mortgages and debts, and the replacement of short leases with long-term leases. Much agricultural rehabilitation was accomplished by this agency, despite the fact that appropriations were too low for the size of the task.

THE NEW DEAL AND LABOR

A number of major reforms reflected the sympathetic attitude of the government toward the demands of labor.

Labor and the NRA. Section 7-A of the National Industrial Recovery Act guaranteed that (1) employees had the right to organize and bargain collectively, (2) no worker could be compelled to join a company union, and (3) no one could be barred from employment because of his union membership. Labor was expected to benefit from the NRA codes which established minimum wages, prohibited the speed-up, and forbade the employment of children under sixteen. A great surge of unionization resulted. In 1935, however, the act was declared unconstitutional.

National Labor Relations Act (July, 1935). The National Labor Relations Act re-enacted the provisions of Section 7-A of the NIRA and established the National Labor Relations Board. Employers were forbidden to interfere with labor's right to bargain collectively, to refuse to bargain with unions, and to discriminate against union members. The NLRB could issue "cease and desist" orders against employers who violated the law. It was difficult to enforce the law until its constitutionality was upheld by the Supreme Court in 1937; thereafter the strength of organized labor increased rapidly.

Fair Labor Standards Act (1938). The Fair Labor Standards Act enacted minimum wages and maximum hours for labor engaged in interstate commerce or in the production of goods involved in interstate commerce. In 1938 as many as 12 to 13 million workers were subject to these regulations. Maximum working hours per week were set at 44, to be reduced to 40 after two years. Minimum wages per hour started at 25 cents and were to be raised to 40 cents by 1945. With the coming of war, however, the minimum-wage regulations of the Fair Labor Standards Act were far below actual wages and the law was inoperative. After the war the minimum wage was raised to 75 cents an hour.

Other Labor Legislation. The National Employment Service Act (1933) effected co-operation between the federal government and local employment offices. The Walsh-Healey Government Contracts Act (1936) regulated working conditions in factories holding government contracts amounting to $10,000 or more. The Railroad Retirement Act (1935) provided government management of pension systems for railroad employees.

Rise of the CIO. A controversy within the American Federation of Labor split that organization in November, 1935, when eight union leaders founded a rival group—the Committee for Industrial Organization. The CIO conducted a campaign for members in the mass production industries. It was highly successful in the automobile and steel industries, securing recognition as sole bargaining agent for employees in these industries. By 1942 the CIO had a membership of about 5 million out of a national total of 13 million in all unions.

RESULTS AND MEANING OF THE NEW DEAL

In 1939 the national income (in terms of 1929 dollars) was 84.5 billion dollars as compared with 82.9 billion dollars in 1929. However, the population had increased over 10 million and the productivity of the nation's industrial plant had grown. The New Deal failed to alter appreciably the distribution of the national income, for the proportion going to wages and salaries rose only from 65.5 per cent in 1929 to 68.2 per cent in 1939. It is impossible to determine precisely to what extent the New Deal measures, natural forces of recovery, and the stimulation of war demands were responsible for the nation's recovery from the depression.

Reform and Rehabilitation. Government action instituted major reforms in the banking structure and the securities market. In its agricultural program the New Deal fostered soil conservation, flood control, scientific farming, and the rehabilitation of rural areas. The federal government not only relieved unemployment but also established minimum wage and maximum hour regulations in important segments of the economy. Plans for the attainment of social security were drawn up. In some regions, notably in the Tennessee Valley, the regeneration of an entire area was attempted.

Deficit Finance. The expansion of government services required vastly increased expenditures: the federal debt rose from 16 billion to 40 billion dollars in the 1930's. The administration held that deficit financing was as justifiable in a period of depression as in wartime.

The Decline of Laissez-Faire. The New Deal represented the first broad effort in American history to promote economic recovery by means of government action. This effort necessitated abandonment of the time-honored policy of laissez-faire, but there were many precedents for the controls imposed by the New Deal. Federal regulations date back to the Interstate Commerce Act (1887) and the Sherman Antitrust Act (1890). Laws to promote the public welfare were common in the states and local communities during the nineteenth century. The New Deal did not represent a drastic break with the past; it extended and applied speedily historical principles and methods that had been adopted many years before.

REVIEW QUESTIONS

1. What were the basic purposes of the New Deal programs for industry, agriculture, and labor?
2. What relief measures were initiated during the period 1933-1935 to aid the unemployed?
3. Summarize and evaluate the activities of the Works Progress Administration.
4. In what ways did the New Deal attack the problems of low-cost housing, slum clearance, and home finance?
5. What were the purposes of the New Deal monetary program? When and how did the United States abandon the gold standard? Why was the gold content of the dollar reduced?
6. What were the purposes and provisions of the Glass-Steagall Act? The Securities Exchange Act?

7. How was the National Industrial Recovery Act designed to hasten recovery? How successful was the NRA?
8. What antimonopoly measures were taken by the New Deal?
9. Outline the activities of the TVA.
10. What were the purposes and provisions of the first Agricultural Adjustment Act? How successful was this act?
11. What did the New Deal do to make credit available to farmers?
12. Outline the program of the Farm Securities Administration.
13. How was labor aided by the NRA? The National Labor Relations Act? The Fair Labor Standards Act?
14. Explain the statement that the New Deal was not a revolutionary movement in the economic history of the United States.

31

AMERICA AND WORLD ECONOMICS

Although the United States was still a debtor nation to the extent of 3,686 million dollars in 1914, the amount of American capital invested abroad was increasing rapidly. World War I transformed the nation into a creditor power: European-owned American securities were returned to the United States; American private and public loans to Europe during the war totalled about 12 billion dollars.

AMERICAN FOREIGN INVESTMENTS SINCE 1914

Capital continued to flow out of the country as the foreign investments of Americans (excluding government loans) rose from 6,955.6 million dollars in 1919 to 17,009.6 million dollars in 1929. The latter amount was estimated to be equally divided between portfolio and direct investments. Unfortunately many of the portfolio investments were unsound and for nonproductive purposes; investment firms were frequently more interested in their underwriting profits than in the security of the investments. In the 1920's many American companies extended their economic interests, establishing plants abroad in order to capture foreign business and to avoid tariff barriers.

The Depression Decade. After World War I, foreign nations found it difficult to meet their obligations to the United States. Their exports to the United States were hampered by the new tariff rates. Increased competition from the American merchant marine reduced their income from transportation services. American investments abroad decreased in 1928 and virtually ended with the coming of the depression. In the

1930's American investors lost almost 11 billion dollars in foreign securities. (Loans to European governments in default on payments to the government of the United States were forbidden by the Johnson Debt Default Act of 1934.) American investments abroad in 1940 totalled 10,771 million dollars; the three leading areas for investment, in the order of their importance, were Canada and Newfoundland, South America, and Europe. At the same time, however, foreign investments in the United States were valued at 9,695 million dollars.

WAR DEBTS AND REPARATIONS

Following World War I the United States attempted to recover the 12 billion dollars it had loaned to European governments during the war. The debtors found it hard to repay the loans and urged the United States to treat them as a contribution to the common cause. In any event most of the money had been used to buy American goods. The United States agreed to debt reductions but insisted upon the general principle of repayment. The reductions, which ranged from 23 per cent for Great Britain to 75 per cent for Italy, were largely nullified by the postwar deflation.

The German reparations debt of 33 billion dollars (the amount set in 1921) was too much for Germany to pay, and she soon defaulted. The United States, though insisting that the war debts of the Allies and the question of reparations were entirely separate matters, did assist in scaling down the German obligations to facilitate payment. In actuality, the Allies turned over to the United States a considerable share of the reparation payments received from Germany. In 1924 the Dawes Plan reduced German reparations and granted Germany a loan of 200 million dollars in gold from the United States and the Allies. The Young Plan in 1929 again reduced the German debt and provided that the amount of annual payments would depend upon American reductions in the Allied debts. The United States rejected this plan.

With the onset of the depression, Germany defaulted and, in the face of general economic breakdown, President Hoover proposed a one-year moratorium on all intergovernmental payments. In 1933 token payments were made to the United

States by Great Britain and Italy, acknowledging existence of the debt but postponing settlement. As previously mentioned, the Johnson Act (1934) forbade loans to foreign powers in default to the United States. Much resentment and ill-will between America and European nations resulted from the war debts question.

INTERNATIONAL TRADE

The process of continued industrialization profoundly affected the foreign trade of the United States. A decline in the proportion of exports of foodstuffs and raw materials was accompanied by an increase in the export of manufactures. Meanwhile the proportion of raw materials imported rose and the proportion of manufactures declined. In general the United States imported raw materials and exported manufactured commodities.

Importance of Foreign Trade. Because of a high degree of self-sufficiency, foreign trade has not been so important to the United States as it has been to other nations. In the period between the two world wars the value of neither exports nor imports ever exceeded 8 per cent of the national income. Yet some agricultural and industrial producers depended upon an export market; the United States still had to import such commodities as raw silk, rubber, tin, sugar, coffee, and tropical fruits.

Balance of Trade. American exports continued to exceed imports, and this fact, coupled with the outflow of capital invested abroad, added to the creditor position of the nation. In the 1920's, with international trade hampered by high tariffs and other restrictions, European debtors had to use their diminishing stocks of gold to pay for imports from the United States. These gold payments were offset largely by ever increasing American loans and investments abroad. The latter caused an intensification of an already dangerous situation and could not continue indefinitely. As has been noted, when the depression came the export of American capital stopped and trade collapsed.

Reciprocal Trade Program. The New Deal administration proposed to reduce tariffs through reciprocal trade agreements.

An amendment to the Smoot-Hawley Tariff, the Trade Agreements Act of 1934, permitted the President to conclude agreements raising or lowering tariff rates by not more than 50 per cent. By 1949 the United States had reached agreements with 29 nations (purchasing two-thirds of American exports) to reduce the tariff and eliminate other trade barriers. The general effect was to make international trade freer, though it is impossible to trace all the far-reaching consequences of the various trade agreements. The foreign trade of the United States increased from 1934 to 1937, declined in 1938 and 1939, and expanded rapidly after the outbreak of World War II. The improvement in world commerce was no doubt partly due to the reciprocal trade agreements, but also reflected the general betterment of economic conditions.

ISOLATIONISM AND NEUTRALITY

Following World War I there was a resurgence of American isolationism. Many Americans felt that collective security had failed miserably, and they resented the attitudes of European nations towards the question of the war debts. The great majority believed in safeguarding the neutrality of the United States and avoiding involvement in future wars.

In 1935 a neutrality act prohibited temporarily the sale of munitions to all nations at war and empowered the President to forbid the passage of American citizens (except at their own risk) on the vessels of belligerents. A second measure extended the arms embargo and banned loans to belligerent powers. In January, 1937, existing legislation was extended to include factions participating in a civil war. A "permanent" neutrality act (May, 1937) retained the bans on loans and on the sale of munitions, but explicitly forbade Americans to travel on the vessels of any country involved in war. The law also established a cash-and-carry policy for the sale of non-embargoed goods to belligerents.

THE OUTBREAK OF WAR

World War II, which broke out in Europe in August, 1939, doomed American isolationism and the hope for neutrality, and provided a tremendous stimulus to the American economy. The United States made a pretense of neutrality until the Japanese attack on Pearl Harbor (December 7, 1941), but the government had long been aiding the Allied Powers on the assumption that their cause was vital to American security.

Modified Neutrality. Shortly after the outbreak of war, American neutrality laws were revised to permit the belligerents to purchase American arms and munitions. The cash-and-carry principle was retained. In March, 1941, a lend-lease program was set up, authorizing the sale, exchange, or loan of war equipment to any nation whose defense the president considered vital to the United States. By means of this measure the United States became fully engaged in economic warfare.

Organization for Defense. In 1940 a Council of National Defense (six cabinet members meeting with a National Defense Advisory Commission) was established. This organization was soon superseded by the Office of Emergency Management, which had two subordinate agencies, the Office of Production Management and the Office of Price Administration. William S. Knudsen became head of the OPM in January, 1941, and the chief organizer of war production. In September, 1941, President Roosevelt established the Supply, Priorities, and Allocations Board to expedite war preparations.

Industrial Expansion. During the period between the outbreak of World War II and the attack on Pearl Harbor, American industrial output was doubled. This achievement was made possible by the defense program, the European demand for American goods, and an increasing domestic demand for consumers' goods. Expansion was accompanied by increasing employment, rising prices and wages, and an increase in exports from 3,177 million dollars in 1939 to 5,147 million in 1941.

REVIEW QUESTIONS

1. Show how the United States was transformed into a creditor power during World War I.
2. What happened to American investments abroad in the 1930's?
3. To what extent did the United States obtain payment of war debts from European powers?

4. In what ways did the United States help in settling the reparations issue?
5. How has the character of American foreign trade changed since 1914?
6. How important to the United States was foreign trade in the 1920's?
7. Describe and evaluate the reciprocal trade program.
8. By what means did the United States try to insure its neutrality in the 1930's? Indicate the steps leading to the abandonment of neutrality.
9. Outline the national organization for defense in the years 1939-1941.

32

ECONOMIC PROBLEMS OF WORLD WAR II

Within three years after Pearl Harbor the United States had developed its productive facilities and techniques to an unprecedented degree, providing enormous quantities of supplies for its allies while sustaining armed forces of nearly twelve million Americans at home and in all parts of the world.

ECONOMIC MOBILIZATION

The conversion of the United States from a peacetime to a total war economy involved gigantic problems: (1) existing facilities had to be converted to war production, and new plants were necessary; (2) raw materials had to be procured and properly allocated; (3) a much greater labor supply was needed. The accomplishment of this huge task necessitated central planning and control in a degree far greater than had been previously known in America.

Administrative Organization. The Office of Emergency Management was the large executive organization in charge of defense efforts. Chief among the OEM agencies was the War Production Board, created in January, 1942. The WPB co-ordinated government controls over production, procured vital materials, and greatly stimulated war production. Other agencies under the OEM included the Office of Lend-Lease Administration, the Office of Defense Transportation, the Office of Civilian Defense, the Board of Economic Warfare, the War Shipping Administration, and the National War Labor Board.

Conversion to War Production. Thousands of plants that normally made peacetime goods participated in war production. In addition the government spent 16 billion dollars for new war plants. The production of many goods for civilian use, such as automobiles, refrigerators, radios, and certain electrical appliances was stopped. From 1939 to 1944 the proportion of the national product allocated to war uses rose from 2 to 40 per cent; in the period 1940-1945 the United States spent 186 billion dollars on munitions. In addition it provided its allies with goods and services under the Lend-Lease program amounting to 49 billion dollars. The extent of economic expansion during the war is indicated by the fact that from 1939 to 1945 the national income rose from 72,532 million dollars to 181,731 million, and the gross national product from 90,426 million to 213,429 million. The expansion in certain industries was phenomenal: with the average of the period 1935-1939 used as a base of 100, the index of production of raw materials reached 148 in 1943; of fuels, 145 in 1944; of food, 136 in 1945.

Procurement of Raw Materials. In 1939 Congress appropriated 100 million dollars for each of the five succeeding years for the purpose of accumulating stockpiles. Progress was slow until May, 1940, but thereafter the United States increased its imports of such vital goods as tin, tungsten, manganese, and rubber. Export restrictions were imposed in July, 1940, to prevent some commodities from reaching the Axis Powers. The nation's production of vital materials was rapidly increased, and conservation was effected through salvage, the use of substitutes, and the curtailment of production of civilian goods.

IRON. The unprecedented demand for steel resulted in a shortage of iron. This situation was alleviated somewhat through greater utilization of scrap and restrictions on the production of nonessential goods. By 1943 (the peak year of production) the output of iron ore was a third greater than it had been in 1940.

ALUMINUM. An acute shortage of aluminum in the early part of the war was met by great expansion of production. From 1940 to 1943 the nation's output of aluminum increased 347 per cent.

RUBBER. The seizure of the East Indies by the Japanese deprived the United States of almost all of its natural rubber supply. This shortage was met by rigid conservation and governmental development of a synthetic rubber industry. Production of synthetic rubber rose from virtually nothing in 1940 to 22,000 long tons in 1942 and more than 750,000 tons in 1944. Supplies were adequate for military needs, but the supply of rubber for civilian use was rigidly limited.

PETROLEUM. The great demand for gasoline and fuel oil was met by increased production (almost 25 per cent greater in 1944 than in 1940), by strict rationing, and by the construction of pipe lines which eliminated some of the hazardous transport of oil by sea.

Domestic Transportation. War brought a tremendous burden to the nation's transportation facilities: total freight movement increased over 66 per cent from 1940 to 1944. In 1944 the railroads handled about 70 per cent of the freight volume, and also quadrupled the number of passenger-miles reported for 1940. The Office of Defense Transportation, established in 1941, supervised air transport, inland and coastal shipping, pipe lines, and automobile transport.

Shipping. There was a shortage of merchant vessels because of the increased volume of shipping and German submarine warfare. During the war the United States built 53 million tons of shipping, thus controlling over one-half of the total shipping of the world.

RATIONING AND PRICE CONTROL

The government immediately attacked the problem of inflation, resulting from huge government expenditures, full employment, and the increasing scarcity of civilian goods. The Price Control Act (January, 1942) established the Office of Price Administration with authority to fix maximum prices, to control rents, and to impose penalties on violators of the law. During 1942 the OPA began to ration tires, gasoline, sugar, and coffee. By mid-1943, 95 per cent of the nation's foodstuffs was rationed and maximum prices and rents had been established. There was much criticism of the OPA, but this agency did cut the cost of the war to the American people and insured a fair distribution of consumer goods.

The Office of Economic Stabilization was created under the Anti-Inflation Act (October, 1942) to supervise the limitation of wages and salaries and the curbing of prices and rents not yet controlled. Greater co-operation in combatting inflation was obtained by the Office of War Mobilization, organized in May, 1943.

LABOR AND THE WAR

From 1940 to 1945 the total labor force of the United States rose from 54 to 64 million, an increase of more than 18 per cent. The additional labor force was drawn from the unemployed men (9,000,000 in 1939), young people, the aged, and women. From 1939 to 1944 there was a 20-per-cent increase in the average work week. The number of organized workers grew from 11 million in 1941 to 14.5 million in 1945. New problems in labor relations had to be met, such as the training of inexperienced workers, urban congestion and inadequate housing (during 1940-1946, urban population increased by almost 9 million), absenteeism, and a high incidence of sickness and nervous exhaustion.

Labor Disputes. At the start of the war, labor and management agreed to prevent work stoppages in essential industries, to settle disputes by peaceful methods, and to abide by decisions of a war labor board. The National War Labor Board was organized to settle disputes and to try to adjust wages to the cost of living. In 1942 the record was good and few man-hours of labor were lost. In July, 1942, the Little Steel formula was adopted, allowing labor a 15-per-cent increase to make up for the higher cost of living. The next year, however, strikes cost three times the amount of time lost in the previous year, and in June, 1943, the Smith-Connally War Disputes Act was passed. This law required unions to give thirty days' notice before a strike vote could be taken, empowered the president to seize war industries threatened by work stoppages, made it a criminal offense to foment or aid strikes in government-operated industries, and forbade unions to make contributions to political campaigns. The number of man-days of labor lost due to strikes was cut by about 5 million in 1944.

WAR FINANCE

The United States financed the war through heavy taxation and extensive borrowing. Measures to control inflation reduced the cost of the war, as did the investment of savings in government bonds. The budgets for 1941-1945 exceeded a total of 317 billion dollars, of which 88 per cent went for war purposes. The federal debt rose from 48.9 billion dollars in 1941 to 258.7 billion in 1945.

Taxation. Taxes were used to fight inflation as well as to provide revenue. The category of individuals paying income taxes was expanded to include all persons earning 500 dollars or more in a year, and surtaxes ranged from 19 to 88 per cent. A method of withholding taxes from salaries and wages was begun in 1943. An excess profits tax was levied on corporate income, and heavier excise taxes were adopted. More excise taxes were levied, and rates were increased. Total receipts from taxes in the period 1941-1945 approximated 138.5 billion dollars.

Loans. From May, 1941, to January, 1946, the government sold securities amounting to 185.7 billion dollars. It is estimated that private individuals bought 53 billion dollars' worth of this amount, while banks and corporations absorbed the rest. In view of the great increase in savings during the war and the fact that 17 per cent of the bonds purchased by individuals prior to September, 1945, had been presented for redemption, the record was not outstanding.

COST OF THE WAR

The total cost of World War II will never be accurately established, but it has been estimated as high as over 1 trillion dollars.

Money. Continuing expenditures (interest on war debts, pensions, care of veterans, grants and credits for rehabilitation, etc.) have been and are raising the cost of the war substantially. For the United States the monetary cost during the period of fighting exceeded 325 billion dollars. Of this amount about 50 billion dollars had been provided the Allies under the Lend-Lease Acts. It has been predicted by the National Industrial Conference board that by 1972 the cost of the war to the United States alone will have reached 700 billion dollars.

Casualties. World War II lasted until May 8, 1945 in Europe and three months longer in the Pacific area. Fifty-seven nations, Allied and Axis, had fought in the war, and the total number of military personnel killed exceeded fifteen million. The United States had a peak manpower in the armed forces of 12.5 million, and 292,100 lives were lost. In all, Americans suffered over one million casualties.

REVIEW QUESTIONS

1. What were the major problems in economic mobilization? Outline the administrative organization established to accomplish the task.
2. How was conversion to war production accomplished? What steps did the government take for the procurement of vital materials?
3. Discuss the wartime measures taken by the United States to control inflation. How successful were they?
4. How was the need for a larger labor supply met? To what extent did labor disputes hamper the war effort?
5. How did the United States finance the war? Discuss the relative importance of taxation and loans.

33

THE AMERICAN ECONOMY AT MID-CENTURY

At the end of World War II the American people were optimistic over the prospects of peace and international harmony. The United States sought to avoid mistakes of the World War I period and took a leading part in the establishment of the United Nations. It was several years before disillusionment set in, and only slowly and reluctantly did the American people grasp the realities of the postwar divisions and cold war rivalries.

THE PROBLEMS OF RECONVERSION

Some anxiety was felt about the cessation of war spending and the possibility of a return of the depression. These fears were groundless, however, for the period since World War II has been one of great economic growth and in general the most sustained period of prosperity in United States history.

Demobilization. In October 1944, the United States changed the Office of War Mobilization into the Office of War Mobilization and Reconversion, an agency intended to coordinate efforts at reconversion. At the end of the war the government hastened to end controls, to terminate war contracts, and to convert to peacetime activities. In the postwar reaction, amidst gloomy predictions of widespread unemployment, glutted markets, and deflation, price controls were dropped, taxes were reduced, and new labor legislation was enacted. In the years that followed, however, the nation's most difficult domestic problem proved to be inflation rather than deflation. The great demand for consumer goods and the continuing heavy export trade gave impetus to reconversion, and by mid-1947 the transition had been virtually completed. In the postwar years the economy expanded rapidly, there was relatively little unemployment, and the country enjoyed prosperity.

Truman's Domestic Program. Immediately after Japan's surrender President Truman proposed an extensive domestic program which involved considerable long-range economic planning. Among the proposals which were later called the Fair Deal were: (1) an increase in the minimum wage from forty to sixty-five cents an hour; (2) broader social security; (3) a permanent Fair Employment Practices Commission; (4) a full employment program; (5) slum clearance and public housing; (6) regional flood control and hydroelectric projects; (7) the nationalization of atomic energy; (8) national health insurance; (9) federal aid to education; (10) and the St. Lawrence Seaway. Some of these proposals were enacted into law, most were changed through compromise, and others were defeated.

Inflation. Accumulated civilian demand and the continued heavy flow of goods abroad caused shortages and price increases. The War Production Board, replaced by the Civilian Production Administration in October 1945, began to lift priorities before the war ended, and after V-J Day wartime controls and rationing quickly disappeared.

Congress debated the extension of OPA and price controls and finally passed a weak measure that Truman vetoed; thus most price controls came to an end in July 1946. Despite shortages of some goods and the deliberate withholding of goods from the market in expectation of higher prices, the cost of living index increased by only 3 per cent between V-J Day and July 1946. A sharp increase in prices in July 1946, particularly of meat, led to enactment of a weak price control bill which was utilized to control meat prices until October 1946. In November 1946, all controls on prices, except for rents, rice, and sugar were discontinued. The postwar efforts of the Truman administration to control prices were both unsuccessful and productive of much criticism from varied sources.

Other governmental measures to control inflation, consisting mainly of credit restrictions and wage stabilization efforts, were quite inadequate. The wholesale price index (with the 1935-1939 average as a base of 100) rose from 116.1 in 1946 to 161.5 in 1955; the retail price index rose from 139.3 to 171.9.

Industrial Productivity. All branches of the American economy shared in the general expansion and prosperity of the years following World War II. Only a mild and brief recession was experienced at the end of the war before industrial productivity began to take advantage of the great domestic demand for consumer goods. The following table provides both general and specific indexes of industrial expansion from 1930-1950.

INDUSTRIAL GROWTH, 1930-1950
(Indexes of Production 1947-1949 = 100)

Year	Total Industrial	Non-durable Goods	Durable Goods	Auto-mobiles	Television Sets
1930	49	51	45	56*	...
1940	67	69	63	74*	...
1944	125	99	159	...	...
1945	107	96	123	2*	...
1947	100	99	101	...	70
1948	104	102	104	93	...
1949	97	99	95	122	217
1950	112	111	116	159	561

* Estimated.
SOURCE: *Statistical Abstract of the United States,* 1957, pp. 484–5.

The housing and automobile manufacturing industries expanded phenomenally and exerted great influence on the entire economy. National production in 1950 was twice as great as the average for the years 1935-1939, and the employment index (with 1939 as a base of 100) rose to 147.6 in 1949 and then to 150.6 in 1950. The national income increased from 180.3 billion dollars in 1946 to 236.6 billion dollars in 1950; in the same period profits after taxes jumped from 13.9 billion dollars to 22.8 billion dollars, and gross private savings increased from 29.3 billion dollars to about 38 billion dollars. Important indications of recent social change have been an increase in the percentage of the national income earned by middle-income families and a decrease in the percentage earned by people in the highest income brackets.

Agricultural Productivity. American agriculture responded to the stimulus of war demands and experienced prosperity. Farm production rose as restrictions of the 1930's were abandoned, and farm income reached the record high of over 14 billion dollars in 1943. Farm prices continued to rise after World War II until 1948. American exports of relief shipments of farm goods, financed largely by United States aid programs, were largely responsible for the postwar prosperity of American farmers.

Industrial Warfare. Reconversion to a peacetime economy was accompanied by a considerable amount of industrial warfare. Inflation resulted in much labor unrest. In 1946 there were 4,700 strikes, and more man-hours were lost in that year than in the entire period of the war. In the fall and winter of 1945-1946, the United Auto Workers and the United Steel Workers struck; in both cases sizeable wage increases and other benefits were won by the unions. Sizeable work stoppages followed in the electrical, meat packing, and mining industries. The Truman administration, utilizing wartime powers, effected compromises which gave labor part of what it demanded and paved the way for price increases to manufacturers and producers.

Truman's handling of the railroad strike of May 1946 was very displeasing to labor. Upon the threat of a strike, the president invoked the Smith-Connally Act and seized the railroads. All but two of the brotherhoods accepted the compromise worked out. When the engineers and the trainmen went on strike, Truman appealed to Congress for extreme powers to handle strikes that endangered the public welfare; the president requested power to draft strikers into the armed forces, to destroy strikers' seniority rights, and to levy heavy fines on union leaders. As the strikers gave in before this pressure, the House of Representatives passed the measure the president wanted but the Senate did not act on it.

A result of widespread antilabor sentiment was the passage in July 1947 of the Labor Management Relations Act (the Taft-Hartley Act). An aroused Congress overrode President

Truman's veto to enact this very controversial measure, which was to be a major political issue for years to come. The Taft-Hartley Act amended the National Labor Relations Act in many respects: unions could now be sued for breach of contract (and for consequent damages) if they participated in jurisdictional strikes and boycotts; the closed shop was outlawed and the union shop was permitted only under strict regulations; unions were forbidden to make contributions for political purposes and if any officer were shown to be a Communist were to be deprived of their rights under the Wagner Act; a cooling-off period of sixty days was required before a strike or a lockout could be called, and the government could obtain against a union an injunction which would postpone for eighty days any strike that would affect the national health or safety.

AMERICA AND WORLD ECONOMICS

The United States assumed leadership during and after the war in relief and recovery measures and in the promotion of greater international economic cooperation.

Recovery from World War II. The purposes of American postwar efforts have been varied: to provide military and civilian goods to our Allies; to provide relief and to aid reconstruction after the war; to aid refugees and displaced persons; to resist Communist aggression; to provide technical and economic aid for underdeveloped nations; to relieve emergencies arising from natural disasters, etc. In December 1942, the United States set up an Office of Foreign Relief and Rehabilitation. The next year the United Nations Relief and Rehabilitation Administration (UNRRA) was organized with each participant contributing 1 per cent of its national income. The United States was the largest contributor, providing 72 per cent originally and 78 per cent later of the total cost. By the time UNRRA discontinued operations in December 1947, the United States had contributed 2.7 billion dollars. Additional post-UNRRA interim aid raised the total to 3.5 billion dollars. The most important aid under this program went to eastern Europe, China, Italy, and Austria.

The International Bank for Reconstruction and Development, established at Bretton Woods, New Hampshire, in 1944, was organized to make capital available for long-term investment. A related organization, the International Monetary Fund, was intended to facilitate international payments. By mid-1949 the World Bank had loaned over 700 million dollars to eleven nations; by June 30, 1961 the bank had made loans totalling 15.7 billion dollars. Several interim emergency devices were also used immediately after the war; the Export-Import Bank of Washington, a United States agency created in 1934, was provided with increased resources to aid European reconstruction; Great Britain was granted a loan of 3.7 billion dollars in 1946. The efforts of these agencies did not fully meet the needs of postwar Europe which was demoralized and threatened with bankruptcy.

Continuation of Foreign Aid. Several factors motivated the United States to extend its foreign aid commitments: (1) inflation reduced the amount of goods that could be purchased with the aid provided; (2) the winter of 1947 left western Europe exhausted and on the verge of collapse; (3) the aggression of Communist Russia threatened the security of central and western Europe.

TRUMAN DOCTRINE. Faced with the threat of Communist seizures of power in Greece and Turkey, Congress provided military and economic aid to these countries in 1947. By 1950, 629 million dollars had been provided and the Communist threat was halted.

MARSHALL PLAN. In April 1948, the United States set up the Economic Cooperation Administration to study the resources and needs of European nations and to promote economic integration among them. In the next three years ECA provided 12 billion dollars to participating nations. The results were gratifying; industrial production in Marshall Plan nations rose 64 per cent and their economies were stabilized.

POINT IV AND ECONOMIC DEVELOPMENT. In 1949 President Truman proposed a plan to provide United States aid to underdeveloped countries. Emphasis was placed on technical assistance, especially in the fields of agriculture, public health, and education. Most of the aid was made available directly to needy nations from the United States. Some assistance was provided through such United Nations agencies as the World Health Organization (WHO), the Food and Agriculture Organization (FAO), and the United Nations Educational, Scientific, and Cultural Organization (UNESCO).

From July 1, 1945 to June 30, 1962 the United States had provided military technical and economic assistance to foreign countries to the extent of about 100 billion dollars. The figures in the following table include expenditures in such multilateral programs as NATO, CENTO, and SEATO.

FOREIGN MILITARY AND ECONOMIC AID BY THE UNITED STATES
July 1, 1945 to June 30, 1962
(in millions of dollars)

	Economic	Military	Total
Europe	$28,872.7	$15,939.8	$44,812.5
Far East	13,743.2	8,417.3	22,160.5
Middle East	6,218.5	4,550.5	10,769.0
South Asia	6,359.7	715.8	7,075.5
Latin America	6,195.5	616.1	6,811.6
Africa	1,664.7	112.0	1,776.6

Foreign Trade. The important position of the United States in the world economy is also to be seen in the character of post-war commerce. American exports were supported by the extension of loans, credits, and other aid to foreign countries. The United States, which at mid-century produced about 40 per cent of the total world output of goods and services, exported approximately 20 per cent of the total world exports during 1951-1955. While foreign commerce is not so important to the United States economy as it is in other countries, some American producers depend heavily on foreign markets. The value of United States exports in 1960 was (in millions of dollars): crude materials, 2,586; food-stuffs, 2,756; manufactures, including semimanufactures, 14,958.

American imports have risen during and after World War II: 1941-45, the average value was 3.4 billion dollars; 1946-50, 6.5 billion; 1954, 10.2 billion; 1957, 12.9 billion dollars. The demands of the domestic market are great and the United States is entirely dependent on imports for natural rubber, tin, industrial diamonds, coffee, cocoa, and tea. Also about 90 per cent of the nickel, cobalt, chromite, and manganese used by the

United States has to be imported. In 1960 imports by categories were thus valued (in millions of dollars): crude materials, 3,014; foodstuffs, 3,288; semimanufactures, 3,092; finished manufactures 5,258.

Trade Policy. The reciprocal trade agreements program, which was begun in 1934, has been continued to date with some alterations and has generally worked well. By the original law, the President could raise or lower existing rates by 50 per cent. The agreements that were made contained a "most-favored-nation" clause. Congress passed a law in 1945 authorizing reductions of rates of that date by another 50 per cent. In 1955 the President was empowered to reduce duties by another 15 per cent. As the program has developed, the average of rates has fallen sharply.

In 1947 a General Agreement on Tariff and Trade, concluded by twenty-two nations at Geneva, represented a new and broader approach to freer international trade. Another agreement was reached in 1952. As a result, by 1957 the average ad valorem duties on imports had dropped to 11 per cent; the average of duties had been 40.8 per cent in 1908, 27 per cent in 1913, 52 per cent in 1930, and 37.3 per cent in 1939.

The progress of economic integration in west Europe, exemplified particularly by the European Common Market, coupled with the threat of higher tariffs on American goods and the loss of European markets for American goods, led to the enactment of President Kennedy's Trade Expansion Act of 1962. This measure gave authority: (1) to reduce existing tariff duties as much as 50 per cent on categories of items (rather than on individual items); (2) to remove duties entirely on categories when the United States and Common Market countries together produced 80 per cent of the world's total output; and (3) to provide aid to American companies and laborers injured by foreign competition in the home market. The Trade Expansion Act by a House amendment refused "most-favored-nation" treatment to any Communist country.

THE ECONOMY AT MID-CENTURY

The invasion of South Korea by North Koreans, begun on June 25, 1950, was followed by United States and United Nations intervention. This police action lasted three years and cost the United States 54,000 lives, 103,000 wounded and over 90 billion dollars. However, the Korean War did stimulate the American economy and produced a greatly accelerated defense program.

At the end of the Korean action there was a downswing in the business cycle which caused concern over the possibility of a serious recession. The 1953-1954 slowup was temporary, and the rest of the decade witnessed expansion and prosperity for the most part. The following indexes provide basic facts concerning America's economic growth since World War II.

POPULATION GROWTH

Date	Numbers (in millions)	Per Sq. Mile	Percent increase over last census
1930	122.7	40.6	16.1
1940	131.6	43.6	7.2
1945	139.4	. . .	. . .
1950	151.7	49.9	14.5
1955	165.3	. . .	. . .
1960*	179.2	49.6	19.0

* Includes Alaska and Hawaii for the first time

CIVILIAN LABOR FORCE

Year	CLF (millions)	Year	CLF (millions)
1945	52.8	1953	61.9
1946	55.3	1954	60.9
1947	57.8	1955	62.9
1948	59.1	1956	64.7
1949	58.4	1957	65.0
1950	59.7	1958	64.0
1951	60.8	1959	65.6
1952	61.0	1960	66.4

Source: U. S. Dept. of Commerce

OUTPUT PER MAN-HOUR
(1909 = 100)

Year	Agriculture	Manufacturing	Total
1919	104.8	115.0	112.8
1929	114.8	198.1	140.3
1939	138.9	232.5	171.7
1949	184.5	280.1	209.6
1959	342.6	385.5	305.6

Source: U. S. Dept. of Labor

AVERAGE HOURLY EARNINGS 1939–1960

Industry or Activity	Dollars per hour 1939	1960
Farm	.16	.97
Textiles	.46	1.62
Lumber products	.49	1.99
Furniture	.52	1.88
Retail trade	.54	1.78
Paper products	.59	2.32
Chemicals	.65	2.55
Machinery	.75	2.60
Telephone	.82	2.32
Bituminous mining	.89	3.26
Automobiles	.93	2.83

CONSUMER PRICE INDEX

(1947-1949 = 100)

Year	Index	Year	Index
1946	83.4	1954	114.8
1947	95.5	1955	114.5
1948	102.8	1956	116.2
1949	101.8	1957	120.2
1950	102.8	1958	123.5
1951	111.0	1959	124.6
1952	113.5	1960	126.5
1953	114.4		

GROSS NATIONAL PRODUCT

Year	GNP (billions)	Year	GNP (billions)
1945	369.1	1953	425.5
1946	321.7	1954	416.8
1947	321.1	1955	449.7
1948	333.6	1956	459.2
1949	334.2	1957	467.8
1950	362.3	1958	459.7
1951	392.0	1959	490.6
1952	406.8	1960	504.4

NATIONAL INCOME BY SELECTED INDUSTRIES
(Millions of Dollars)

Industry	1953	1955	1957	1960
Agriculture, forest, fisheries	17,498	16,084	16,365	17,161
Mining	5,208	5,609	6,238	5,516
Manufacturing	97,953	104,490	112,476	121,544
Wholesale and retail trade	49,753	55,000	60,350	68,768
Transportation	15,754	15,781	17,208	17,816
Services	29,201	33,740	39,978	50,000
All industries, total	305,573	330,206	366,943	417,054

SOURCE: U. S. Dept. of Commerce

AMERICA'S GREAT ACHIEVEMENT

Some 350 years after the founding of the first permanent settlement in English America and 180 years after the winning of American independence, the United States has become the wealthiest and most powerful country in the world. The nation has grown in size to 180 million people; America's productive capacity has risen to first place among the nations. Once only an outpost of Western Europe, America has become the great bastion and hope in the struggle for survival of western civilization.

The rapid expansion of American productivity and the growth of both national and per capita income have permitted the development of a very high standard of living, both quantitatively and qualitatively. Not only have economic goods become increasingly available to the people, but Americans have also increasingly enjoyed such benefits as better medical care, longer life expectancy, extensive educational opportunities and more leisure time. These spectacular evidences of progress lead to the conclusion that the great achievements of the American economy represent one of the greatest success stories in human history.

REVIEW QUESTIONS

1. Explain the principal problems of the United States during the reconversion period.
2. How did the United States government deal with inflation? How successful was this policy?
3. How successful was organized labor in securing gains for itself immediately after World War II?
4. Why and how was the Taft-Hartley law passed? How was this a departure from previous policies?
5. Describe United States contributions to the recovery of foreign nations from World War II.
6. Explain reasons for and effects of American aid to foreign countries since 1945.
7. Explain trends in American foreign commerce in recent years. How has United States trade policy changed since 1945?

FINAL EXAMINATION

1. Which of the following did *not* contribute to the rise of modern capitalism? (a) Calvinism (b) revival of trade (c) feudalism (d) the nation-state.
2. What was the most important reason for the migration of the greatest number of persons to America? (a) desire for religious freedom (b) opportunity to obtain good land (c) desire for democracy (d) opportunity for investment.
3. Which of the following was *not* an important national purpose of English colonization in America? (a) procurement of raw materials (b) relief of overpopulation in England (c) development of American manufacturing (d) development of colonial trade.
4. Which of the following conditions was least characteristic of the economy of New Spain in America? (a) paternalism (b) free trade (c) the encomienda system (d) commercial monopoly.
5. The colony begun largely through the efforts of a private company was (a) Maryland (b) Pennsylvania (c) Rhode Island (d) New Netherland.
6. Which of the following was *not* begun as a proprietary colony? (a) Carolina (b) Massachusetts (c) Maryland (d) Pennsylvania.
7. In which colony was a communal arrangement attempted temporarily? (a) New Plymouth (b) New York (b) Connecticut (d) Pennsylvania.
8. Which of these factors was least characteristic of land tenure in colonial New England? (a) scattered holdings (b) relatively small holdings (c) quitrent obligations (d) organization into villages.
9. Primogeniture was most common in (a) Virginia (b) Pennsylvania (c) Massachusetts (d) Connecticut.
10. Which of the following was most characteristic of early New England agriculture? (a) the large plantation (b) commercial agriculture (c) subsistence farming (d) cultivation of staples.

11. Which product was *not* an important staple of the southern colonies before 1775? (a) tobacco (b) cotton (c) rice (d) indigo.
12. The most serious hindrance to colonial commercial activity was (a) inadequate money supply (b) difficulty of transport (c) general dislike of English goods (d) insufficient warehouses.
13. Which of the following was *not* a part of England's mercantile policy? (a) the encouragement of colonial production of raw materials (b) the exclusion of foreigners from the trade of the empire (c) the development of colonial self-sufficiency (d) the "enumeration" of vital colonial products.
14. The greatest volume of colonial trade was carried on with (a) England (b) France (c) West Indies (d) southern Europe.
15. The basic reason for the triangular trade of colonial New England was (a) hostility toward the mother country (b) a great American demand for slaves (c) an opportunity to market tobacco (d) the necessity of paying for imports of English goods.
16. The most widespread opposition to English policy in America was aroused by (a) writs of assistance (b) the Stamp Act (c) the Sugar Act (d) the Proclamation of 1763.
17. Which of the following was *not* a result of the French and Indian War? (a) elimination of France from America (b) acquisition of Louisiana by England (c) increased expense and administrative responsibility for England (d) English determination to revitalize the mercantile system.
18. During the Revolutionary War the Continental Congress obtained the most money from (a) foreign loans (b) domestic loans (c) taxation (d) issuance of paper money.
19. Which of the following was the most basic cause of the depreciation of Continental paper money during the Revolutionary War? (a) Congress did not impose sufficient taxes (b) inability to secure foreign loans (c) shortages of goods (d) the people preferred English currency.
20. Which of the following important powers did the Continental Congress lack? (a) to borrow money (b) to make treaties and declare war (c) to regulate interstate commerce (d) to issue paper money.

21. Which line of American economic activity underwent the most extensive reorganization immediately after the Revolutionary War? (a) commerce (b) agriculture (c) finance (d) manufacturing.
22. Which of the following groups was *not* prominently associated with the agitation for a strong federal government? (a) merchants and businessmen (b) large landowners (c) followers of Daniel Shays (d) owners of Continental paper currency.
23. Which of the following was *not* one of Hamilton's financial proposals? (a) assumption of state debts (b) nonpayment of arrearages of interest on the national debt (c) bimetallism (d) issuance of new government bonds.
24. In which of the following years was the national debt lowest? (a) 1815 (b) 1836 (c) 1801 (d) 1857.
25. Which was invented first? (a) Jethro Wood's plow (b) Cyrus McCormick's reaper (c) Eli Whitney's cotton gin (d) Morse's telegraph.
26. Which of the following was least influential in encouraging the development of cotton production in the period 1790-1825? (a) development of cotton manufacturing (b) technological advances (c) development of a foreign market (d) increasing importation of slaves.
27. Which state was the leading producer of cotton in 1850? (a) Mississippi (b) Alabama (c) South Carolina (d) Georgia.
28. Which port handled the greatest amount of cotton in 1860? (a) New Orleans (b) Charleston (c) Memphis (d) Mobile.
29. About how many slaves were there in the South in 1860? (a) 2½ million (b) 3 million (c) 3½ million (d) 4 million.
30. In which of the following decades did the largest number of immigrants arrive in the United States? (a) 1820's (b) 1830's (c) 1840's (d) 1850's.
31. During the period 1820-1860, the largest increase in the number of workers occurred in (a) manufacturing and mechanic arts (b) agriculture (c) domestic and personal service (d) professions.
32. The first organizations of American workers were formed by the (a) farmers (b) skilled workers in the trades (c) seamen (d) unskilled laborers.
33. Which of the following was *not* a pre-Civil War gain of labor? (a) a 10-hour work day was established for gov-

ernment employees (b) the right to strike for lawful purposes was recognized (c) wages rose about 100 per cent during the period 1800-1860 (d) the use of injunctions against unions was forbidden by law.

34. Which of the following was *not* included in the Gallatin Plan? (a) federal construction of canals (b) a north-south turnpike from Maine to Georgia (c) federal aid to railroad projects (d) East-West turnpikes.
35. From which of the following did the railroads receive the most public aid in the period before the Civil War? (a) local governments (b) the states (c) the federal government.
36. The best commercial route to the interior was controlled by which city in the second quarter of the 19th century? (a) Philadelphia (b) Boston (c) New York (d) Charleston.
37. The trend of federal land policy in the period 1783-1860 was to (a) lower the price and the minimum acreage that could be bought (b) raise the price and the minimum acreage (c) raise the price and reduce the acreage to be sold (d) reduce the price and raise the minimum acreage.
38. During the period 1783-1815, which of the following did *not* discourage the development of manufacturing in the United States? (a) dependence on Europe (b) scarcity of labor (c) lack of capital (d) European wars.
39. What was the principal cause of the South's failure to develop industry before 1860? (a) the South invested surplus capital in northern manufacturing or in foreign industry (b) the South lacked the necessary raw materials (c) the South had little surplus capital for investment in manufacturing (d) there was an inadequate supply of labor in the South.
40. The first successful textile mill in America was founded by (a) Patrick Tracy Jackson (b) Samuel Slater (c) Paul Moody (d) Francis Cabot Lowell.
41. Which of the following was *not* an advantage of corporate form of business? (a) unlimited liability (b) broadly distributed ownership (c) ability to attract large funds (d) a greater degree of permanence than in other forms of organization.
42. Which of the following ranked first in value among man-

ufactured products in 1860? (a) iron products (b) woolen goods (c) flour (d) cotton goods.

43. Which of the following did *not* contribute to commercial expansion during the period 1789-1807? (a) the opening of trade with new areas (b) the outbreak of European war (c) the increase of American tonnage registered for foreign trade (d) English Orders in Council.
44. The expansion of American trade in the 1840's and 1850's was encouraged by (a) the demise of the Second Bank of the United States (b) the increasing production of woolen goods for export (c) European wars and revolutions (d) the invention of the typewriter.
45. The United States financed its excess of imports over exports in the pre-Civil War period in several ways. Which of the following was *not* one of those ways? (a) specie exports (b) investment of surplus American funds abroad (c) performance of various services (d) earnings of foreign investments in America.
46. Our most valuable foreign trade in the pre-Civil War period was with (a) England (b) France (c) Cuba (d) British North America.
47. Next to raw cotton the most valuable American export in 1860 was (a) cotton manufactures (b) tobacco (c) wheat and flour (d) lumber and wood manufactures.
48. The most valuable American import in 1860 was (a) coffee (b) woolens (c) sugar (d) cotton manufactures.
49. The period 1792-1834 is known as the silver period of our monetary history because (a) silver dollars were minted throughout the period and served as the principal coins of the country (b) overvalued silver coins drove gold out of circulation (c) the market ratio of gold to silver rose higher than the fixed mint ratio (d) there was a great shortage of gold.
50. Which of the following was *not* one of the functions of the Bank of the U. S. as proposed by Alexander Hamilton? (a) to create a safe depository for government funds (b) to establish a central financial institution separated from commercial banking (c) to provide a fiscal agent for the government (d) to establish an agency empowered to issue paper money.
51. The period of the panic of 1819 was characterized by (a) general expansion of English loans and credits to American businessmen (b) depression in manufacturing

enterprises but continued prosperity for American agriculture (c) the extension of loans by the Bank of the United States to relieve business distress (d) widespread unemployment and imprisonment for indebtedness.

52. Which of the following was *not* a contributing factor in the economic expansion of the 1830's? (a) an increase in the supply of loanable capital (b) the distribution of the entire Treasury surplus in 1837 (c) speculation in land (d) easy credit policies.
53. A pre-Civil War southern economic condition was that of (a) a scarcity of labor and capital (b) broad distribution of money income (c) rapidly growing cotton textile manufacturing (d) an active shipping enterprise.
54. The most important issue in the North-South antagonism in the generation before the Civil War was that of (a) federal support of internal improvements (b) the extension of slavery in the territories (c) free silver (d) a liberal homestead policy.
55. Which of the following arguments was the most basic factor in the South's opposition to the tariffs of 1828 and 1832? (a) the tariffs violated states' rights (b) high duties on cotton and tobacco would hurt the South's export business (c) it was highly probable that the North intended to abolish slavery (d) the tariff would raise the prices of manufactured goods.
56. The South expected to benefit during the Civil War from the fact that (a) the South produced over one-half of the nation's wealth (b) two-thirds of the real property of the country was in the South (c) European governments generally sympathized with the South (d) over one-half of the nation's railroad mileage was in the South.
57. Northern agricultural production during the Civil War was *not* increased by (a) the Homestead Act (b) labor-saving machinery (c) the loss of southern markets (d) an unusual demand for goods at home and abroad.
58. Northern labor was generally at a disadvantage during the Civil War because (a) wages rose somewhat more slowly than prices (b) the government was very hostile to labor organization (c) conversion to war production resulted in considerable unemployment.
59. The Union government raised the greatest amount of money to finance the Civil War through (a) loans (b)

increased taxes (c) issuance of paper money (d) sale of property.

60. The South suffered the greatest loss of capital during and immediately after the Civil War through (a) seizure of plantations by the Union government (b) destruction of property by Union armies (c) abolition of slavery (d) loss of foreign commerce.
61. Which of the following acts provided for the establishment of public agricultural colleges? (a) Homestead Act (b) Morrill Act (c) Timber Culture Act (d) Carey Act.
62. Which of the following statements does *not* apply to agricultural history during the period 1860-1910? (a) the acreage under cultivation quadrupled (b) the value of farm property increased five-fold (c) the number of farms was tripled (d) the production of leading crops increased substantially.
63. The mechanization of agriculture during the period 1860-1910 resulted in (a) a decrease in the farmer's real income (b) a decline in per capita production of farm products (c) the cultivation of less marginal land (d) a reduction in the number of workers required in farming.
64. Scientific farming was *not* encouraged during the period 1860-1910 by (a) the development of agricultural education (b) increased public aid and interest (c) the existence of much unoccupied cultivable land throughout the period (d) the development of keen competition in a period of declining prices.
65. Which of the following contributed most importantly to agrarian discontent during the period 1865-1900? (a) foreign competition damaged the farmer's home market (b) increased productivity resulted in farm surpluses and declining prices (c) liberal credit policies encouraged farmer indebtedness (d) the resumption of free and unlimited coinage of silver.
66. Which of the following was *not* a part of the program of the Grange? (a) public regulation of railroads (b) free silver (c) farmer co-operatives (d) farmer-owned harvester works and plow factories.
67. Three of the following were advocated in the platform of the People's Party in 1892. Which was not? (a) issuance of greenbacks (b) a graduated income tax (c) removal of public land from control by the railroads (d) governmental ownership of railroads.

68. Which of the following acts extended the authority of the Interstate Commerce Commission over telephone and telegraph companies? (a) the Mann-Elkins Act (b) the Hepburn Act (c) the Elkins Act (d) the Physical Valuation Act.
69. The holdings of foreign investors in American securities in 1914 were worth about (a) 1 billion dollars (b) 2½ billion dollars (c) 5 billion dollars (d) 7 billion dollars.
70. Which of the following was *not* an encouragement to industrialism in America after the Civil War? (a) technological advance (b) expansion of the railroad system (c) an abundance of natural resources (d) a scarcity of domestic capital.
71. The history of labor in the United States during the period 1860-1900 was characterized by (a) a three-fold increase in the number of employed persons (b) an increase in the proportion of agricultural labor (c) a decrease in the proportion of non-agricultural labor.
72. The value of American manufactures exceeded the value of agricultural products in (a) 1880 (b) 1890 (c) 1900 (d) 1910.
73. A number of industries developed in the Middle West after the Civil War. Which of the following was *not* an important industry in that area? (a) iron and steel (b) small-metal manufactures (c) meat-packing (d) flour-milling.
74. After the Civil War southern New England specialized in the manufacture of (a) jewelry (b) farm machinery (c) railroad locomotives (d) petroleum products.
75. Which of the following industries did *not* develop importantly in the Far West? (a) lumbering (b) petroleum refining (c) canning of food products (d) iron and steel.
76. Notable development took place in which of the following industries in the South after the Civil War? (a) lumbering (b) woolen textiles (c) meat-packing (d) printing and publishing.
77. The percentage of industrial power provided by electricity in 1940 was roughly (a) 30 per cent (b) 40 per cent (c) 50 per cent (d) 60 per cent.
78. The energy pattern in the twentieth century has been characterized by (a) the continued dominance of coal as an energy source, but a relative decline in the importance

of coal (b) the rising importance of electricity, two-thirds of which has been consistently derived from water power (c) rapid growth in the importance of petroleum until World War II and steady decline thereafter (d) the elimination of natural gas as an important energy source.

79. Which of the following industries held first place in the monetary value of its production in 1860? (a) iron and steel (b) flour-milling (c) cotton textiles (d) meat-packing (e) railroad equipment.
80. The industry which ranks first today in the monetary value of its production is (a) flour-milling (b) chemicals (c) products of steel works (d) railroad equipment (e) meat-packing.
81. Textile manufacturing since the Civil Was has been accompanied by (a) a decline in the number of southern cotton mills, but a sharp increase in the amount of production (b) an increase in the output of the woolen industry which has generally ranked second to cotton in monetary value of its production (c) the absence of tariff protection for all textiles but woolens (d) a more rapid increase in the production of woolen goods than in the production of any other textile during the period 1865-1914.
82. In 1890 which of the following forms of business combination was outlawed? (a) the merger (b) the holding company (c) the trust (d) the cartel.
83. The form of combination in which the stock of a number of corporations was turned over to a board of trustees to effect unified management was known as (a) the trust (b) the holding company (c) the merger (d) the pool.
84. A company that owns a controlling share of the stock of subsidiary corporations in a single line of business is known as (a) a trust (b) a pool (c) a holding company (d) a merger.
85. Which of the following was *not* an advocate of the business philosophy of Herbert Spencer? (a) E. L. Youmans (b) J. B. Clark (c) W. G. Sumner (d) H. D. Lloyd.
86. Which of the following was demanded most frequently by American businessmen even though it was contradictory to the general belief in laissez-faire? (a) a centralized banking system under private control (b) non-interference with business combinations (c) the protective

tariff (d) government regulation of railroads to eliminate discriminatory practices.

87. Which of the following acts determined that the word *person* was to apply to corporations as well as to individuals? (a) Sherman Antitrust Act (b) Hepburn Act (c) Federal Trade Commission Act (d) Clayton Antitrust Act.
88. The largest number of prosecutions under the Sherman Antitrust Act took place in the administration of (a) T. Roosevelt (b) W. McKinley (c) W. H. Taft (d) W. Wilson.
89. The dissolution of which of the following was *not* ordered by the United States Supreme Court? (a) United Shoe Machinery Company (b) Standard Oil of New Jersey (c) Northern Securities Company.
90. Which of the following factors did *not* encourage the organization of labor unions in the period after the Civil War? (a) the concentration of labor in urban centers (b) fear of the effects of mechanization (c) the existence of a public opinion which generally favored labor organization (d) the development of huge impersonal corporations.
91. Which of the following factors did *not* contribute to the rapid decline of the Knights of Labor? (a) T. V. Powderly was not an aggressive leader (b) association with the Haymarket riot caused public disapproval (c) the union obstinately refused to compromise and engaged in too many strikes (d) the union operated for about a decade as a secret society.
92. Which of the following statements was true about the American Federation of Labor in the 19th century? (a) it was a federation of industrial unions (b) it gave official support to the Democratic Party (c) it favored avoidance of association with radicalism (d) it made a constant effort to unionize unskilled laborers.
93. In the period 1865-1913 the per capita real income of the United States rose about (a) 100 per cent (b) 75 per cent (c) 50 per cent (d) 25 per cent.
94. Which of the following was *not* an important gain of labor in the period before World War I? (a) limitation of child labor by Congressional action (b) establishment of an eight-hour day for federal government workers (c) relative decline in the number of child laborers in the

early twentieth century (d) minimum-wage legislation for women workers in Massachusetts.

95. The expansion of American foreign commerce during the period 1860-1914 was encouraged by (a) declining agricultural production which permitted greater attention to industrial expansion (b) development of an American merchant marine large enough to handle the increased volume of trade (c) improvement of banking and credit facilities which made the financing of foreign trade easier (d) a low United States tariff.
96. Which of the following statements is true about American foreign commerce in the period 1860-1914? (a) increasing exports greatly exceeded increasing imports (b) a remarkable degree of self-sufficiency permitted the nation to import less and less (c) the monetary value of exports of manufactured items was greater than the value of agricultural exports throughout the period (d) the importation of raw materials declined.
97. In the period 1860-1914 about what proportion of American ocean-borne commerce was handled by American ships? (a) 100 per cent (b) 75 per cent (c) 25 per cent (d) 10 per cent.
98. Which of the following represented the most drastic change in the United States policy of tariff protection? (a) the Dingley Tariff (b) the Payne-Aldrich Tariff (c) the Underwood-Simmons Tariff (d) the McKinley Tariff.
99. Which of the following was referred to as "the crime of '73"? (a) demonetization of silver (b) the Specie Resumption Act (c) the Bland-Allison Act (d) the panic of 1873.
100. In 1873 there was little immediate opposition to the discontinuance of bimetallism because (a) silver was undervalued at the United States mint (b) western farmers were not in favor of inflation at that time (c) by the terms of the Bland-Allison Act the government was obligated to buy as much silver as under the bimetallic system (d) the production of silver had been steadily declining.
101. In the 1870's the demand for the resumption of silver coinage arose because (a) the market value of silver in terms of gold was increasing (b) western farmers believed that silver coinage would curb inflation (c) the commercial ratio of silver to gold had risen above 16 to 1 and it would have been profitable to coin silver at the

mint ratio (d) businessmen in general wanted a large volume of currency in circulation.

102. Which of the following statements was *not* true about the National Banking system in the early period of its existence? (a) the comptroller of the currency was responsible for investigation and approval of applicants for membership (b) the banks had limited liability (c) capitalization was determined by the size of the city in which each bank was located (d) charters were limited to a period of 20 years.
103. Which of the following trends indicates *directly* that the standard of living in the United States rose from 1860 to 1914? (a) the phenomenal expansion of industry (b) increasing economic concentration (c) per capita real income more than doubled (d) the growth of the national income.
104. Three of the following were basic purposes of the "new imperialism." Which was not? (a) promotion of national security (b) procurement of vital resources (c) control of overseas markets (d) procurement of foreign capital for domestic investment.
105. In 1897 the largest foreign investments of the United States were in (a) Europe (b) Mexico (c) Canada and Newfoundland (d) Asia.
106. In 1914 the largest foreign investments of the United States were in (a) Europe (b) Canada and Newfoundland (c) Cuba and the West Indies (d) South America.
107. Which of the following was *not* annexed by the United States at the end of the Spanish-American War? (a) Cuba (b) Puerto Rico (c) Guam (d) Philippine Islands.
108. Three of the following were principles of the Open Door policy. Which was not? (a) no power should interfere with any treaty port or vested interest within its sphere of influence in China (b) the Chinese tariff should apply within the foreign powers' spheres of influence (c) foreign powers should withdraw from leaseholds in Manchuria (d) no power should discriminate against foreigners in determining harbor and railroad charges within its sphere of influence.
109. Which of the following was *not* a means of financing World War I used by the United States? (a) sale of bonds (b) an income tax (c) issuance of paper money (d) excise taxes.

110. The most important method of financing World War I used by the United States was (a) procurement of foreign loans (b) increased taxation (c) increased tariff rates (d) domestic loans.
111. Despite problems of reconversion after World War I, the United States experienced prosperity until the middle of 1921. One of the reasons for this was (a) war production continued at a high level (b) while foreign demand for American goods declined, civilian production increased (c) government spending continued at a high level (d) labor made spectacular gains in the postwar period.
112. Which of the following did *not* contribute importantly to industrial expansion during the period 1923-1929? (a) increasing automobile production (b) increasing purchasing power of the agricultural population (c) growth of the construction business (d)expansion of the electrical industry.
113. Organized labor lost strength in the 1920's partly because (a) laissez-faire was abandoned (b) the prolonged deflation was accompanied by declining wages (c) "welfare capitalism" declined in this decade (d) the government was unsympathetic to labor.
114. Which of the following was an important economic force or condition in the 1920's? (a) the general adoption of low tariffs (b) the increase in American consumption but at a slower rate than the increase in productivity (c) the decrease in bank borrowings of American stock brokers during the period 1927-1929 (d) expansion of the purchasing power of American agriculture.
115. In the period 1929-1932 the total national income declined from an estimated $85 billion to about (a) $55 billion (b) $47 billion (c) $25 billion (d) $37 billion.
116. Three of the following policies were utilized during the Hoover administration. Which was not? (a) the President's Committee for Unemployment Relief (b) increased expenditures for public works (c) the Reconstruction Finance Corporation (d) the Civilian Conservation Corps.
117. The first Agricultural Adjustment Act gave the president authority to (a) issue up to 5 billion dollars of legal-tender United States notes (b) coin an unlimited amount of silver at any ratio to gold which might be decided upon (c) reduce the gold content of the dollar up to 60

per cent (d) control the prices of goods purchased by the farmers.

118. Which of the following agencies was created primarily to regulate the sale of stocks and bonds? (a) SEC (b) FCC (c) ICC (d) NRA.

119. Three of the following characterized the 1930's. Which did not? (a) restriction of speculative expansion of banks in the Federal Reserve system (b) the abandonment of silver purchases by the government (c) the development of federal hydroelectric projects (d) the adoption of federal minimum-wage legislation.

120. Which of the following agencies was most active in the promotion of rural resettlement? (a) Agricultural Adjustment Act (b) Farm Credit Administration (c) Farm Securities Administration (d) Reconstruction Finance Corporation.

121. By 1939 the national debt had risen to about (a) $25 billion dollars (b) $30 billion dollars (c) $35 billion dollars (d) $40 billion dollars.

122. In the 1920's American foreign investments (excluding government loans) increased about (a) $10 billion (b) $5 billion (c) $20 billion (d) $15 billion.

123. In the 1930's foreign nations found it difficult to meet their obligations to the United States because (a) the United States tariff duties were high (b) the American merchant marine provided greater competition for foreigners than previously (c) the United States defaulted in payment of foreign debts (d) American investments abroad increased.

124. Which of the following statements represented the most common attitude of the people of the United States regarding American loans to Europe during World War I? (a) the United States should cancel the debts (b) the United States should agree to debt reduction but insist on the general principle of repayment (c) the United States should demand that the Allies turn over German reparations payments to it (d) the United States should strictly oppose the postponement of debt payments.

125. Through which of the following did the United States raise the most money during World War II? (a) increased taxation (b) paper money (c) foreign loans (d) domestic loans.

ANSWERS TO EXAMINATION QUESTIONS

1. (c)
2. (b)
3. (c)
4. (b)
5. (d)
6. (b)
7. (a)
8. (c)
9. (a)
10. (c)
11. (b)
12. (b)
13. (c)
14. (a)
15. (d)
16. (b)
17. (b)
18. (d)
19. (c)
20. (c)
21. (a)
22. (c)
23. (b)
24. (b)
25. (c)
26. (d)
27. (b)
28. (a)
29. (d)
30. (d)
31. (a)
32. (b)
33. (d)
34. (c)
35. (a)
36. (c)
37. (a)
38. (d)
39. (c)
40. (b)
41. (a)
42. (d)
43. (d)
44. (c)
45. (b)
46. (a)
47. (c)
48. (b)
49. (b)
50. (b)
51. (c)
52. (b)
53. (a)
54. (b)
55. (d)
56. (c)
57. (c)
58. (a)
59. (a)
60. (c)
61. (b)
62. (a)
63. (a)
64. (c)
65. (b)
66. (b)
67. (a)
68. (a)
69. (d)
70. (d)
71. (a)
72. (b)
73. (b)
74. (a)
75. (d)
76. (a)
77. (d)
78. (a)
79. (b)
80. (c)
81. (b)
82. (c)
83. (a)
84. (c)
85. (d)
86. (c)
87. (a)
88. (d)
89. (a)
90. (c)
91. (c)
92. (c)
93. (c)
94. (a)
95. (c)
96. (a)
97. (d)
98. (c)
99. (a)
100. (a)
101. (c)
102. (b)
103. (c)
104. (d)
105. (b)
106. (b)
107. (a)
108. (c)
109. (c)
110. (d)
111. (c)
112. (b)
113. (d)
114. (c)
115. (d)
116. (d)
117. (b)
118. (a)
119. (b)
120. (c)
121. (d)
122. (a)
123. (a)
124. (b)
125. (d)

SELECTED REFERENCES FOR FURTHER READING

Part I: General

Beard, Charles and Mary. *Rise of American Civilization.* 2 vols. New York: Macmillan Co., 1927.

Bogart, E. L., and Thompson, C. M. *Readings in the Economic History of the U.S.* New York: Longmans, Green & Co., 1916.

Farrand, L. *Basis of American History.* New York: Harper & Brothers, 1904.

Flugel, F., and Faulkner, H. U. *Readings in the Economic and Social History of the United States 1773-1929.* New York: Harper & Brothers, 1929.

Gras, N. S. B., and Larson, H. M. *Casebook in American Business History.* New York: F. S. Crofts & Co., 1939.

Hacker, L. M. *Triumph of American Capitalism.* New York: Simon and Schuster, Inc., 1940.

Hulbert, A. H. *Soil and Its Influence on the History of the U.S.* New Haven: Yale University Press, 1930.

Huntington, E. *The Red Man's Continent.* New Haven: Yale University Press, 1919.

Kellogg, C. E. *The Soils that Support Us.* New York: Macmillan Co., 1941.

McCarty, H. H. *The Geographic Basis of American Economic Life.* New York: Harper & Brothers, 1940.

Osborn, F. *Our Plundered Planet.* New York: Grosset & Dunlap, 1948.

See, H. *The Economic Interpretation of History* New York: Adelphi Co., 1929.

Seligman, E. R. A. *The Economic Interpretation of History.* New York: Columbia University Press, 1922.

Semple, E. C. *American History and Its Geographic Conditions.* (Rev. ed.) New York: Houghton Mifflin Co., 1933.

Part II: The Colonial Period to 1783

Adams, J. T. *The Founding of New England.* Boston: Little, Brown & Co., 1921.

Andrews, C. M. *The Colonial Period in American History.* 4 vols. New Haven: Yale University Press, 1934–1937.

Beard, C. A. *An Economic Interpretation of the Constitution of the U.S.* New York: Macmillan Co., 1913.

Beer, G. L. *The Old Colonial System.* 2 vols. Gloucester: Peter Smith, 1912.

———. *The Origins of British Colonial System.* Gloucester: Peter Smith, 1907.

Bidwell, P. W., and Falconer, J. I. *History of Agriculture in the Northern United States before 1860.* Washington, D. C.: The Carnegie Institute of Washington, D. C., 1925.

Bridenbaugh, C. *Cities in Revolt.* New York: Knopf, 1955.

Carrier, L. *The Beginnings of American Agriculture.* New York: McGraw-Hill Book Co., 1923.

Channing, E. *History of the U.S.* Vols. I–III. New York: Macmillan Co., 1905–1912.

Cheyney, E. P. *European Background of American History.* New York: Harper & Brothers, 1904.

East, R. A. *Business Enterprise in the American Revolutionary Era.* New York: Columbia University Press, 1938.

Gray, L. D. *History of Agriculture in the Southern United States.* 2 vols. Washington, D. C.: The Carnegie Institute of Washington, D. C., 1933.

Haring, C. H. *The Spanish Empire in America.* New York: Oxford University Press, Inc., 1947.

Harper, L. A. *The English Navigation Laws.* New York: Columbia University Press, 1939.

Hawk, E. Q. *Economic History of the South.* New York: Prentice-Hall, Inc., 1934.

Hibbard, B. H. *A History of the Public Land Policies.* Gloucester: Peter Smith, 1939.

Hull, W. I. *William Penn and the Dutch Quaker Migration to Pennsylvania.* Swarthmore: Swarthmore College, 1935.

Jernegan, M. W. *Laboring and Dependent Classes in Colonial*

America, 1607–1783. London: Cambridge University Press, 1931.

Lipson, E. *The Economic History of England.* 3 vols. New York: Macmillan Co., 1915–1931.

Middleton, A. P. *Tobacco Coast: A Maritime History of Chesapeake Bay in the Colonial Era.* Newport News: Mariners' Museum, 1953.

Miller, J. C. *Origins of the American Revolution.* Boston: Little, Brown & Co., 1943.

Morris, R. B. *Government and Labor in Early America.* New York: Columbia University Press, 1946.

Nettels, C. *The Roots of American Civilization.* New York: F. S. Crofts & Co., 1938.

Osgood, H. L. *The American Colonies in the Seventeenth Century.* 3 vols. New York: Macmillan Co., 1904–1907.

———. *The American Colonies in the Eighteenth Century.* 4 vols. New York: Macmillan Co., 1924–1925.

Parkman, F. *The Old Regime in Canada.* Boston: Little, Brown & Co., 1873.

Phillips, U. B. *American Negro Slavery.* New York: D. Appleton & Co., 1921.

———. *Life and Labor in the Old South.* New York: D. Appleton & Co., 1929.

Schlesinger, A. M. *Colonial Merchants and the American Revolution.* New York: Columbia University Press, 1918.

Smith, A. E. *Colonists in Bondage: White Servitude and Convict Labor in America, 1607–1776.* Chapel Hill: University of North Carolina Press, 1947.

Tryon, R. M. *Household Manufactures in the U.S., 1640–1860.* Chicago: University of Chicago Press, 1917.

Wertenbaker, T. J. *The Planters of Colonial Virginia.* Princeton: Princeton University Press, 1922.

Part III: The Agricultural Era, 1783–1865

Abbot, W. J. *The Story of Our Merchant Marine.* New York: Dodd, Mead & Co., 1919.

Albion, R. G. *The Rise of New York Port.* New York: Charles Scribner's Sons, 1939.

Ambler, C. H. *History of Transportation in the Ohio Valley.* (Limited edition.) A. H. Clark, 1932.

Balinky, A. *Albert Gallatin: Fiscal Theories and Policies.* New Brunswick: Rutgers University Press, 1958.

Beard, C. A. *The Economic Origins of the Jeffersonian Democracy.* New York: Macmillan Co., 1915.

Bidwell, P. W., and Falconer, J. I. *History of Agriculture in the U.S., 1620–1860.* Washington, D. C.: The Carnegie Institute of Washington, D. C., 1925.

Bond, B. W. *The Civilization of the Old Northwest.* New York: Macmillan Co., 1934.

Channing, E. *History of the United States.* Vols. IV–VI. New York: Macmillan Co., 1927–1932.

Clemen, R. A. *The American Livestock and Meat Industry.* New York: Ronald Press Co., 1923.

Cole, A. H. *The American Wool Manufacture.* 2 vols. Cambridge: Harvard University Press, 1926.

Coman, K. *Economic Beginnings of the Far West.* 2 vols. New York: Macmillan Co., 1912.

Copeland, M. T. *The Cotton Manufacturing Industry in the United States.* Cambridge: Harvard University Press, 1912.

Dorfman, J. *The Economic Mind in American Civilization.* Vol. I. New York: The Viking Press, Inc., 1946.

Dunbar, S. *History of Travel in America.* 4 vols. Indianapolis: The Bobbs-Merrill Company, Inc., 1915.

Ferguson, E. J. *Power of the Purse: A History of American Public Finance, 1776–1790.* Chapel Hill: University of North Carolina Press, 1961.

Gray, L. D. *History of Agriculture in the Southern U.S. to 1860.* 2 vols. Washington, D. C.: The Carnegie Institute of Washington, D. C., 1933.

Green, C. M. *Eli Whitney and the Birth of American Technology.* Boston: Little, Brown & Co., 1956.

Gregg, Josiah. *Commerce of the Prairies.* (ed.) Max Moorhead, Norman: University of Oklahoma Press, 1954.

Hammond, B. *Banks and Politics in America from the Revolution to the Civil War.* Princeton: Princeton University Press, 1957.

Harlow, A. F. *Old Towpaths.* New York: D. Appleton & Co., 1926.

Henlein, P. C. *Cattle Kingdom in the Ohio Valley.* Lexington: University of Kentucky Press, 1959.

Jones, F. *Middlemen in the Domestic Trade of the United States.* Urbana: University of Illinois Press, 1937.

Kirkland, E. C. *Men, Cities, and Transportation.* 2 vols. Cambridge: Harvard University Press, 1948.

Kuhlmann, C. B. *Development of the Flour-Milling Industry in the U.S.* New York: Houghton Mifflin Co., 1929.

MacGill, C. E., et al. *History of Transportation in the U.S. before 1860.* Washington, D. C.: The Carnegie Institute of Washington, D. C., 1917.

McGrane, R. C. *The Panic of 1837.* London: The Cambridge University Press, 1924.

Nettels, C. P. *The Emergence of a National Economy, 1775–1815.* New York: Holt, Rinehart and Winston, 1962.

Nevins, A. *Ordeal of the Union.* 2 vols. New York: Charles Scribner's Sons, 1947.

Perkins, B. *Prologue to War: England and the United States, 1805–1812.* Berkeley: University of California Press, 1961.

Phillips, U. B. *American Negro Slavery.* Gloucester: Peter Smith, 1918.

———. *History of Transportation in the Eastern Cotton Belt to 1860.* New York: Macmillan Co., 1908.

———. *Life and Labor in the Old South.* Boston: Little, Brown & Co., 1929.

Pratt, J. W. *The Expansionists of 1812.* New York: Macmillan Co., 1925.

Randall, J. G. *The Civil War and Reconstruction.* Boston: D. C. Heath & Co., 1937.

Robbins, R. M. *Our Landed Heritage: The Public Domain, 1776–1936.* Princeton: Princeton University Press, 1942.

Schachner, N. *Alexander Hamilton.* New York: Appleton-Century-Crofts, Inc., 1946.

Schafer, J. *The Social History of American Agriculture.* New York: Macmillan Co., 1916.

Sellers, J. B. *Slavery in Alabama.* University: University of Alabama Press, 1950.

Smith, W. B., and Cole, A. J. *Fluctuations in American Business, 1790–1860.* Cambridge: Harvard University Press, 1935.

———. *Economic Aspects of the Second Bank of the United States.* Cambridge: Harvard University Press, 1953.

Stampp, K. M. *The Peculiar Institution.* New York: Knopf, 1956.

Taylor, G. R. *The Transportation Revolution.* New York: Rinehart & Co., Inc., 1951.

Wade, R. C. *The Urban Frontier: The Rise of Western Cities, 1780–1830.* Cambridge: Harvard University Press, 1959.

Walters, R. *Albert Gallatin.* New York: Macmillan Co., 1957.

Ware, N. *The Industrial Worker.* New York: Houghton Mifflin Co., 1924.

Part IV: Industrial America

Barger, H. *The Transportation Industries, 1889–1946.* New York: National Bureau of Economic Research, 1951.

Barrett, D. C. *The Greenbacks and Resumption of Specie Payments, 1862–1879.* Cambridge: Harvard University Press, 1931.

Baruch, B. M. *American Industry in the War.* New York: Prentice-Hall, Inc., 1941.

Blaisdell, D. C. *Government and Agriculture.* New York: Farrar, Straus & Young, Inc., 1940.

Bonbright, J. C., and Means, G. C. *The Holding Company.* New York: McGraw-Hill Book Co., 1932.

Brandeis, L. D. *Other People's Money.* New York: Frederick A. Stokes Co., 1914.

Brissenden, P. F. *The I.W.W., a Study of American Syndicalism.* New York: Columbia University Press, 1919.

Buck, S. J. *The Granger Movement.* Cambridge: Harvard University Press, 1913.

Burns, A. F. *Production Trends in the U.S. since 1870.* New York: Macmillan Co., 1934.

Clarkson, G. B. *Industrial America and the World War.* New York: Houghton Mifflin Co., 1923.

Clemen, R. A. *The American Livestock and Meat Industry.* New York: Ronald Press Co., 1923.

Cole, A. H. *The American Wool Manufacture.* 2 vols. Cambridge: Harvard University Press, 1926.

Commons, J. R., et al. *History of Labour in the U.S.* 4 vols. New York: Macmillan Co., 1918–1935.

Corey, L. *The House of Morgan.* G. Howard Watt, 1930.

Craf, J. R. *A Survey of the American Economy, 1940–1946.* New York: North River Press, 1947.

Dale, E. E. *The Range Cattle Industry.* Norman: University of Oklahoma Press, 1930.

Dick, E. *The Sod House Frontier.* New York: Appleton-Century-Crofts, Inc., 1937.

Douglas, P. H. *Real Wages in the United States, 1890–1926.* New York: Houghton Mifflin Co., 1930.

Epstein, R. C. *The Automobile Industry.* New York: The McGraw-Hill Book Co., 1928.

Faulkner, H. U. *The Decline of Laissez Faire.* New York: Harper & Brothers, 1951.

Frederick, J. H. *Commercial Air Transportation.* New York: Rinehart & Co., Inc., 1942.

Giddens, P. *The Birth of the Oil Industry.* Harrisburg: Pennsylvania Historical Committee, 1938.

Harlow, A. F. *Steelways of New England.* New York: Creative Age Press, Inc., 1945.

Hendrick, B. J. *Andrew Carnegie.* 2 vols. New York: Doubleday & Co., Inc., 1932.

Hibbard, B. H. *A History of the Public Land Policies.* New York: Macmillan Co., 1924.

Hogan, W. T. *The Development of American Heavy Industry in the Twentieth Century.* New York: Fordham University Press, 1953.

Hutchins, J. G. B. *The American Maritime Industries and Public Policy, 1789–1914.* Cambridge: Harvard University Press, 1941.

Kemmerer, E. W. *The ABC of the Federal Reserve System.* Princeton: Princeton University Press, 1938.

Kennedy, E. D. *The Automobile Industry.* New York: Reynal & Hitchcock, 1941.

Kirkland, E. C. *Men, Cities, and Transportation.* 2 vols. Cambridge: Harvard University Press, 1948.

Kuhlmann, C. B. *The Development of the Flour-Milling Industry in the U.S.* New York: Houghton Mifflin Co., 1929.

Laidler, H. W. *Concentration in American Industry.* New York: Thomas Y. Crowell Co., 1931.

Leonard, W. N. *Railroad Consolidation under the Transportation Act of 1920.* New York: Columbia University Press, 1946.

Levinson, E. *Labor on the March.* New York: Harper & Brothers, 1938.

Lewis, C. *America's Stake in International Investments.* Washington, D. C.: The Brookings Institution, 1938.

Lyon, L. S., et al. *The National Recovery Administration.* Washington, D. C.: The Brookings Institution, 1935.

Millis, H. A., and Brown, E. C. *From the Wagner Act to Taft-Hartley.* Chicago: University of Chicago Press, 1950.

Mills, F. C. *Economic Tendencies in the U.S.* New York: National Bureau of Economic Research, 1932.

Mitchell, B. *Depression Decade.* New York: National Bureau of Economic Research, 1947.

Mitchell, W. C. *Business Cycles.* New York: National Bureau of Economic Research, 1913.

Moley, R. *After Seven Years.* New York: Harper & Brothers, 1939.

Moulton, H. G., and Pasvolsky, L. *War Debts and World Prosperity.* New York: Century Company, 1932.

Nelson, D. M. *Arsenal of Democracy: the Story of American War Production.* New York: Harcourt, Brace & Co., 1946.

Nevins, A. *Ford: The Times, the Man, the Company.* New York: Macmillan Co., 1954.

———. *John D. Rockefeller: The Heroic Age of American Business.* 2 vols. New York: Charles Scribner's Sons, 1940.

Nevins, A., and Frank E. Hill. *Ford: Expansion and Challenge (1915–1933).* New York: Charles Scribner's Sons, 1957.

Osgood, E. S. *The Day of the Cattleman.* Minneapolis: University of Minnesota Press, 1929.

Regier, C. C. *The Era of the Muckrakers.* Chapel Hill: University of North Carolina Press, 1932.

Rickard, T. A. *A History of American Mining.* New York: McGraw-Hill Book Co., 1932.

Ripley, W. Z. *Railroads, Finance and Organizations.* New York: Longmans, Green & Co., 1915.

———. *Railroads, Rates, and Regulations.* New York: Longmans, Green & Co., 1912.

———. *Main Street and Wall Street.* Boston: Little, Brown & Co., 1927.

Shannon, F. A. *The Farmer's Last Frontier: Agriculture 1860–1897.* New York: Farrar, Straus & Young, Inc., 1945.

Soule, G. *Prosperity Decade from War to Depression 1917–1929.* New York: Rinehart & Co., Inc., 1947.

Stocking, G. W., and Watkins, M. W. *Cartels or Competition.* New York: The Twentieth Century Fund, 1948.

Taft, P. *The A. F. of L. in the Time of Gompers.* New York: Harper & Bros., 1957.

Taussig, F. W. *Tariff of the United States.* New York: Putnam, 1931.

Veblen, T. B. *Theory of Business Enterprise.* New York: Charles Scribner's Sons, 1904.

Ware, N. J. *The Labor Movement in the United States.* New York: D. Appleton Co., 1929.

Watkins, M. W. *Industrial Combinations and Public Policy.* New York: Houghton Mifflin Co., 1927.

Webb, W. P. *The Great Plains.* Boston: Ginn & Co., 1931.

Wecter, D. *The Age of the Great Depression.* New York: Macmillan Co., 1948.

Whitney, S. N. *Antitrust Policies.* 2 vols. New York: Twentieth Century Fund, 1958.

Williams, B. H. *Economic Foreign Policy of the United States.* New York: McGraw-Hill Book Co., 1929.

INDEX

Mary Fran Harden